Reading Between the Lines

eXtreme teaching
rigorous texts for troubled times

Joe L. Kincheloe and Danny Weil
General Editors

Vol. 2

PETER LANG
New York • Washington, D.C./Baltimore • Bern
Frankfurt am Main • Berlin • Brussels • Vienna • Oxford

Marion E. Neville-Lynch

Reading Between the Lines
A Balanced Approach to Literacy

PETER LANG
New York • Washington, D.C./Baltimore • Bern
Frankfurt am Main • Berlin • Brussels • Vienna • Oxford

Library of Congress Cataloging-in-Publication Data
Neville-Lynch, Marion E.
Reading between the lines: a balanced approach to literacy /
Marion E. Neville Lynch.
p. cm. — (Extreme teaching, rigorous texts for troubled times; v. 2)
Includes bibliographical references.
1. Reading (Secondary). 2. Reading (Adult education).
3. Reading comprehension. I. Title. II. Series.
LB1632 .N36 428.4'071'2—dc21   2002013588
ISBN 0-8204-5759-0
ISSN 1534-2808

Bibliographic information published by **Die Deutsche Bibliothek**.
Die Deutsche Bibliothek lists this publication in the "Deutsche
Nationalbibliografie"; detailed bibliographic data is available
on the Internet at http://dnb.ddb.de/.

Cover design by Lisa Barfield

© 2005 Peter Lang Publishing, Inc., New York
275 Seventh Avenue, 28th Floor, New York, NY 10001
www.peterlangusa.com

All rights reserved.
Reprint or reproduction, even partially, in all forms such as microfilm,
xerography, microfiche, microcard, and offset strictly prohibited.

Dedicated to my students

The City University of New York
Brooklyn College
New York City Technical College
York College

Dear Students,

Reading Between the Lines invites you to share in a "virtual" classroom experience to improve your reading skills. *Fourteen* lessons of instruction are presented and, when followed, will definitely yield the benefits you desire—to become a more efficient reader. In these lessons you have the opportunity to engage in a learning experience with students who have worked collaboratively, shared their work, exchanged ideas, and expanded their knowledge and ability to become efficient readers. You exam their work in the form of examples illustrated throughout *Reading Between the Lines*. These examples demonstrate the remarkable progress students made as they followed the reading strategies outlined in this Handbook. Thus, from these examples, you obtain a sense of the thinking of the students and their collaborative efforts as illustrated in these examples presented throughout this text. To place these examples in context, a student Annotated Bibliography is included in *A Conversation With the Author*. My task is to facilitate this book discussion, encourage you to adapt various techniques and think in ways that will improve your reading skills. Thus, your experience in this "virtual classroom" is based on reflection, collaboration, and engagement. I know that you will sometimes feel challenged, but I am sure you will find this experience rewarding and satisfying as you improve your reading skills using the program outlined in *Reading Between the Lines*.

Sincerely,
Marion E. Neville-Lynch

Contents

Acknowledgments xi
Introduction: A Conversation With the Author xiii
    How This Book Is Organized xiii
    What You Can Expect: Authentic Reading Experiences xiv
Student Annotated Book Reviews xv
    Allen, P.G. (1990). *Spider Woman's Granddaughters* xv
    Alvarez, J. (1991). *How the Garcia Girls Lost Their Accents* xv
    Axline, V. (1964). *Dibs in Search of Self* xviii
    Morrison, T. (1987). *Beloved* xx
    Morrison, T. (1973). *Sula* xxi
    Tan, A. (1990). *The Joy Luck Club* xxii

CHAPTER ONE
YOUR LANGUAGE, CULTURE, KNOWLEDGE, AND EXPERIENCE 1
Lesson 1: Your Personal Matrix 1
    How Does My Personal Matrix Function With Reading? 3
Lesson 2: Interactive Readers 5
    Reading Assessments 6
    Learning Styles 8
    Self-Motivation 9
    Assess Your Reading Experience 10
    Monitoring Your Emotional Responses to Text 10
    Monitoring Your Thinking 11
    Relaxation for Readers 17
    An Autosuggestion Technique 17
    A Relaxation Technique 18
Lesson 3: Previewing Text 19
    Expository Text 19
    Textbook Chapters 20
    Essays 21
    Marginal Notes 21
    Formulating Questions Before Reading 21

A Practice Preview 23
Imaginative Literature 26
General Guidelines. 26
Key Story Components 26
Asking Questions. 27

CHAPTER TWO
UNDERSTANDING AUTHORS' LANGUAGE. 31
Lesson 4: Authors' Purpose and Point of View 31
Topic. 32
Choice of Language 33
Authors' Personal Matrix. 33
Unfamiliar Vocabulary. 33
Transitional Words and Phrases. 36
Denotations and Connotations 39
Figurative Language. 43
Lesson 5: Deconstructing Paragraphs 46
Literal Comprehension 46
Thesis 47
Interpretive Comprehension 52
Critical Comprehension. 55
Affective Comprehension 57
Paragraph Patterns 59
Simple Listing 60
Compare and Contrast 61
Cause and Effect 62
Persuasive Argument 63
Summarizing Authors' Language 66

CHAPTER THREE
ALTERNATIVE WAYS OF THINKING ABOUT READING. 67
Lesson 6: Thinking Outside of the Box 67
What is Lateral Thinking 67
Lateral Thinking and Reading Strategies. 68
Lesson 7: The Concept Web. 69
Creating a Concept Web 69
The Writing-Web-Rewriting Process 70
Create Your Concept Web 81
Lesson 8: Semantic Maps 82
Expository Text 82
Student Semantic Map 83
Imaginative Literature 85
Character Analysis 87
Lesson 9: Reading Aloud 90

CHAPTER FOUR
JOURNAL WRITING 93
Lesson 10: Recalling, Reflecting, Rethinking Context 93
    Journal Formats 93
Lesson 11: Journal Entries 94
    Themes and Thesis 95
    Summary Annotations 98
    Commentary Annotations 99
    Question Annotations 100
    Character Maps and Analysis 101
    Extended Journal Entries 103
    Alternative Journal Entries 115

CHAPTER FIVE
READING AND WRITING ANALYTICALLY 119
Lesson 12: The Summary 119
    Guidelines for Writing the Summary 120
    Summary Scoring Guide 121
    Expository Text With Concept Webs 122
    Imaginative Literature With Concept Webs 125
Lesson 13: Evaluating Text 129
    The Critique 131
    Critique Scoring Guide 131
    Expository Text 132
    Imaginative Literature 135
    Synthesis 137
    Synthesis Scoring Guide 138
Lesson 14: Test Taking 141
    Essay Exams 141
    Directive Verbs in Essay Exams 142
    Preparation for Essay Exams 143
    Writing a Practice Essay Exam 145
    Objectives Exams 146
    Studying for Objective Exams 147
    Multiple Choice Tests 147

CHAPTER SIX
READING SELECTIONS: FREEDOM AND CHOICE 149
    Overview 149
    Preparation Before Reading 151
    Concept Webs for Freedom and Choice 151
    The Declaration of Independence 152
    Elizabeth Cady Stanton (1848): Declaration of Sentiments and Resolutions 156
    Frederick Douglass (1852): "What to the Slave Is the Fourth of July?" 160

Chief Seattle (1854): Chief Seattle's 1854 Oration 168
John F. Kennedy (1961): President's Inaugural Address 171
Martin Luther King, Jr. (1963): Letter From Birmingham City Jail 175
Shirley Chisholm (1969): Equal Rights for Women........................... 183
Doris Lessing (1987): Group Minds 186
Shirley Jackson (1947): The Lottery... 195
George Orwell (1948): 1984, Part I 203
Syntheses of Readings 207

Bibliography... 209

Acknowledgments

Writing this book has meant engaging the sum total of my Personal Matrix: my knowledge, cultural background, language, and experiences. Thus, it is appropriate that I thank all of those with whom I have had contact to complete this endeavor. I quickly acknowledge, however, that the shortcomings herein, are due to my interpretations of what all so generously gave to encourage this project. I would like to acknowledge those individuals whose input has been critical; some who encouraged me to begin this project and others who have been with me to see this project to its completion.

I thank Marie Buncombe, colleague and friend whose encouragement has been from the very beginning. Appreciation goes to two colleagues Jacqueline DeWeever and Ken Bruffee both who read my initial outline and offered suggestions. A deep sense of thanks and appreciation for the following colleagues and friends: For Milga Morales, colleague and friend who read my manuscript, offered suggestions and helped me keep my sense of humor; for the friendship and encouragement of Glenne Martin; for Jean E. Davis, Esq. who graciously gave me a "crash course" to navigate technology; and Nick Irons, Director and Darshani Kahanda at the Brooklyn College Faculty Academic Technology Center who patiently helped me with technical concerns; for Wilda Gallagher who helped format the design I envisioned for this book; for my sons, James A. Lynch, Esq., an avid reader and writer, and Derek Lynch, an educator, both read and reread chapters as "prospective readers" for *Reading Between the Lines*—therefore, their suggestions have been invaluable.

For Chris Meyers, at Peter Lang for his patience in providing the time needed to complete this project; and Bernadette Shade, Production Supervisor, who was always available and helpful. Last, and in a separate category, I wish to thank Joe Kincheloe, a colleague, friend, and editor at Peter Lang Publishers Inc. He believed in this project and without hesitation encouraged me to begin in earnest; Shirley Steinberg, also a colleague, friend and editor at Peter Lang Publishers who kept me focused and on my "toes." Both these editors have been a treasure and kept me going. And, to my students who have been a joy and an inspiration throughout my career.

The author gratefully acknowledges the permission to reprint selected texts from the following:

"Letter from Birmingham City Jail, April 16, 1963" by Rev. Martin Luther King, Jr. Reprinted by arrangement with the estate of Martin Luther King, Jr., c/o Writer's House as agent for the proprietor New York, NY. Copyright © 1963 Martin Luther King Jr., copyright renewed 1991 Corretta Scott King.

"Group Minds" from PRISONS WE CHOOSE TO LIVE INSIDE by Doris Lessing. Copyright © 1988 Doris Lessing. Reprinted by kind permission of Jonathan Clowes Ltd., London, on behalf of Doris Lessing. Reprinted by permission of HarperCollings Publishers Inc.

"The Lottery" from THE LOTTERY AND OTHER STORIES by Shirley Jackson. Copyright © 1948, 1949 by Shirley Jackson. Copyright renewed 1976, 1977 by Laurence Hyman, Barry Hyman, Mrs. Sarah Webster, and Mrs. Joanne Schnurer. Reprinted by permission of Farrar, Straus and Giroux, LLC. "The Lottery" by Shirley Jackson. © 1948, 1949 by Shirley Jackson. Copyright by United Kingdom, Linda Allen, 1949 Green Street, Suite 5, San Francisco, California 94213. FSG Permissions, Hill and Wang North Point Press Faber & Faber, Inc.

Introduction

A Conversation With the Author

> What is reading but silent conversation?
> —W.S. Landor

Reading Between the Lines is an instructive handbook, designed as a bridge to improve your reading skills and help you to become an efficient and critical reader. It suggests alternative ways of thinking about reading and helps you focus your attention on important skills which efficient readers automatically employ as they read. In addition to basic reading skills, you will learn how to utilize your *Personal Matrix*, which you, as a reader bring to the text. Your Personal Matrix includes your cultural background, ethnicity, your traditions, experiences, prior knowledge, and your emotional responses. Each is independently important and collectively they represent your Personal Matrix and play a significant role in the way you interact with a text. The bottom line is, as the reader, your point of view has value. How you respond to an author's language will determine how effective you will be in constructing meaning. It also means reading interactively and thinking critically. Throughout this book, strategies will be introduced to help you make a conscious effort to engage your Personal Matrix along with your reading skills to become an efficient reader.

How This Book Is Organized

A series of lessons are presented to help you improve your reading behavior and critical thinking skills to read expository text (informational) critically, and techniques to read imaginative literature (fiction). You are guided through 14 lessons carefully designed to provide concrete suggestions, which will improve your reading technique. To begin, an emphasis is placed on helping you understand how your feelings and responses to text will indeed influence the ways in which you interpret what you read. Chapter One introduces the concept of your *Personal Matrix*, which influences your interaction with text. In this chapter we also include discussions on previewing textbooks, expository text, and imaginative literature. The approach to expository text and imaginative literature is decidedly different and understanding how to approach each will aid in your goal to become a more efficient reader. In Chapter Two we discuss how authors use language systematically to convince readers to believe a particular point of view. To help you have a comprehensive understanding of your readings, we present strategies to identify authors' language methods. In addition, ways to deconstruct paragraphs are also explored to identify main ideas and ways in which these ideas are supported. Chapter Three focuses on alternative ways of thinking about reading through various modes to monitor your thinking. Specific techniques will be introduced: concept webs, semantic maps, and reading aloud. In Chapter Four, the focal point is on journal writing; you are guided in ways to write summary annotations, commentary, question annotations, and character analysis. Many student examples are provided to guide you. Chapter Five connects reading to writing analytically through summarizing, evaluating, critiques, and synthesis. In addition, test taking is discussed: that is, essay exams and multiple choice with examples to indicate how to combine your reading and writing skills in this important area. Chapter Six, consists of a themed-based selection of readings arranged to connect authentic extended text to reading strategies outlined in *Reading Between the Lines*. At the end of each reading, questions are given to suggest ways to connect reading strategies to the readings. Thus, from previewing to journal writing, evaluating and synthesizing will all be applied to the Selection of Readings.

What You Can Expect: Authentic Reading Experiences

First, and foremost, if you follow the strategies discussed in this Handbook, you will be a more efficient reader. During this learning experience, you will need to let go of old patterns and ways of thinking which do not serve you as an efficient reader. That is, in order to see and interpret your readings from a broader perspective, you transform your thinking. You are guided to engage in the process of using alternative ways of thinking—you learn to trust your thinking and rely on your skills and ability to understand the readings. You are encouraged to read as often as possible as this is the way to improve your reading. Reading passages and doing the exercises provided in *Reading Between the Lines* is a means to apply and practice the suggested reading strategies giving you the mechanism to apply the strategies and prepare to use them automatically during your reading experience. However, if you confine your reading to these passages and exercises, you will not get the desired results—i.e., to be a more efficient reader you need to read extended text. The passages are only intended to practice the reading strategies; they cannot take the place of an authentic reading experience. Therefore, in order to get the most from this Handbook, it is important to engage in authentic reading experiences and as you do so, you will automatically begin to apply the reading strategies to your authentic reading experiences.

At the end of Chapter Five theme-based reading selections are provided so that you can apply the reading strategies to extended text. You may also wish to consider reading one of the novels listed below in the Student Annotated Book Reviews *that correspond to the many reading and writing examples* presented throughout this Handbook. If you are enrolled in a course, use this Handbook in conjunction with your textbooks.

Student-Annotated Book Reviews

Allen, P. G. (1990). *Spider Woman's Granddaughters*. New York: Ballantine Books.

Student Annotation/Spider Woman's Granddaughters

Spider Woman's Granddaughters is a group of essays written by Native American women. These women are members of different tribes and their stories are about their tribal traditions. Their stories are from the oral tradition of the tribes and do not follow the same way of thinking that Western stories might. In the Native Indian way of thinking, the individual is important within the tribe so that the stories emphasize one's place in the group. The stories come from tribal traditions and the stories are about survival of the whole tribe instead of the individual. In this sense, being set apart from the group does not seem to be of value to Native Americans. In Western stories, the emphasis may be on the individual as a hero. I liked the stories because it gave me a chance to learn how different Native Americans view things.

Alvarez, J. (1991). *How the Garcia Girls Lost Their Accents*. New York: Penguin Books.

Student Annotation/How the Garcia Girls Lost Their Accents

How the Garcia Girls Lost Their Accents, is about four girls and their parents who live in the Dominican Republic and then move to America. The four girls, Carla, Sandra, Yolanda, and Sofia have very strict parents, Laura and

Carlos. The girls always have to go out with chaperons and come home early. Sofia was always the daring one and always had all the boyfriends; her sisters would ask her for advice. Once she came home late with her boyfriend and was punished. When her father discovered letters she received from her boyfriend, he read them and was furious because of the sexual nature of some of the letters. Sofia felt her privacy had been violated and left home and married a German man. Sofia always looked as if she was heading for trouble but always ends up lucky. Yolanda was shy around men but had lovers and wrote poems about her encounters. Sandra, the prettiest, was very insecure about herself: she uses drugs to get skinny and ends up in the hospital. Carla was the oldest and always got what she wanted by screaming and crying and ordering her parents to give in to her. She was the bossy one but all the sisters were spoiled. I believe the strongest of the girls is Sofia because she tried to face her problems and work them out. Sandra was the weakest, taking drugs in order to look skinny. I enjoyed reading this book because I could reflect on the life of these girls and relate it to my own; reading about Sofia was like reading about myself. Sometimes it was difficult to keep my interest, but I made it more interesting by pretending each of the four girls was my friend and Laura and Carlos my parents. While reading, I pictured the whole scene in my head which made it fun. It turned out to be a great book.

Student Annotation/How the Garcia Girls Lost Their Accents

In the novel, *How the Garcia Girls Lost Their Accents*, the author Julia Alvarez narrates the story of a family: Carla, Sandra, Yolanda, Sofia, and their parents Laura and Carlos. This story took place in the Dominican Republic when it was ruled by a dictator called Trujillo. Carlos, the Garcia's girls' father was wealthy and well educated and this was the reason why he was wanted by the dictator. He had to escape with his family to the United States where the lives of the girls changed totally. The reason why they immigrated to the United States and how the girls were Americanized, what they have lost, and what they found is discussed in this book.

The Garcia de la Torre was a very well-known and wealthy family in the Dominican Republic. They lived in a compound where all the extended family lived. Living so close to each other enabled them to share their belongings with the rest of the family. For example, children were able to stay for meals at whatever table they were closest to; they went home just to take their bath and to go to bed. However, the Garcia de la Torre social relationships were totally different. They always maintained distance and cold relations with their maids, even though servants were treated with humanity and consideration. For example, the children were forbidden to go to the maids' bedrooms under any circumstances. On the other hand, there was also a big difference between men and women. The men were the ones to work, pay bills, etc. The women have to stay do housework and take care of the children. The women were seen as something inferior to men. Living in this kind of society, the young women were not allowed to go out without a chaperon.

In spite of the girls being so young when they got to the United States, the new culture and lifestyle was not difficult to influence and they adjusted quickly. The mother, Laura, began to speak to the girls in English making the girls forget their native language. For example, after many years in the United States, when Yolanda went to the Dominican Republic she did not know the meaning of some words in Spanish like "Antojos" and needed someone to translate it for her.

I think that the strongest of the four girls is Sofia because she had a strong will and she was very determined. The way she reacted showed us that even though she was raised with very strict parents, she always did what she wanted or planned. For example, when she stood her ground with her father when he found her love letters. I feel that the weakest of the four girls is Sandra. She was a very sensitive person and this characteristic made her weak. For example when she saw Mrs. Fanning kissing her father she was very hurt and hoped that she could forget what she saw.

This book, *How the Garcia Girls Lost Their Accents*, I did not like at all. The novel is easy to interpret, is written in simple language, but I did not like the structure of the book. It was not written in chronological order. It went back and forward. The book began with Yolanda being a middle-aged women and it ended with her being a child. I felt that the book was missing something and I think that the missing thing was it did not make the characters enjoyable. The book did not give me the thirst to continue reading to find out what was going to happen later to the characters.

Student Annotation/How the Garcia Girls Lost Their Accents

The book, *How the Garcia Girls Lost Their Accents*, by Julia Alvarez was not a wonderful book to read. The book talked about how the Garcia girls were caught between the old world, the Dominican, and the new world, America. Overall, the book was not a good book to read, but there were some good things about it too. Julia Alvarez used very simple language that made it easy to read. She also used proverbs that are very common among Dominican people. In addition, she reflected a good aspect of Dominican parents—they are very strict and concerned about family image and reputation. That is why the girls had to be chaperoned whenever they went some place. Another thing I did not like was the order of the stories—it did not make much sense. She started writing stories from 1989 then through 1956. Also, there were a couple of things she should have made clear about the Dominican Republic in order to make the reader better understand what was happening in the story. I am Dominican and many of the things she stated in the book I do not agree with, and are not true. She does not seem to have much knowledge of what she is writing about in her book. She needed to explain better the kind of government the Dominican Republic had at that time, and the type of president Trujillo was. For instance, in the chapter, "The Blood of the Conquistadors," she states that Trujillo, the president of the Dominican, did not like skilled workers. Trujillo liked skilled people, but these professionals either had to be under his control or be pushed out of the country. Definitely, this book I would not recommend anybody to read.

Axline, V. (1964). *Dibs in Search of Self*. New York: Ballantine Books.

Student Annotation: Dibs in Search of Self

Dibs is a true story about a five-year-old child in need of love. Dibs was the son of two worldly successful intellectuals. His father was a scientist and his mother was a doctor. Dibs was an unexpected surprise to these "intellectuals." So from infancy forward he had trouble fitting into their lives. They were very rich so Dibs had everything money could buy but love was not one of those things. Having achieved their worldly goal of success in their fields, they thought they had accomplished everything and so forgot their humanity and grew cold. Dibs was not shown love and he withdrew into a world of his own —not speaking, appearing not to gather knowledge yet gathering much more than was thought. Dibs, having been deprived by his parents of the natural love, affection, care that is shown to a child felt left out and unwanted. Because of this he did not have self-confidence—didn't even recognize himself as his own person always referring to himself as "you" rather than "I." He lived in his own world and hid from the facts of the real world, because his parents did not have the attachment and affection towards him which would enable them to be patient enough to guide him. He kept all inside because no one gave him the initiative to really express himself. He was unhappy but while he was keeping everything in, he was gathering a lot of knowledge. He did not talk and did not act his age, and so he appeared retarded. But his knowledge was above what is expected of a child his age. He just needed someone as patient and caring and real as Virginia Axline, the psychologist, who helped him open the locked doors. The beauty of this story is how a psychologist helps him come out of his shell and finds that he is a very unusual boy.

INTRODUCTION   xix

Student Annotation/Dibs in Search of Self

Dibs is a child who has many emotions locked inside of him. He is very unhappy and angry. These emotions have made him like this. It seems as if no one has ever given or shown him love or attention. He shows people, or rather, gives the impression that he is a "slow" child. But in reality, he is very, very smart. He is like a sponge, constantly absorbing information around him. Or more like a computer, he has all this knowledge inside, but only lets it out when he wants to (with the help of Virginia Axline). He has a sneaky way about finding out things. Although he gives the impression that he is unaware of what is going on around him, he really knows what is going on. I see his parents as two people who are more worried about what other people are thinking about them, instead of paying attention to Dibs. They are more worried about their lives, their jobs, lifestyle. They have no room for Dibs. These parents don't listen.

Virginia Axline, the psychologist, really amazes me. From what I have read, she is very patient. Even if she wants to say or do what she really feels, if it is for the benefit of Dibs, she will refrain from it. She takes her time with Dibs. She is very experience in the work that she does and does not get ahead of herself as most people in her profession would. Virginia Axline is rewarded by the way Dibs acts. I would say that she is comfortable with him and enjoys helping him and the progress he makes. I wish I knew someone like her. This was a very good book because it was the true life story of a troubled boy who overcame his problems.

Student Annotation/Dibs in Search of Self

The characteristics of Dibs makes this a very interesting story. He is a little boy, who has locked himself from any form of activities with other children. He is a little boy, very intelligent and aware of what is going on but just disguises himself from others. Dibs is also unique: the manner in which he does things, crawling around on the floor listening tentatively and learning. One can observe that he is a brilliant boy. Dibs feels left out, needs more love from his parents. He also needs attention—that is the reason why he locked himself away from everybody. His parents are to be blamed for his strange behavior; although they are quite intelligent and respected. They are intelligent and have good professions—his mother is a doctor and his father is a well-recognized scientist. When Dibs was born and they found out the child was a boy, they were disappointed. The mother seems to be a cold person, she neglects Dibs and is ashamed of him because she thinks he is mentally retarded. Virginia Axline, the psychologist, is an independent, intelligent person with a lot of patience. In her discussions with Dibs, she tries to make him feel independent and reliable. She also takes a lot of time with him to really find out why he is behaving in a strange manner.

Morrison, T. (1987). *Beloved*. New York: Alfred A. Knopf.

Student Annotation/Beloved

Beloved by Toni Morrison is a great book. Although the book takes place after slavery, it is really all about how slaves were treated and the effects of the slave experience on their lives when they were free. Throughout the novel, memories of the slave experience are always present in the minds of the characters and these memories actually affect their actions in the present. As they attempt to create a new life, the past shapes their behavior and the characters seem to be caught in a never-ending cycle of the horrible effects of slavery. *Beloved* really takes you on a journey with the characters to try to work out these horrible memories that hound them. How they do this is very weird because it involves a ghost. In this story, the main character, Sethe has unconditional love of a mother for her child so she kills her child in order for her not to go through all the hell of slavery. I loved the way Morrison used the ghost character Beloved to help the reader understand slavery. Beloved was a "ghost" and sometimes acted like a young girl and then sometimes like a little two-year-old child. Although *Beloved* was a big challenge for me, it is a book that I definitely highly recommend to my friends to read.

Student Annotation/Beloved

Beloved is a novel that consists of twenty-eight chapters and three parts. Each chapter is introduced without a title. In my opinion the good points of this book is that Toni Morrison lets you name your own title for the chapter. This is good because sometimes the chapter involves more than a title could indicate. *Beloved* was a very interesting novel for me because as I read many questions came into my mind to know what was going on, and to know what was going to happen next. Well, that made me more excited and with more intentions to finish reading the novel. As you read the chapters your questions were answered. Something that I had to keep in mind was that the novel, *Beloved*, was written with many flashbacks and at first, was difficult to follow and understand. Meanwhile, I knew I had to read carefully and imagine what was really going on in the novel. Some bad points of this novel was the ending because I expected the novel to end differently with the appearance of Halle even though he was crazy. I also expected Beloved to kill her mother, Sethe.

I really enjoyed this novel and I would recommend it to my friends and anybody. They will see that this novel is very special and enjoyable.

Student Annotation/Beloved

The novel *Beloved* by Toni Morrison is about a ghost who was killed by her mother Sethe because Sethe did not want her daugther, Beloved, to go through what Sethe went through as a slave. When Beloved died, her spirit did not. After a while, Beloved comes back in "human flesh" to be with her mother. I enjoyed reading this book so much that I wish they would make a movie out of this. This book had the present, past, and future all at once which made it confusing but yet exciting. Toni Morrison does not give her information right then and there, she give it little by little which makes it mysterious and I get curious so I keep turning pages and won't stop until I find out what I have to find out. This is what I love about this book. It never made me go to sleep, or get bored not even once. What made it interesting for me is that it was about a ghost and slavery which, in my case, I have never read those two combinations. I am planning to read all of Morrison's exciting books.

Morrison, T. (1973). *Sula*. New York: Penguin Books.

Student Annotation/Sula

Sula is about a young woman who seems to be living in her own little world. She does whatever pleases her. She doesn't mean any harm when she sleeps with a lot of men; she sleeps with husbands and the wives definitely do not like her. Other people in the town think she is evil. There's something interesting to Sula about love making, she is very curious and I think she is always looking for something. The person who seems to satisfy her curiosity is a man named Ajax. Ajax and Sula are a perfect match. Ajax was curious about Sula and Sula is also curious about him; this brought them together. I think she was looking for love from Ajax that she did not find in her mother. Actually, Sula's mother loved her; but she said she did not *like* Sula. To Sula, it didn't make a difference. All she wanted to do was to explore things. I think Sula found love in Ajax; she just did not want to admit it. When she prepared for Ajax, cleaning the house for him, these are signs of love.

Student Annotation/Sula

Sula is a novel about a woman who chooses to do what she wants to do when she wants to do it. She grows up in a small town and has a best friend, Nel, and

xxii   INTRODUCTION

they do everything together. But as Sula grows up the people are all afraid of her. When she is grown, she leaves town and when she returns the people are afraid of her and say she is evil. In the meantime, we are introduced to many other characters and it makes the story exciting to learn about everybody's life. Sula seems to be very confused about where she belongs in Medallion. She returns and acts just like a child would. Doing the first thing that comes to her mind without thinking about the consequences. She doe not realize how much she is hurting her best friend Nel. Everyone she has come into contact with, she has hurt or used them in a terrible way. She hurt Eva, her grandmother, by disrespecting her and locking her up. She hurts Nel by sleeping with her husband, and she just wanted to use Jude by sleeping with him and leaving him. Sula's mother never showed or expressed any kind of affection for Sula and I think this was a major reason why Sula came on the way she did. When she finally found someone who she could talk to as well as love, and receive love in return, the person left her. Sula was hurt by this but at least she lived long enough to know love expressed and shown.

Student Annotation/Sula

Sula is about the relations with people in a small town where she grows up. Sula is a very complicated person. She does not seem to know what she wants. Sula had a best friend Nel and even though they were always with each other, their relationship was based on need. But Sula did some mean things to Nel. They needed each other for companionship and love because of the lack of maternal love. The strengths of their relationship was based on their private secret and Nel's ability to think for Sula. Nel trusted Sula until Sula slept with her husband. Sula's relationships with other characters in the story are just as complicated. There are all sorts of accounts of her not getting along with her mother, grandmother, or any of the townspeople. I liked this story very much but it was hard to like Sula because she was only for herself.

Tan, A. (1990). *The Joy Luck Club*. New York: Ballantine Books.

Student Annotation/The Joy Luck Club

The Joy Luck Club is a novel about the relationship between four mothers and four daughters. The story tells of each mother's life in China and then life in the United States with their daughters. The daughters and mothers always seem to have a lot of problems with each other. Some of the problems were because the mother wanted things for their daughters but the daughters just wanted to be Americans. Each chapter focused on the relationship of a mother and daughter. In the chapter, *Rules of the Game*, Waverly Young was very good at playing chess but she resented her mother taking credit for what she did. In the story, *Two Kinds*, the daughter Jing Mei had a problem with her mother because her mother wanted her to be a good piano player and Jing Mei resented this. She obeyed her mother because it was unthinkable for her to be disobedient. Lena St. Clair also had problems with her mother because her father was Irish and could not speak Chinese so Lena had to be the translator for her father and mother. Lena would translate what they said but would sometimes lie to keep peace between her parents. Lena realized that her mother was crazy and suffered a lot. The last daughter, Rose Hsu Jordan was not able to make decisions and she always had problems with her mother over this. Many of the problems that mothers and daughters had, came from what the mothers wanted for the daughters and what the daughters wanted for themselves. I really enjoyed this book but had difficulty remembering the names of all the characters.

Student Annotation/ The Joy Luck Club

The Joy Luck Club is about immigrant Chinese families and their daughters born in America. The mothers try to pass on Chinese traditions by telling their daughters stories and explain life's purpose. All the mothers and daughters had some kind of problem and most of the problems were because the mothers were traditional and their daughters were American. Lena St. Clair grew up in a a household where her mother and father could not communicate because the father was Irish. And Lena finds it difficult to communicate with her mother. Waverly Jong's problem is that she always wants to do things her own way and is constantly angry with her mother. I think she is just selfish. Rose Hsu Jordan is a weak person and cannot make decisions for herself. Her mother is trying to teach her how to make her own decisions. Jing Mei Woo could never understand her mother's advice. In the end, the mothers are able to get through to the daughers and the problems are solved. I liked this novel because the problems are things that happen in any family. But there were a lot of Chinese names to learn.

Summary Annotation/The Joy Luck Club

I loved reading all of these stories in *The Joy Luck Club*. The four mothers tell their daughters stories to warn them of dangers and teach their daughters the Chinese traditions. The daughters personalities were shaped by the way the mothers taught them. The mothers were always trying to help the daughters but sometimes the daughters did not understand. For example, one daughter,

Rose, found it difficult to speak up for herself and had low-self esteem. She would listen to everybody but her own heart. Her mother, An-Mei, taught Rose to be strong and to speak up for herself. Waverly Jong's mother, Lindo, taught her to choose and be the best in everything in life and that is exactly what Waverly grew up to be successful. Jing-Mei did not have any confidence in her abilities and her expectations were low. I think her mother was too hard on her always trying to get Jing-Mei to do things. The last daughter, Lena, allowed her husband to take advantage of her. She followed in her mother's footsteps because her father took advantage of her mother. Her mother helps her see that she is in a bad marriage and Lena finally gets a divorce. In the end the mothers helped the daughters overcome their problems. I was happy with these stories because I could see my family in some of the stories.

Chapter One

Your Language, Culture, Knowledge, and Experience

> To speak, means above all to assume a culture, to support the weight of a civilization, every dialect is a way of thinking.
> —Franz Fannon

Lesson 1: Your Personal Matrix

The emphasis in this book is unique, as it requires that, as you read, you recognize the specific strengths you bring to the reading experience. That is, your cultural background, ethnicity, traditions, experience, and prior knowledge all form your *Personal Matrix* and the point from which you are guided to interpret and construct meaning from text. In addition, your emotional responses to text will also add to how you understand information, construct meaning, and each are discussed in this Chapter. For example, you bring a wealth of knowledge and experiences from your cultural background, which includes its traditions, values, and beliefs. You may also relate to a specific linguistic group, i.e., your primary language or regional dialect that has unique expressions and customs of communicating. In addition, your prior knowledge is formed by your interaction within your community, formal schooling, from discussions on current events, reading newspapers, and other media outlets such as the Internet. Thus, who you are, all that you have observed, studied, learned, or experienced add to your Personal Matrix. Your Personal Matrix influences your perceptions and judgments of events, and all can be a source of strength for you to become an efficient reader. In other words, you come to any text with a great deal of personal and valuable knowledge and experience that influences how you interpret your readings. You need to be aware of how to use your own Personal Matrix to your advantage in interpreting your readings.

Let's examine what a Personal Matrix means by looking at an obvious example of our use of language. Depending on which area of the country you are from or what part of the world you are from, you have a regional dialect that is unique to that region of the country or world. To illustrate this further, consider how you use language within the context of your cultural group. You have knowledge of the dialect and nuances of the region in which you reside, and this enables you to use language and communicate with ease. You engage in a conversation with someone, you listen to the words he or she says but you also pay close attention to nonverbal clues such as gestures. These clues are unique to your tradition or culture. For example, during a conversation, the raising an eyebrow might indicate surprise, skepticism, or disapproval. An upturned lip may indicate disgust or may signal a question about what is stated. Shifting from one foot to another may indicate boredom, or it may indicate impatience with the speaker; looking someone straight in the eyes as they speak may indicate attentiveness or in another cultural context it may indicate disrespect; nodding one's head throughout the conversation may indicate agreement or in another cultural context impatience; and so on. All of these are nonverbal gestures which help to convey the "tone of voice" and intent of the speaker and listener giving additional meaning to the conversation. The conversation is interactive and both the speaker and the listener influence the interpretations of the conversation. This means that your worldview, your Personal Matrix, permits you to be aware of the nuances and subtleties of the language in context and enables you to communicate with others. If you miss these nonverbal clues you may not completely understand important aspects of the conversation. The interaction is similar between an author and reader. In the same manner, an efficient reader must also recognize nuances of "text language" and its implied meaning. Therefore, think of your Personal Matrix as an added strength you bring to the reading experience which influences the way you interpret any text.

As readers enter a "dialogue" with an author, very often you find that your own experiences confirm what you have read. Here is where your Personal Matrix is invaluable. On the other hand, if the information in the text differs from your experiences, you may have difficulty interpreting the content. The reader need not be stuck, for the greatest power readers have is their own imagination and ingenuity. And both are plugged into your Personal Matrix. What to do then? You can ask creative questions which can liberate a reader, for example, "What if . . . ?" and suspend judgment. You then begin to develop alternative ways to help you construct meaning. Alternative ways of thinking are discussed in detail in Chapter Three.

One's Personal Matrix, then, is where efficient readers begin to understand an author's tone of voice and intent and shades of meaning of author's language. Understanding the author's language, going beyond the stated meaning of the text, will enable you to draw the right inferences for a comprehensive interpretation of what you read. Thus, efficient readers are not only analytical and critical about the text; efficient readers automatically engage their Personal Matrix and their imagination as they actively interact with text.

How Does My Personal Matrix Function With Reading?

To illustrate the role of your Personal Matrix in constructing meaning, read the following excerpt from *The Joy Luck Club* by Amy Tan in which she discusses how family "stories" reinforce family values. As you read this passage keep in mind the following questions:

- What aspects of this event can you relate to your culture and traditions?
- What are some of your family "stories" which help to teach, discipline, warn, and pass on family values?
- If there were a member of your family whom everyone believed disgraced the family, how is it handled?
- How are these stories similar to ones in your family?
- How are they different?
- What seems to be some of the expectations for this family?
- In a situation in your family similar to the one described, what would the expectations in your family?
- What are the consequences in your family if these expectations are not met?

Remember, reading is a focused dialogue with the author in which you, as reader, are always asking questions. Your questions help you anticipate events, predict outcomes, and follow the line of the story. Read the passage with these questions in mind and draw upon your Personal Matrix to answer the questions.

Passage 1:

1. When I was a young girl in China, my grandmother told me my mother was a ghost. This did not mean my mother was dead. In those days, a ghost was anything we were forbidden to talk about. So I knew Popo wanted me to forget my mother on purpose, and this is how I came to remember nothing of her. The life that I knew began in the large house in Ningpo with the cold hallways and tall stairs. This was my uncle and auntie's family house, where I lived with Popo and my little brother.

2. But I often heard stories of a ghost who tried to take children away, especially strong-willed little girls who were disobedient. Many times Popo said aloud to all who could hear that my brother and I had fallen out of the bowels of a stupid goose, two eggs that nobody wanted, not even good enough over rice porridge. She said this so that the ghosts would not steal us away. So you see, to Popo we were also very precious.

3. All my life, Popo scared me. I became even more scared when she grew sick. This was in 1923, when I was nine years old. Popo had swollen up like an overripe squash, so full her flesh had gone soft and rotten with a bad smell. She would call me into her room with the terrible stink and tell me stories. "An-Mei," she said, calling me by my school name. "Listen carefully." She told me stories I could not understand.

4. One was about a greedy girl whose belly grew fatter and fatter. This girl poisoned herself after refusing to say whose child she carried. When the monks cut open her body, they found inside a large white winter melon.

5. "If you are greedy, what is inside you is what makes you always hungry," said Popo.

6. Another time, Popo told me about a girl who refused to listen to her elders. One day this bad girl shook her head so vigorously to refuse her auntie's simple request that a little white ball fell from her ear and out poured all her brains, as clear as chicken broth.

7. "Your own thoughts are so busy swimming inside that everything else gets pushed out," Popo told me. Right before Popo became so sick she could no longer speak, she pulled me close and talked to me about my mother. "Never say her name," she warned. "To say her name is to spit on your father's grave." *The Joy Luck Club: "An-Mei Hsu: Scar"* Vintage Books, 1991 p. 33–34

The questions should have been helpful to you to understand this passage. What other questions came to you as you read this passage? We ask questions to anticipate events and predict outcomes. Now consider your Personal Matrix to construct meaning. Look at two of the family "stories" in the above passage which warn and discipline; for example:

- Forbidden to speak of a disgraced family member
- Warning that disobedient children could be stolen

Under similar circumstances, in you tradition, what "family stories" would have been used to warn and discipline? What action would be taken if someone disgraced the family? For disobedience?

If asking questions is insufficient to clarify issues, you might draw a diagram to help you understand the dynamics of events. While this method might take some time, it will enable you to understand a text's meaning. In this case, you could compare your personal experiences with those in the passage.

COMPARE AND CONTRAST

Your Traditions	Joy Luck Club's Traditions

Under "Your Traditions," list examples of your family traditions that are different from the traditions described in *The Joy luck Club*, and list these traditions described. Are there common "elements" which seem to reflect both cultural experiences? Your Personal Matrix will help you understand others.

Doing a simple analysis of this kind enables you to understand the dynamics and interaction of the characters. The characters have their own lives that the author wants you to see and experience. It permits you to comfortably step into another worldview and easily navigate the story's terrain. As you compare and contrast the similarities and differences between your tradition and those discussed, the diagram provides an invaluable focal point to construct meaning of the text. If events contradict your experiences, the diagram provides background information to ask the critical questions, broaden your knowledge base from this new information, and seek alternative means of thinking about the topic. Always begin with your Personal Matrix to understand others point of view.

Lesson 2: Interactive Readers

Efficient readers are fundamentally interactive readers. As stated earlier, as in any conversation, interactive readers are engaged in a focused dialogue with the author, i.e., the text is a written conversation, which is cause for excitement since the author must confront your Personal Matrix if he or she wishes to make his or her message understood. Interactive reading enables you to experience and comprehend text in ways you may not have done so before;

you reflect, respond, and react to the text—responding in writing, asking questions, anticipating events, and being fully engaged as you read. This also means assessing your reading behavior, monitoring your thinking and emotional responses. The reading process then becomes transformative: it adds to your knowledge base, expands your existing Personal Matrix, changes how you think, and broadens your perspective and view of the world.

Reading Assessments

We can assess our reading skills whenever we read and are particularly sensitive to this when we are formally tested, e.g., taking class exams, high school regents exams, SAT, GED, and so on. However, it is our personal assessments as we read which are most helpful and usually lead us to want to improve our skills and take steps to become efficient readers. Read the following student assessments regarding their reading experiences.

> I enjoy reading because of its imagery. Using your imagination is very important that is why I like to read poetry and drama. I read newspapers and magazines occasionally.

> I enjoy reading any type of books. If I have to read long passages, it is harder for me to understand what I read and to form it into my own words or to write an essay about that subject. While reading out loud to my children, I understand what I read better.

Both students enjoy reading. The first student simply identifies the types of reading she enjoys but does not identify any particular area of concern. The second student's assessment clearly indicates that she is aware of the challenges she is confronted with when she reads. Many students have difficulty reading long passages, particularly expository text. In this Chapter, we address these concerns. You are guided through a series of lessons to learn how to prepare and preview before reading, and structure your reading in manageable sections to gain the most from your reading experience. In addition, strategies are also suggested to help you write expanded essays.

Other students indicate that they also enjoy reading but have different concerns:

> During my early upbringing, I was never really encouraged to read, but at a later stage, about the age of eleven, I became interested in reading, which was a difficult period for me being that I was never your typical reader.

> My experience with reading has been much like a roller coaster. I am not considered your everyday reader, but I Do read on occasion. I mainly like to read topics that have a direct relation to me. For example, I like to read books on great black forefathers. I seldom read books that don't relate to my existence. Take

for example I am presently reading a book by Alex Haley on the life of the late Malcolm X.

Reading and me don't mix. My main problem in reading is my listening and comprehension skills. As I read, I find I have to read the passage twice or even three times before I get a good understanding of what I read.

I enjoy reading interesting topics such as sports, weather, or comedy. If the topic is boring I will eventually lose interest and towards the middle of the story stop reading. In high school I read several shakesphere plays but I wasn't interested in shakesphere at the time. I failed most of the tests because I hardly read the books.

The above students were very good at assessing their difficulties during the reading process: vocabulary, lack of interest, and difficulty in comprehending. These students' assessments also bring out three very important aspects of an efficient reader: what you bring to the reading experience is important, how you relate to the reading, and self-motivation—all are necessary to attain your goal to become an efficient reader. These assessments also help to explain how one's Personal Matrix, i.e., prior knowledge, interest, self-motivation, and the like, are all necessary to attain your goal. Finally, in the following assessments, students emphasize a love of reading but reveal that vocabulary is difficult because English is their second language.

I enjoy reading. I like to read books and I have not had any reading classes but I have had a class in English-as-a-Second Language. Now I read a book called *Die for Me*. This is a very interesting book about high schools students. One of them was killed and they tried to find out who did it. When I read this book I don't have any problem in understanding but sometimes it is very difficult for me to read because I don't have enough vocabulary. So for me vocabulary is the biggest problem.

I enjoy reading because I like to do it. I like to spend many hours reading. I'm living in America only one year and I have not read too many books here. But in my life, I've read many Russian books. Best of all I like classical books and authors such as Chekhov and Tolstoy. My favorite book is *War and Peace* by Tolstoy. This book is about war and love and I liked this book.

Reading has played a great part in my life, because I never used to read a lot until I came to the United States. In Jamaica we had books in school but I wasn't a good reader, so now I am trying to read everything to make up what I didn't fulfill in my early days.

This is my second time that I am taking the reading class. I read when professors assign the reading assignments. I rarely read the newspaper or magazines. I usually read in Chinese, my native language.

This final assessment is included as an example of a student who, after taking my reading course, gained confidence and feels she is now an efficient reader.

> I have taken two reading courses to help build my vocabulary. I like reading because it expands my knowledge: things that I am ignorant about are cleared up when I read and replaced with answers. Reading also helps me to think critically about the topic I am reading so that I will have informed opinions to develop arguments. I read the newspaper to have some knowledge of what is going on around me. Books have taught me about the morals of characters and the struggles they have gone through to achieve the things they want.

These student assessments clearly indicate that they enjoy reading but find it a struggle because of the areas in which they are having difficulty. They have clearly identified what makes reading enjoyable, are willing to read a variety of books when it is interesting, and enjoy reading books to which they can relate to incorporate their prior knowledge. They assess their needs to be self-motivation, vocabulary building, writing about reading, and expanding their ideas. Reading aloud was also helpful for comprehension. All the concerns expressed in the students assessments are addressed throughout *Reading Between the Lines*. In the above discussion on Personal Matrix, the importance of beginning with oneself was stressed; thus the first step is to assess your reading experience as outlined below.

Learning Styles

Thus far, we have defined an efficient reader as one who understands that one's Personal Matrix is a critical component in constructing meaning and interpreting readings. And as you actively interact with text, monitoring your thinking and emotional responses, you construct an in-depth analysis of your readings. Another characteristic of an efficient reader is to know "how" you learn best; that is, your learning style. Your learning style is your unique way of processing information in order to construct meaning and attain knowledge. There are many different characteristics to describe and define learning styles; therefore how your learning style is defined will depend upon which test you take, what measures have been identified on a particular test. For example, some tests focus on the best environment for the learner, i.e., morning, evening, bright light, soft light, air quality, and so on. Other tests may identify personal characteristics. For example, learning styles tests may determine whether you are an independent learner or dependent learner; others may identify whether you prefer competitive situations or cooperative learning. Or you may take a test which indicates you prefer organizing material using linear patterns or you may prefer nonlinear patterns—as discussed in Chapter Three.

Then there are learning style tests which measure whether you prefer hands-on learning, or visuals or auditory means. The characteristics measured can be rather broad. However, an exhaustive discussion on learning styles is not the purpose here. The purpose here is for you to become aware of particular ways in which you prefer to process information and acquire knowledge. Since *Reading Between the Lines* requires that you try alternative ways of thinking and approaches to your reading experience, it is most important that you remain flexible: monitor the environmental factors which help you to study, for example, the time of day you prefer. Incorporate the reading strategies outlined in the chapters applying them as suggested, combining the strategies with ones you currently use, or you may adapt the strategies to accommodate your preferred way of learning. Ultimately, you will find that the strategies outlined in this Handbook are techniques to your goal—to become a more efficient reader.

Self-Motivation

What really is self-motivation? What kinds of skills do self-motivated people have? We generally associate self-motivation to areas such as business and sports but it is equally as important in the area of reading. An important characteristic of an efficient reader is to be self-motivated, that is, having a strong will to win, persistent in your efforts, and flexible to alter your present course and try new approaches to reading. It means being open minded, willing to meet new challenges knowing you can win. It is putting new learning into action, in this case putting the reading strategies to the test, realizing that mistakes are only stepping stones on your way to achieve your goal. To increase your knowledge and learning and become an efficient reader, it begins with completing what you start, and applying the suggested reading strategies to your authentic reading experiences. In addition, it is being motivated to read as often as possible…any material, whatever interests you. Moreover, efficient readers are highly motivated because they set a purpose for reading. That is, whether it is to gain additional information about a topic, to acquire new knowledge, or simply for enjoyment or gain additional insights. The fact that you are reading *Reading Between the Lines* indicates that you are self-motivated. The important point is that you maintain your self-motivation to achieve your goal. Thus, it is important that for whatever material you read, set a purpose for reading the material. Setting a purpose for reading means to know why you are reading. Setting a purpose for reading is discussed at length under Lesson 3: Previewing Text. But begin this process now with a general purpose for reading and completing *Reading Between the Lines*. Before conducting any of the exercises, test the validity of the reading strategies, ask, *"Does this read-*

ing strategy really work?" Then apply the strategy to the exercises and to the extended text in Chapter Six, Reading Selections, and to all other materials you may be reading.

Since you have chosen this Handbook to help you read more efficiently, it is safe to assume that one characteristic you clearly express is that of an independent learner. This would suggest that you direct your learning without immediate outside rewards or feedback from others. On the other hand, your feedback from the strategies in *Reading Between the Line* will be immediate: as you apply the reading strategies you will see the difference in how you interpret readings and the expansive way in which you write. Reading strategies suggested in this Handbook can be practiced as suggested or easily modified to accommodate your particular learning style. Maintain a degree of flexibility in adapting techniques to your particular learning style. Therefore, the key is to remain flexible and get to know your comfort zone and how you can incorporate new ways of knowing and thinking to get the results you want. In this way, identifying your personal learning style may be helpful—but only as a point of reference to be aware of what you have been doing as you seek ways to make changes. If you wish to obtain a more definitive evaluation of your learning style, self-scoring learning style tests may be found on the Internet.

Assess Your Reading Experience

Take ten or fifteen minutes to write a paragraph to reflect and assess your own reading experience. Think about how you learned how to read, how you approach reading assignments in school, the kind of material you read on your own and how you feel about reading in general. Consider the following points as well: your experiences with reading, in general how you respond to textbook material, your emotional responses when reading imaginative literature—the kind of material which motivates you—your approach to reading, i.e., learning style, and if you find the act of reading enjoyable or stressful. This assessment is important to help you identify your particular strengths and areas you need to change or enhance to become a more efficient reader.

Monitoring Your Emotional Responses to Text

In addition to your Personal Matrix, an awareness of your emotional reactions to reading material is critical. Why are emotional reactions so important? Authors use language to convey a specific "tone"—how the writing sounds to you and how it makes you feel—so that we might respond in a particular way. The tone of voice of the writing can convey feelings corresponding to serious, critical, funny, sad, shock, excitement, and the like. This is not unusual because tone of voice influences our perceptions and how we relate to others daily. Your reactions will help you construct meaning. In fact, contrary to what you may have been taught, you must be able to trust your feelings to go beyond the stated meaning of a text. The tone of voice of the text appeals to your senses providing clues to recognize the author's intent.

Reading is a dynamic process; it exposes you to new ideas, expands your Personal Matrix and provides provocative ideas to consider and decide whether this is something you value. Thus, emotional responses are fundamental to your interpretations. Emotional responses sensitize the reader to the message of the author to construct a comprehensive, aware interpretation. It is the readers' awareness, empathy, and responses toward characters, events, conditions, issues, etc., that enables you to do so.

The following chart illustrates elements of emotional responses and corresponding strategic questions readers should keep in mind to monitor your emotional responses to the text. When you ask these questions, you are monitoring your reactions to the language of the text.

ELEMENTS OF EMOTIONAL RESPONSES AND READING STRATEGIES

Identifying Your Emotional Responses	Sample Strategic Questions to Help Monitor Your Emotional Responses to Text
Recognizing your emotional responses as it happens	How does this writing make me feel? What does it remind me about? How does it relate to my Personal Matrix?
Handle your responses appropriately; become keenly aware of how language affects you	How is this related to my experiences? How are my responses related to the topic? What words or phrases in this text are causing me to feel this way? What is this leading me to believe?
Empathize with others helps to build your awareness and response to text	How is the character responding or acting to the events, issues, etc. What events are causing the character to respond in this way? How would I respond to these events or issues, etc.?

Monitoring Your Thinking

As you monitor your emotional reactions, you should also be aware of what you are "*thinking*." The process of monitoring your thinking is called *metacog-*

nition. I know, sounds like a roadblock, but simply put it is the process of being aware of your thinking. Being aware of our thinking and our emotional responses is what efficient readers do automatically. Both these processes are of equal importance. The diagram below illustrates how monitoring our thinking and our emotional reactions influence our interpretations in constructing meaning.

METACOGNITION	+	EMOTIONAL RESPONSES	=	INTERPRETATION
What does the author state?	→	How does it make me feel?	→	Now, what do I believe?
What does it mean?	→	How do I feel?.	→	Why? Etc.

How Can We Monitor Our Thinking and Emotional Responses?

To demonstrate how you can learn to monitor your thinking and emotional reactions to text, let's begin with a music exercise. First, read over the questions listed below, then listen to a music selection and as you listen to the selection, answer the questions.

Exercise A: Music Selection Questions

1. As you listen to your selection, jot down words or phrases to describe how the music makes you feel.
2. After listening, use your notes to write a paragraph to describe the feelings you connected to the musical selection. Be as descriptive as possible and include the following points:
   • It made me feel _____
   • It reminds me of _____
   • These pictures came to mind as I listened _____
   • I like it because _____
   • I did not like it because _____
   • I was able to relate this music to my following experiences _____
   • My thoughts were on _____

Suggestions for Music Selections

• Jazz
• Classical music (from any tradition)
• American Country/Western

- Hip Hop
- Folk music (from any tradition)
- Your preference

In the same way that you were able to monitor your responses to the musical selection, you should also be aware of your thinking and emotional responses when reading. Now monitor your thinking and emotional responses to a reading passage.

Exercise A—Directions:

- Read the following passage to monitor your thinking and emotional responses to the text.
- Underline words or phrases to which you strongly react.
- Use the context of the passage to determine what the boldface words mean.

Before beginning this exercise, read the questions to monitor your thinking and emotional responses. You may also wish to read Lesson 3: Previewing Text for suggestions to use symbols and marginal notes. Then answer the questions and record your reactions to the passage.

Monitor Your Emotional Reactions to the Passage:

1. Describe your emotional responses to the words and phrases underlined.
2. How did this help you understand the tone of voice of the passage?

Monitor Your Thinking as You Read the Passage:

1. Use the clues in the text to define the boldface words and note your definition in the margin.
2. What are your thoughts as you read this passage?
3. How would you describe the person telling the story?
4. Write a paragraph to describe your emotional reactions to the passage.

Passage 2:

1. As the seasons passed, the young men of the village could not fail to see that Blue Bird was maturing and that her growing beauty was remarkable. But this fact troubled her grandmother greatly, and she

felt the need of someone with whom to share the responsibility for the girl until she should be safely married. Knowing well how some reckless young men played at courtship, she feared for Blue Bird. She must be warned at once that many a girl had come to ruin by taking their smooth wooing seriously and the grandmother was the only one to tell her. "I shall have a talk with her tomorrow." But each day she put it off, dreading the ordeal. "I am too old for this; would that her mother were here," she said to herself. "Or perhaps I should simply give the girl away in marriage now, to some kind and able householder, to be a co-wife. Then she can be honorably married before any trouble can befall her. Yes, that would be best."

2. But just whom to give her to was a puzzle. And what wife would want her? Being co-wife was not necessarily bad, provided the man was kind. She had been a co-wife herself. But then, she was the wife's sister and therefore was well received. In fact, as she remembered now, it was that elder sister who had offered to take her into the family. Ah, but Blue Bird had no sister in this camp circle. A head wife might resent her. That too must be considered. Slowly and timidly the old woman turned the problem over in her mind many times. But she had not yet acted when Blue Bird said to her one day, "Grandmother, one of the young men at the courting place has been urging me to marry him. His name is Star Elk."

3. The old woman shook her head **emphatically**, "No! No! Not that one. It would be good for you to marry, grandchild. We are so alone and helpless without a man to provide for our home. But not that one. Only last night the women around the campfire were talking about him. 'He is no hunter,' they said. 'He takes no interest in anything. Always he has been headstrong and unfriendly, even as a boy,' they said. That is not the kind of man for you, grandchild."

4. "But I have told him I would marry him, Grandmother." The silence that followed was **ominous**. When the old woman again found her voice, she said, "Ah, if only you had told me he was courting you so I could have warned you, grandchild. Since you have promised already, there is nothing I can do. Once she gives it, an honorable Dakota woman does not break her word to a man. Those who make false promises are ever after derided. To give your word is to give yourself." With that she stumbled out of the little **tipi** and began to wail in a **quavering** voice that following **lament**: "Ah, my son! Ah, my daughter-in-law! You left me alone to struggle on. What can I do, frail and full of years as I am?" Far into the night she wailed.

5. Blue Bird's marriage was **inevitable** now. But even after **resigning** herself to it, the grandmother went about with a heavy heart. "If only I had had someone to help me arrange a suitable marriage for

her," she muttered to herself from time to time. That the girl might run off with Star Elk was a dreaded possibility, even while there was a feeble hope that perhaps the young man had been misrepresented as altogether undesirable. Perhaps he was not that bad after all, and perhaps he would soon do the honorable thing—marry the girl openly, with tribal approval.

6. The most glamorous kind of marriage was by purchase. A woman who married in that way was much respected, for it meant that she had kept herself so unattainable that the man, who wanted her at all costs, thought nothing of giving horses for her, even at the risk of her rejecting him publicly. "I do not aspire to that for my poor orphaned grandchild," the grandmother said. "All I ask is a valid marriage, and then I should die happy." He might come to live with them to take her to his people openly. Whichever way, it should be planned and aboveboard, and then Blue Bird would be respected." (Excerpt from "Blue Bird's Offering," Ella Cara Deloria in *Spider Woman's Granddaughters*, Paula Gunn Allen, ed., New York: Ballantine Books, 1990, pp.102–104)

Here is another brief exercise to read interactively. Read the following passage about marriage, make marginal notes, record meaning for vocabulary words, and describe your thinking and emotional responses to the text.

Passage 3:

1. This is how I became betrothed to Huang Taitai's son, who I later discovered was just a baby, one year younger that I. His name was Tyan-yu—tyan for "sky," because he was so important, and *yu*, meaning "leftovers," because when he was born his father was very sick and his family thought he might die. Tyan-yu would be the leftover of his father's spirit. But his father lived and his grandmother was scared the ghosts would turn their attention to this baby boy and take him instead. So they watched him carefully, made all his decisions, and he became very spoiled.

2. But even if I had known I was getting such a bad husband, I had no choice, now or later. That was how backward families in the country were. We were always the last to give up stupid old-fashioned customs. In other cities already, a man could choose his own wife, with his parents' permission of course. But we were told stories of sons who were so influenced by bad wives that they threw their old, crying parents out into the street. So Taiyuanese mothers continued to choose their daughters-in-law, ones who would raise proper sons, care for the

old people, and faithfully sweep the family burial grounds long after the old ladies had gone to their graves.
3. Because I was promised to the Huangs' son for marriage, my own family began treating me as if I belonged to somebody else. My mother would say to me when the rice bowl went up to my face too many times, "Look how much Huang Taitai's daughter can eat." My mother did not treat me this way because she didn't love me. She would say this biting back her tongue, so she wouldn't wish for something that was no longer hers.
4. I was actually a very obedient child, but sometimes I had a sour look on my face—only because I was hot or tired or very ill. This is when my mother would say, "Such an ugly face. The Huangs won't want you and our whole family will be disgraced." And I would cry more to make my face uglier.
5. "It's no use," my mother would say. "We have made a contract. It cannot be broken." And I would cry even harder. (Amy Tan "Lindo Jong: The Red Candle," in *The Joy Luck Club*. New York: Vintage Books, 1990, pp. 51–52)

Questions to Consider:

1. What were your thoughts about the mother?
2. What were your thoughts about the daughter?
3. Describe your emotional reactions regarding words or phrases you felt strongly about.
4. What was your overall emotional reaction to this passage?
5. What did this passage lead you to believe?
6. What else might this passage suggest?
7. Can you identify aspects of your Personal Matrix that helped you understand this passage?

Your Personal Matrix regarding family traditions and marriage will have a direct impact on your interpretation and evaluation about these passages. You may agree or disagree with the point of view expressed, but being open to the author's "voice" and awareness of your own Personal Matrix enables you to create a broader understanding of the topic and adding to what you already know. Consequently, you begin to think differently about a topic and perhaps even your own worldview changes. As you have seen, monitoring your thinking and emotional responses is important to understanding text. And this self-monitoring should become an automatic practice during your reading process.

Relaxation for Readers

Why relaxation techniques? A major consideration to become an efficient reader is to remain relaxed, flexible, and willing to change. Persistence, patience, and focused attention will definitely yield results. An efficient reader may at times find reading a challenge but can, at the same time, derive enjoyment and satisfaction. However, the reading experience should not be stressful: stress interferes with the reading process. Studies conducted indicate that anxiety interferes with the reading process and makes it difficulty to process information. And, readers who experience high levels of anxiety need much more time to construct meaning from text. In this Handbook we do not focus on these studies but will briefly describe how anxiety may interfere with the reading process. For example, readers experiencing high levels of anxiety need much more time to construct meaning from text. Overall, research indicates that efficient readers are less anxious readers:

- Perform better on reading tasks
- Spend less time processing information attaining a higher degree of comprehension
- Read more efficiently

Thus, if you are particularly anxious, you sabotage your ability to read efficiently. There are many different relaxation techniques to help you: biofeedback to monitor your bodily responses to stress, autogenic training to relax different parts of the body, guided imagery focusing on pleasant scenes to relax you, to name a few. Outlined here are two relaxation methods: a meditative technique and autosuggestion method to relax the body. I have used both these methods with my students with considerable success. My students found the techniques helpful and their reading skills improved as their level of anxiety decreased significantly. Below are suggestions to help decrease the level of anxiety you may experience to help keep focused.

An Autosuggestion Technique

In the autosuggestion technique you relax the entire body with the suggestions you give yourself. It is a simple technique that you may wish to practice alone or in conjunction with the relaxation technique described below. Very often after a long day, it is generally good to first relax the body, and then begin the relaxation technique described below. You may wish to tape record the process for daily use:

1. Sit in a comfortable position, place your feet flat on the floor, place your hands on your lap, and close your eyes. Begin by gently repeating the following steps silently to yourself. Take your time, repeat each step slowly and go on to the next step as you feel your body relax.
2. Bring your attention to your forehead and feel the tension melting away. I can feel the tension slowly melting away.
3. Now bring your attention to your neck and feel the tension melting away. There is no tension; my neck is completely relaxed.
4. Now bring your attention to your shoulders and feel the tension melting away. There is no tension; my shoulders are completely, totally relaxed.
5. Now bring your attention to your arms and feel the tension melting away. There is no tension; my arms are completely relaxed.
6. Now bring your attention to your hands and feel the tension melting away. There is no tension; my hands are completely relaxed.
7. Now bring your attention to your stomach and feel the tension melting away. There is no tension; my stomach is completely relaxed.
8. Now bring your attention to your thighs and feel the tension melting away; there is no tension, my thighs are completely relaxed.
9. Now bring your attention to your legs and ankles and feel the tension melting away. There is no tension; my legs and ankles are completely relaxed.
10. Now bring your attention to your feet and feel the tension melting away. There is no tension; my feet are completely relaxed.
11. I am now completely relaxed.
12. Wait for approximately one minute; slowly open your eyes.

A Relaxation Technique

The purpose of this technique is to help you relax, focus your attention on your reading to read more efficiently to gain a higher degree of comprehension. It is an adaptation of the Relaxation Response developed by Herbert Benson. It is best not to eat a heavy meal before you begin this technique.

1. Find a quiet place, wear comfortable clothing, and sit with your feet flat on the floor; no high heels.
2. Rest your hands comfortably on your lap.
3. Close your eyes and before beginning, wait for approximately one minute (do not count off the time).
4. Begin repeating "one" silently to yourself.

5. As you repeat the word, other thoughts will come to mind; when you realize you are thinking other thoughts, quietly go back to saying "one." Keep your eyes closed and repeat this for approximately 10 or 15 minutes.
6. If you open your eyes and have not completed the 10 or 15 minutes, close your eyes and continue to repeat "one" until you have completed the 10 or 15 minutes.
7. After approximately 10 or 15 minutes, stop repeating the word "one." Wait for approximately one minute then slowly open your eyes.
8. Practice this technique for 10–15 minutes once in the morning before starting your daily activities and 10–15 minutes in the evening before starting your evening activities—then go about your day relaxed ☺.

It is advisable that you do not try these techniques without the advice and consent of a physician.

Lesson 3: Previewing Text

Authors express their ideas through expository text and imaginative literature. Expository text includes informational material such as textbooks, academic journals, newspapers, magazines, and the like. Whereas imaginative literature involves creative writing, which may also inform the reader, and includes fiction, short stories, novels, plays, poetry. In both expository writing and imaginative literature, before we begin to read, we set a purpose for reading. We do this by *previewing* expository writing and *preparing* to read imaginative literature. Previewing is a way to get a general idea of the content, a quick view of how material is arranged by topic, and an opportunity to review study aids included in the text. All of these help set a purpose for reading. Preparing to read imaginative literature is a way to make predictions and anticipate events. First, we shall outline methods for previewing expository text which are based on the SQ3R method—and then look at ways to prepare to read imaginative literature.

Expository Text

Expository text is informational, and we read such material to learn about a new topic or gain additional information about a topic. Therefore, when we preview expository text, we set a purpose for reading, to become familiar with the material, and set a plan to begin reading. In a course, a textbook is chosen because it has been deemed to be the best to cover a particular subject, and includes topics necessary to learn the content for the course. For that reason, a considerable amount of time is given in choosing textbooks for use in a course. Hence, to understand the direction of the course instruction, previewing the textbook before reading gives you a general idea of what you can expect.

To preview a textbook, follow these steps:

1. Start with the title page, copyright date, table of contents, preface, and introduction to become familiar with the overall structure and topics covered. These are the pages students may generally skip. But reading these will provide you with the "map" for the book.
2. A quick preview of chapters to determine the layout of the chapters—the length, study aids, summary, review questions, and any references.
3. At the back of the book—for additional references, charts, index, glossary, appendices, websites, and other aids. This is particularly helpful when you have to follow up on a topic; these references are a good place to begin.

Textbook Chapters

An effective method for previewing text material is the SQ3R method—Survey, Question, Read, Recite/Write, Review. The following steps to preview chapters is an adaptation of this method. Begin your preview by quickly skimming the entire chapter to get a general idea of how the information is organized then follow the steps outlined below.

1. Read the title and introduction to the chapter that provides the focus, concepts, topics, and so on presented in the chapter.
2. Read all subheadings (boldfaced type); these are the key points and concepts to help you understand the direction and focus of the topic being covered.
3. Turn the subheadings into a question; questions help keep you focused on the topic.
4. As you read, note any additional questions you have.
5. Review study aids, graphs, charts, diagrams, etc.
6. At the end of the chapter read the summary and any review questions.
7. After previewing, for study reading, divide the chapter into manageable sections to read and review; the boldfaced subheadings are good points to divide your reading into segments.
8. Summarize each segment and key points in your own words and note any additional questions.

Essays

When you need current information on a topic you may use expository text such as journal articles, newspapers, research papers, monographs, or other types of manuscripts. Since the Internet has become a major avenue to review source materials, as with all sources, Internet materials should be carefully evaluated to determine the source and validity of the information. The following guidelines are recommended to preview articles and essays.

- Read the introduction and/or first paragraph.
- Read the first and second sentence of each paragraph; the topic of the paragraph may be here).
- Read the subheadings and formulate questions (see below). As you read, keep these questions in mind to prepare answers; if subheadings are not included use the first sentence of paragraphs to generate questions.
- Read the summary or the concluding paragraph.
- Note graphs, charts, diagrams, etc.
- After reading, write a summary of the article in your own words.

Marginal Notes

As you read, write notes in the margin of your book to note important points and these will serve as a study aid for review. If you are accustomed to using marginal notes, you have probably come up with notations that serve you well. You may also wish to flag the pages with post-its. However, if you are not accustomed to using marginal notes, here are some pointers to get started.

- As you read, use a highlighter to underline unfamiliar vocabulary, key terms, or phrases; flag important information with post-its.
- Write notations and questions in the margin: all of your notations will to be helpful when reviewing key terms and information.
- Write question marks, exclamation points, asterisk, to indicate key points for review or points you need further clarification.
- Record specific questions.
- Review these notes at the end of each chapter or segment.
- Be sure to write terms, definitions, and summaries in your own words.

Formulating Questions Before Reading

As we suggested under self-motivation, questions before you read are a good motivation. In the same way, in order to comprehend the author's point of view, as you read formulate questions in anticipation of the discussion and to follow the thinking of the author. The author provides the "road map," and the reader interprets and follows the direction of the author's thinking. Formulating questions before you begin to read enables you to look at options and recognize that there may be a number of positions to take or approaches to a topic to find solutions to problems. You involve your Personal Matrix, experiences to interpret what the author states is "true." Thus asking questions before we begin reading and continually asking questions as we read will help us interpret text. How can you formulate questions before you begin to read? Use the first two sentences of each paragraph or the subheadings. In my research with college students, formulating questions using subheadings has been very effective. Turning subtitles into questions keeps you focused on the topic and answering subtitle questions ensures that you focus on concepts the author has deemed important. For example, when students in my classes experience difficulty with key terms and concepts one method I suggest is to preview and turn subtitles into questions. In one class, they were unfamiliar with the terms as they were used in the text, and after developing questions the reading became accessible to them. That is, they were focused and reading with a purpose to answer specific questions, and questions helped keep them focused on the topic. Examples of the subtitle questions are listed in the table on the next page.

USING SUBTITLES TO FORMULATE QUESTIONS

*Subtitles	Student Questions
1. Developing the Vision to See Through the Cognitive Fog →	1. What is the Cognitive Fog?
2. Making New Forms of Human Being Possible →	2. What forms will it take?
3. Democratic Empowerment via Expansion of the Boundaries of Intelligence: Getting Smarter →	3. How can intelligence be expanded?
4. The Importance of Reading Intertextual Reading? →	4. What is meant by Intertextual Reading?
5. Eugenics, Evolution, and Deaf Education →	5. What is Eugenics? How is it related to Evolution and Deaf Education?

*From *Rethinking Intelligence*, J. L. Kincheloe et al. eds. (1999).

The questions you formulate may not be precisely on target. But formulating questions keeps you focused on the topic and you will be able to determine if the way you framed a question is relevant to the author's point of view. This is very helpful when reading expository text. Critical questions for expository text are:

- What does the author want me to believe and why?
- Why is this significant or important?
- Who benefits if readers believe this?

A Practice Preview

Preview the following excerpt, from *Disobedience as a Psychological and Moral Problem* by Erich Fromm (1981). Preview the passage and formulate questions. Begin your questions with the title, "What does it mean?" When you complete your preview, before reading the essay, you may wish to divide it into segments, e.g., read the first paragraph and write down what it means to you, then read the next two paragraphs, reread when necessary and record your understanding of each segment as you read. As you read, note your marginal notes. Write answers for the questions you formulated. Write down what you have learned during the preview. Read the passage to answer the questions you formulated.

Passage 4:

1. For centuries kings, priests, feudal lords, industrial bosses and parents have insisted that obedience is a virtue and that disobedience is a vice. In order to introduce another point of view, let us set against this position the following statement: *human history began with an act of disobedience, and it is not unlikely that it will be terminated by an act of obedience.*

2. Human history was ushered in by an act of disobedience according to the Hebrew and Greek myths. Adam and Eve, living in the Garden of Eden, were part of nature; they were in harmony with it, yet did not transcend it. They were changed when they disobeyed an order. By breaking the ties with earth and mother, by cutting the umbilical cord, man emerged from a pre-human harmony and was able to take the first step into independence and freedom. The act of disobedience set Adam and Eve free and opened their eyes. They recognized each other as strangers and the world outside them as strange and even hostile. Their act of disobedience broke the primary bond with nature and made them individuals. "Original sin," far from corrupting man, set him free; it was the beginning of history. Man had to leave the Garden of Eden in order to learn to rely on his own powers and to become fully human. . . .

3. Just as the Hebrew myth of Adam and Eve, so the Greek myth of Prometheus sees all of human civilization based on an act of disobedience. Prometheus, in stealing the fire from the gods, lays the foundation for the evolution of man. There would be no human history were it not for Prometheus' "crime." He, like Adam and Eve, is punished for his disobedience. But he does not repent and ask for forgiveness. On the contrary, he proudly says: "I would rather be chained to this rock than be the obedient servant of the gods."

4. Man has continued to evolve by acts of disobedience. Not only was his spiritual development possible only because there were men who dared to say no to the powers that be in the name of their conscience or their faith, but also his intellectual development was dependent on the capacity for being disobedient—disobedient to authorities who tried to muzzle new thoughts and to the authority of long-established opinions which declared a change to be nonsense.

5. If the capacity for disobedience constituted the beginning of human history, obedience might very well, as I have said, cause the end of human history. I am not speaking symbolically or poetically. There is the possibility, or even the probability, that the human race

will destroy civilization and even all life upon earth within the next five to ten years, there is no rationality or sense in it. But the fact is that, while we are living technically in the Atomic Age, the majority o men—including most of those who are in power—still live emotionally in the Stone Age; that while our mathematics, astronomy, and the natural sciences are of the twentieth century, most of our ideas about politics, the state, and society lag far behind the age of science. If mankind commits suicide it will be because people will obey those who command them to push the deadly buttons; because they will obey the archaic passions of fear, hate, and greed; because they will obey obsolete clichés of State sovereignty and national honor. The Soviet leaders talk much about revolutions, and we in the "free world" talk much about freedom. Yet they and we discourage disobedience—in the Soviet Union explicitly and by force, in the free world implicitly and by the more subtle methods of persuasion.

6. But I do not mean to say that all disobedience is a virtue and all obedience a vice. Such a view would ignore that dialectical relationship between obedience and disobedience. Whenever the principles which are obeyed and those which are disobeyed are irreconcilable, and of obedience to one principle is necessarily an act of disobedience to its counterpart, and vice versa. Antigone is the classic example of this dichotomy. By obeying the inhuman laws of the State, Antigone necessarily would disobey the laws of humanity. By obeying the latter, she must disobey the former. All martyrs of religious faiths, of freedom and of science have had to disobey those who wanted to muzzle them in order to obey their own consciences, the laws of humanity and of reason. If a man can only obey and not disobey, he is a slave; if he can only disobey and not obey, he is a rebel (not a revolutionary); he acts out of anger, disappointment, resentment, yet not in the name of a conviction or a principle.

7. However, in order to prevent a confusion of terms an important qualification must be made. Obedience to a person, institution or power (heteronomous obedience) is submission; it implies the abdication of my autonomy and the acceptance of a foreign will or judgment in place of my own. Obedience to my own reason or conviction (autonomous-obedience) is not an act of submission but one of affirmation. My conviction and my judgment, if authentically mine, are part of me. If I follow them rather than the judgment of others, I am being myself; hence the word obey can be applied only in a metaphorical sense and with a meaning which is fundamentally different from the one in the case of "heteronomous obedience." ("Disobedience

as a Psychological and Moral Problem" in *On Disobedience and Other Essays*, by Erich Fromm. New York: The Seabury Press, 1981, pp. 16–19.)

Imaginative Literature

Imaginative literature includes fiction—short stories, novels, plays, poetry, etc. Since imaginative literature is basically read for enjoyment, you allow your imagination to soar, you are open for surprises, are always emotionally involved to gain a better understanding of the human condition and suspend your idea of reality to become fully engaged. It engages our intellect but strongly appeals to our feelings to be open and accepting of what the author suggests and states as "true." That is, in some cases, we must suspend our notions of reality so that we can enjoy the story; at other times, we rely on our personal experiences and our ability to make judgments. The judgments are based on the "reality" within the context of the story; thus, given what the author has constructed, you determine what is suitable. When we watch movies we do this automatically; it requires us to suspend our ideas of reality and make judgments according to the setting and plot the movie defines. It is the same when we read imaginative literature. Whatever the case may be, we are always involved emotionally: we become familiar and at home with the characters, we follow what they are thinking, what they do and say, and how they react to other characters. We know when there is a contradiction between what a character is thinking and the actions she or he takes. We read actively and become emerged in the story. Therefore, instead of previewing, efficient readers try to anticipate events and make predictions.

General Guidelines

General guidelines to help us enjoy and interpret imaginative literature begin by answering the basic who, what, when, where, how questions. To get a clear understanding and enjoy imaginative literature it is also important to identify key story components which appear in fiction.

Key Story Components

- Characters—people, animals, or objects with specific roles in the story; is there one main character or several characters of equal importance?
- Background and Setting—the time, place, background information, situation, conditions, and circumstances in which the story takes place

- Tone of voice—the emotional feeling created by what the characters, think, do, and say. Detailed descriptions of events, situations, and setting will also help to create the tone of voice of the story.
- Plot—events which unfold giving the story its direction
- Theme—the main point of the story or chapter. In complex story plots, there may be more than one theme in a chapter.
- Conflict—the problem, difficulty, predicament, or dilemmas with which characters are confronted and try to solve
- Climax—turning point of the problem, conflicts
- Conclusions—how characters handle problems and solve difficulties with which they are confronted

Asking Questions:

As we read, we make predictions and anticipate events, and ask questions. For example, if a character does something unexpected: "Why is this character doing this?" "Why did he leave the lid off?" etc. We continue to ask questions following the course of events, e.g., "I think this character is going to fool the others, he is not doing what he is saying." Or "He is definitely going to get caught because he left too many clues."

- How are the characters interacting with each other? What is the relationship between the characters?
- What are the characters thinking, saying, and doing? Are their actions/behaviors consistent with their thinking? If not,
- What is the author suggesting by the contradictions characters face between what they think and what they do?
- In what ways have your experiences, your Personal Matrix, helped you understand or believe this story?

Read the questions students formulated as they read the first chapter in *The Joy Luck Club:* Suyuan Woo tells her daughter, Jing-Mei, different versions of a story of how she lost her babies when she fled China during the Japanese invasion. But her daughter is never sure what the stories mean or if they are true. Students wrote the following questions in anticipation of what would be revealed and to try and make sense of what was happening in the story.

Questions:

Student #1: Why does Suyuan always change the end of the stories about the war and her two lost daughters?

Student #2: What happened to the babies when the mother was fleeing Kweilin?

At this point the readers were not able to determine why Suyuan continued to change her story about her lost daughters. Questions such as these are a natural outcome of following events in the story. As these students continue to read they discover the reason for the seemingly distortion of the same story which was clearly a painful event in the life of the mother. Efficient readers ask questions as they read in anticipation of events and for clarification. Questions keep us interested, focused, and help to anticipate events. Therefore, instead of previewing, prepare to read imaginative literature by keeping questions in mind to anticipate events and make predictions. The trick is to continue to ask questions as you read.

Read the following excerpt from *Sula* by Toni Morrison. Monitor your thinking and emotional responses and note the rich figurative language Morrison employs to enliven the events in this story. Make notes in the margin and underline words and phrases which indicate figurative language. After reading, answer the who, what, where, when, and how questions. Write your questions and comments and reread the passage to clarify points. A sample of students' questions appear at the end of this passage.

Passage 5:

1. So late one night in 1921, Eva got up from her bed and put on her clothes. Hoisting herself up on her crutches, she was amazed to find that she could still manage them, although the pain in her armpits was severe. She practiced a few steps around the room, and then opened the door. Slowly, she manipulated herself down the long flights of stairs, two crutches under her left arm, the right hand grasping the banister. The sound of her foot booming in comparison to the delicate pat of the crutch tip. On each landing she stopped for breath. Annoyed at her physical condition, she closed her eyes and removed the crutches from under her arms to relieve the unaccustomed pressure. At the foot of the stairs she redistributed her weight between the crutches and swooped on through the front room, to the dining room, to the kitchen, swinging and swooping like a giant hereon, so graceful sailing about in its own habitat but awkward and comical when it folded its wings and tried to walk. With a swing and a swoop she arrived at Plum's door and pushed it open with the tip of one crutch. He was lying in bed barely visible in the light coming from a single bulb. Eva swung over to the bed and propped her crutches at its foot.

She sat down and gathered Plum into her arms. He woke, but only slightly.

2. "Hey, man. Hey. You holdin' me, Mamma?" His voice was drowsy and amused. He chuckled as though he had heard some private joke. Eva held him closer and began to rock. Back and forth she rocked him, her eyes wandering around his room. There in the corner was a half-eaten store-bought cherry pie. Balled-up candy wrappers and empty pop bottles peeped from under the dresser. On the floor by her foot was a glass of strawberry crush and a Liberty magazine. Rocking, rocking, listening to Plum's occasional chuckles, Eva let her memory spin, loop and fall. Plum in the tub that time as she leaned over him. He reached up and dripped water into her bosom and laughed. She was angry, but not too, and laughed with him.

3. Eva lifted her tongue to the edge of her lip to stop the tears from running into her mouth. Rocking, rocking. Later she laid him down and looked at him a long time. Suddenly she was thirsty and reached for the glass of strawberry crush. She put it to her lips and discovered it was blood-tainted water and threw it to the floor. Plum woke up and said, "Hey, Mamma, whyn't you go on back to bed? I'm all right. Didn't I tell you? I'm all right. Go on, now."

4. "I'm going, Plum," she said. She shifted her weight and pulled her crutches toward her. Swinging and swooping, she left his room. She dragged herself to the kitchen and made grating noises.

5. Plum on the rim of a warm light sleep was still chuckling. Mamma. She sure was somethin'. He felt twilight. Now there seemed to be some kind of wet light traveling over his legs and stomach with a deeply attractive smell. It wound itself—this wet light—all about him, splashing and running into his skin. He opened his eyes and saw what he imagined was the great wing of an eagle pouring a wet lightness over him. Some kind of baptism, some kind of blessing, he thought. Everything is going to be all right, it said. Knowing that it was so he closed his eyes and sank back into the bright hole of sleep.

6. Eva stepped back from the bed and let the crutches rest under her arms. She rolled a bit of newspaper into a tight stick about six inches long, lit it and threw it onto the bed where the kerosene-soaked Plum lay in snug delight. Quickly, as the *whoosh* of flames engulfed him, she shut the door and made her slow and painful journey back to the top of the house.

7. Just as she got to the third landing she could hear Hannah and some child's voice. She swung along, not even listening to the voices of alarm and the cries of the Deweys. By the time she got to her bed

someone was bounding up the stairs after her. Hannah opened the door. "Plum! Plum! He's burning, Mamma! We can't even open the door! Mamma!"

9. Eva looked into Hannah's eyes. "Is? My baby? Burning?" The two women did not speak, for the eyes of each were enough for the other. Then Hannah closed hers and ran toward the voices of neighbors calling for water. (Toni Morrison, *Sula*, pp. 45–48.)

Students' Questions:

1. Did Eva Peace kill her son Plum because she did not want to see him in pain? He was dying very slowly.
2. Why did Eva set her son on fire?
3. Eva was consistent in her actions. She took drastic measures when she cut off her leg for money and now she burned her son. He can't be her baby again—the best thing she could do was to relieve him of his misery and pain.
4. Why did she kill Plum? She should have helped him.

All the students were shocked that a mother would burn her son. It is in the asking of the the right questions that events in a story will become clearer and an in-depth understanding of the characters will emerge. By "right questions," it means thinking creatively, asking what is not expected. Thus, asking questions as you read imaginative literature is a critical skill to understand all elements in the story and characters' development.

Imaginative literature is entertaining and enjoyable, but it also informs us, uplifts our spirit, and makes us think. It opens us to new possibilities, inspires us to reach for higher ideals to elevate ourselves and the human condition, and, very often, has universal appeal. In addition, issues which a group or society may have may be addressed through imaginative literature to help bring clarity to the issues under discussion.

Chapter Two

Understanding Authors' Language

The writer has a feeling and utters it from his true self. The reader reads it
and is immediately infected. He has exactly the same feeling.
—Brenda Ueland

Lesson 4: Authors' Purpose and Point of View

Authors write about a topic with a specific purpose choosing language that will clearly express ideas based on their particular perspective and point of view. It is the authors' intention to convince the reader that they are objective—without biases—but this is generally not the case. Authors come with their beliefs, biases, and their own Personal Matrix which influences their perspective on the topic they write. Their language is chosen to convey a message and is done to elicit a clear response from the reader, that is, to cause you to change or reinforce your beliefs about a particular subject and, perhaps, convince you to take action or not act at all. Therefore, efficient readers must be able to evaluate the language as well as the content and context to determine if the information is supported by sufficient evidence. It is also important to know how the evidence was chosen; this may not always be apparent. The author's purpose may be to describe, explain, or persuade you to believe a concept, idea, or point of view. You will consider the information and form an opinion; or before forming an opinion, you may withhold judgment to research the subject for additional information to have an informed opinion. An efficient reader must always look to determine how facts and opinions are presented and if they are easily distinguishable. What is the author's purpose? What does the author want you to believe and why? Who benefits socially, economically, politically, and so on? Through careful analysis, you will be able to analyze the author's use of language and identify biases, purpose, and intent toward a topic. This is an important skill in constructing meaning. You evaluate the author's point of view through the prism of your Personal Matrix. It is equally important, as you enter the world of the author, to acknowledge his or her reality and be open to the possibilities to expand your prior knowledge whether you agree or disagree with his or her point of view. The diagram below illustrates how authors' Personal Matrices influence their writing.

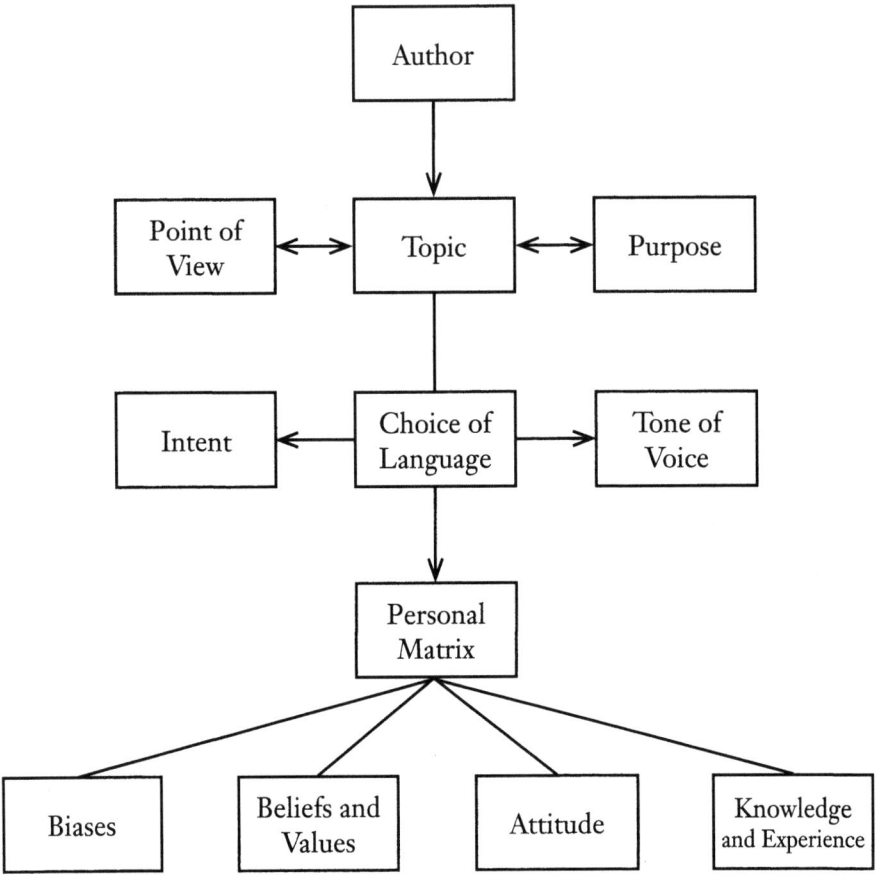

Let us look at each aspect of the diagram to understand the process.

Topic

As this diagram indicates, authors write about a topic with a specific purpose and point of view. They convey their purpose and point of view by telling a story from a particular perspective, and in imaginative literature, use characters to reflect their thinking. Thus, in a story, an author's point of view is presented by what characters do, think, and say (both major and minor characters are considered). Very often, characters are given the task of presenting contrasting viewpoints to give the reader different perspectives on a topic.

In expository text—nonfiction material—authors attempt to convey a sense of objectivity. By objectivity we mean authors' attempt to detach themselves from events and present facts as they see it. You, the reader, will have to determine how objective the material has been presented.

Choice of Language

Authors structure language in a particular way to set a tone—"tone of voice"—to which the reader will respond. The tone of voice may be humorous, sarcastic, dramatic, sad, angry, excited, scholarly, or other in an effort to elicit a particular response from the reader. If you respond to the tone of voice in the writing in a way the author intends, the author's purpose and point of view have been realized. Thus, the author's purpose may be clear, but his or her attitude and biases are closely linked and are not always easily discernible.

Authors' Personal Matrix

Underlying the purpose, point of view, choice of language—which sets the tone and intent—is the authors' Personal Matrix. Authors' Personal Matrix reflects their attitude, biases, beliefs, values, knowledge, and experience about what he or she writes. For the reader, it is important to try to determine how these biases are influencing the writing. On the other hand, your Personal Matrix, your attitude, biases, beliefs, and emotional responses will also determine how you interpret the text. To explore this further, we shall look at language techniques or devices authors use to help readers understand their purpose and point of view.

Unfamiliar Vocabulary

Whether English is your native language or an additional language for you, you will encounter unfamiliar vocabulary. What is key is that you understand how to tackle unfamiliar vocabulary as you read. And the more you read the more your English vocabulary will expand and provide you with greater fluency with the language. The first strategy you may employ to get the meaning of unfamiliar vocabulary is to determine how the word is used in context. Look at the context clues in the sentence that the word appears and then look at the sentences that come before and after and how it relates to the meaning of the paragraph. The author may give you a definite definition within the sentence by setting off the word or phrase with dashes. For example, "It was an auspicious—favorable—occasion for all the recipients." Thus, setting the word off with dashes indicates the author is giving the meaning as it is used in context.

Here are examples of context clues you may use to get the meaning of unfamiliar vocabulary:

- The words in the sentence surrounding the unfamiliar word or phrase
- Look at the sentence before and after the sentence which contains the unfamiliar word or phrase
- Consider the overall meaning of the paragraph and passage
- Words and phrases may be set off with commas or dashes to provide a definition: "He was culpable—responsible for his actions—during the disturbance."
- Make notations in the margin and jot down key terms
- Use the book's glossary and index for specific definitions
- Use your dictionary, paying close attention to context to choose the correct definition
- Use vocabulary workbooks that emphasize root words, prefixes, and suffixes

To apply the above strategies to unfamiliar vocabulary, read the following portions of The Declaration of Independence of the United States, July 4, 1776; the full text is included in Chapter Six, Reading Selections. Preview, read the passage, and apply reading strategies to determine the meaning of boldfaced words. Replace the boldface word with a word or phrase to make the meaning clear. Monitor your thinking and emotional responses.

Vocabulary Exercise:

The United States of America Declaration of Independence written July 4, 1776, declares that humankind is entitled to freedoms which governments cannot deny. The document is a remarkable one, as it speaks to evidence not fully realized by human beings in the colony or elsewhere at the time. The entire document appears at the beginning of the Reading Selections in Chapter Six. At this point, read this excerpt and identify words as used in the context of the document.

Passage 6: The Declaration of Independence

> When in the course of human events, it becomes necessary for one people to **dissolve** the political bands which have connected them with another, and to assume among the powers of the earth, the separate and equal station to which the Laws of Nature and of Nature's God **entitle** them, a decent respect to the opinions of mankind requires that they should declare the causes which **impel** them to the separation.

We hold these truths to be **self-evident**, that all men are created equal, that they are **endowed** by their Creator with certain **unalienable** Rights, that among these are Life, Liberty and the pursuit of Happiness; that, to secure these rights, Governments are **instituted** among Men, **deriving** their just powers from the consent of the governed; that whenever any Form of Government becomes destructive of these ends, it is the Right of the People to alter or to **abolish** it, and to institute new Government, laying its foundation on such **principles** and organizing its powers in such form, as to them shall seem most likely to effect their Safety and Happiness. **Prudence**, indeed, will **dictate** that Governments long established should not be changed for light and **transient** causes; and accordingly all experience hath Shawn that mankind are more disposed to suffer, while evils are sufferable, than to right themselves by abolishing **Despotism**, it is their right, it is their duty, to throw off such Government, and to provide new Guards for their future security.

Such has been the patient **sufferance** of these Colonies; and such is now the necessity which constraints them to alter their former Systems of Government. The history of the present King of Great Britain is a history of repeated injuries and **usurpations**, all having in direct object the establishment of an absolute Tyranny over these States....

Replace the boldfaced words with a synonym—a word that has the same or similar meaning—and state the meaning.

Vocabulary →	Substitutions/Synonym →	Meaning
1. dissolve		
2. entitle		
3. impel		
4. self-evident		
5. endowed		
6. unalienable		
7. instituted		
8. deriving		
9. destructive		
10. abolish		
11. principles		
12. prudence		
13. dictate		
14. transient		
15. sufferance		
16. usurpations		

Now reread the passage with your substitutions to determine if the passage is clearer for you.

Transitional Words and Phrases

Transitional words and phrases—often referred to as signal words—are an author's way of making a transition from one point to another or as a signal to the reader that an important idea or concept is being presented. For example, the author may wish to change the direction of the text or summarize a point, or draw conclusions. There are many categories for transitional words and phrases, too numerous to list them all; thus, a few examples are given to indicate the process and terms which are sometimes used to indicate relationship. You will notice that in many instances terms are employed in more than one process.

TRANSITIONAL WORDS AND PHRASES

Process	Examples of Transitional Words and Phrases
Summarizing Conclusions	In summary, In conclusion, Thus, Finally, Overall, Restate, Therefore
Compare and Contrast	Likewise, Nonetheless, In contrast, Conversely, In the same way, On the other hand, Although, However, But
Cause and Effect	Because, As a result, For these reasons, Therefore, Consequently, Due to, If
Sequence Chronology	First, Further, In the beginning, Then, Next, In addition, Furthermore, Finally, Next, List, Trace, Namely
Examples and Illustrations	For example (e.g.), That is (i.e.), For instance, To cite, To illustrate, To employ
Opinion Reason	Might, Possibly, I think, I believe, Appears to be, Seems to suggests, Usually, Generally,

Preview the following passage and define the boldfaced vocabulary as used in the passage. Identify the transitional words and phrases and use strategies to indicate the meaning of these transitional words and phrases. This excerpt from "The Freedom to Do as One Pleases" is somewhat of a challenge, but an excellent passage to apply skills for previewing. Apply the reading strategies for previewing an essay, then read the passage, write marginal notes, and answer the questions at the end of the passage. Words which are highlighted are those transitional words or phrases and vocabulary which have been defined within the context of the passage and are important to understand the content.

Passage 7:

1. . . . in the case of liberty and freedom. The two words are completely interchangeable. There are three major forms of freedom. **The first** is a freedom that is **inherent** in human nature. We are born with **it** in our possession. **It** is **distinctive** of human beings, just as **rational** or **conceptual** thought and **syntactical** speech are distinctive of human beings. It is, **therefore**, appropriate to speak of **it** as a natural freedom, thus referring to the way in which we possess it.

2. **The second** major kind of liberty is the liberty that is associated with wisdom and moral virtue. It is possessed only by those who, in the course of their personal development, have acquired some measure of virtue and wisdom. **Thus**, possessed, it is appropriately designated as an **acquired freedom**.

3. Described so far in terms of the way in which we possess them, what do these three forms of freedom or kinds of liberty consist in?

4. Our **natural freedom** consists in freedom of the will. It **is freedom of choice**—the liberty of being able to choose . . . Having such freedom, our actions are not instinctively determined or completely conditioned by the impact of external circumstances on our development, as is the case in the behavior of other animals. With this **innate** power of free choice, each human being is able to change his own character creatively by deciding for himself what he shall do or shall become. We are free to make ourselves whatever we choose to be.

5. **Our acquired liberty**, which is sometimes called "moral freedom," consists in our having a will that is **habitually** disposed by virtue to will as it ought. **Virtue**, as we have already seen, is the habitual disposition to desire aright, which means choosing what one needs—the real goods one ought to desire. The **obstacles** or **impediments** to right desire stem from appetites or passions that generate wants in conflict with needs, wants that tempt or **solicit** us to make the wrong

6. **Human bondage**, according to Spinoza, is our enslavement by such appetites or passions—our lower nature. **Human freedom**—moral liberty—lies in reason's control of the passions, made firm by moral virtue, the acquired habitual disposition to make right rather than wrong choices.

7. The freedom to will or choose as one ought could not be acquired by human beings if they did not antecedently possess, as an inherent property of human nature, a free will and the power of free choice. If we cannot choose otherwise, how can we be morally responsible for choosing aright rather than **yielding** to the seductions of pleasure or lust? And if we cannot be held morally responsible for the choices we make, what justification can there be for the praise or blame we accord an individual for his or her character or conduct?

8. Our **circumstantial freedom** consists in our being able to do as we please—our ability to carry out in overt action the decisions we have reached, to do as we wish for our individual good as we see it, rightly or wrongly.

9. Such freedom can be possessed and exercised by individuals of good or bad moral character. The individual's free choice of a line of conduct to pursue, or his decision about a course of action to take, may be morally virtuous or the opposite, but in either case, circumstances either permit him to behave or act as he wishes, or prevent him from doing so. **Accordingly**, the individual is either circumstantially free or unfree.

10. Our natural or **inherent freedom** of will confers upon us the power to choose otherwise—to make, on a particular occasion, a choice different from the one we made. Our circumstantial freedom of action, when we possess it in the fullest measure, confers upon us the ability to act otherwise. We are not only left free by favorable circumstances to enact the choice we made; we are also left free to enact a different, or opposite choice, had we made it.

11. An individual in prison or in chains is circumstantially free to remain in his cell or manacled, should that be his choice. But bars or chains prevent him from going elsewhere or doing otherwise if he wishes to. The **restraints** imposed by imprisonment impair his freedom of action, not his freedom of choice, and not his moral liberty—his freedom to will as he ought. ("The Freedom to Do as One Pleases" in Mortimer Adler, *Six Great Ideas*, 1981, pp. 140–143.

Define the following vocabulary words as used in context or defined by the author:

Vocabulary
1. inherent _____
2. distinctive _____

3. rational _____
4. conceptual _____
5. syntactical _____
6. innate _____
7. yielding _____

Terms defined in the passage
- acquired freedom _____
- natural freedom _____
- inherent freedom _____
- circumstantial freedom _____
- freedom of choice _____
- acquired liberty _____
- virtue _____
- impediment _____
- human bondage _____
- human freedom _____

Summarize the major points.
What is the author's purpose?
What does the author want you to believe?
How would you identify the author's tone of voice?

Denotations and Connotations

Understanding connotative word meanings is particularly important to understand the author's tone of voice in the writing to interpret readings correctly. Therefore, we will take a considerable amount of time on denotative and connotative word meanings. First, complete the following exercises that are designed to point out how your Personal Matrix contributes to your interpretations of text. Complete the exercises without referring to your dictionary.

Part A—Directions:
Read the following word list without spending too much time on any one word. The purpose is to record you initial response.

Respond to each word as follows:
- If, in general, you associate positive feelings with the word, place a check in column 1.
- If, in general, you associate negative feelings with the word, place a check in column 2.
- If the word is unfamiliar to you or you do not have any particular feelings associated with the word, place a check in column 3.
- As you check each word, jot down words or phrases which come to mine to indicate what you associate with the word and how it makes you feel.
- You need not take much time with each word. Simply record your initial response.

CONNOTATIONS

WORD	1 POSITIVE	2 NEGATIVE	3 NEUTRAL/ UNFAMILIAR
WELFARE			
CHARITY			
AID			
FAMILY			
LOVE			
COLLEGE			
SCHOOL			
AMERICA			
TERRORISM			
DEMOCRACY			
SOCIALISM			
SEX			
WOMAN			
FEMALE			
GIRLS			

LADIES			
MAN			
MALE			
BOY			
GENTLEMEN			

Part B—Directions:
Compare Related Words to Your Associations
- How do your associations for the word "female" compare to woman, girls, and ladies?
- How do your associations for the word "male" compare to man, boy, and gentlemen?
- What do you associate with terrorism?
- What do you associate with democracy?
- Make additional comparison with the remainder of the list.

Now look up each word in the dictionary, jot down the first definition, and answer the following questions:

- Were your associations with the word close to the dictionary definitions?
- Did your associations completely change the dictionary definitions? If so, use your Personal Matrix and reflect to determine what experiences, traditions, etc., may influence what you associated with the word.

The Impact of Connotation in Writing

As you completed the exercise, you may have discovered that dictionary definitions can pose some difficulty since there can be several meanings with shades of differences. Denotation refers to the dictionary definition of a word. If you look up the word "scale" in the dictionary you will find several meanings for it. You have to determine which definition fits the context of what you are reading. What is missing from the dictionary definitions are the meanings we have come to associate with the word and these associations are usually not listed in a dictionary. Thus, connotative word meanings are what the word suggests and what a society or group has come to associate with the word—it is an expanded definition of the word and goes beyond dictionary definitions. Thus, understanding the connotative word meaning is critical to clearly understand an author's intent.

Connotations develop through use in popular culture, music, theater, mass media, television, and other societal context. Thus, connotations help authors convey their ideas based on key assumptions held by members of a society. Therefore, understanding the difference between denotative/connotative word meanings is important to a reader so that you recognize the power and intent of the words authors choose. In addition, authors basically develop their writing for readers' responses to be emotional in nature; and this can be so even in academic textbooks such as those one might read in a history textbook. A concrete example of this would be the use of the word "liberation" as opposed to the word "invasion" which connotes a dramatically different emotional impact on you, the reader. What do these words mean to you? You were able to demonstrate this with the word list exercise at the beginning of this section.

To help heighten your awareness of connotation in writing, try the following exercise.

Exercise C—Connotation and Writing
Choose a topic from each category in the chart below and write a descriptive paragraph without naming the object. For example, if you choose the category *Fruit*, and choose "Apples," as your topic, you cannot include the word "apple" in your paragraph. Be as descriptive as possible using words and phrases that appeal to the senses to help the reader identify your topic.

Fruit	**Vegetables**	**Furniture**	**Feelings**	**Colors**
Apples	Carrots	Chair	Joy	Orange
Oranges	Beets	Table	Love	Yellow
Papayas	Broccoli	File Cabinet	Hate	Red
Bananas	Potatoes	Sofa	Happy	Green

Share your paragraph with someone and ask the person to read it to name the category of your paragraph. Ask the reader to identify words and phrases that appealed to his or her senses and how these made him or her feel.

Figurative Language

Authors use figurative language to create lively images to help readers visualize the text for a clearer understanding. Figurative language helps create vivid imagery for the reader, enlivens imaginative literature, makes it more interesting, comparing and contrasting similar and dissimilar objects, or perhaps giving life to inanimate objects. Other figurative expressions, such as idioms, are used and understood in relation to a cultural context. For example, a common American idiomatic expression—figure of speech—"You cannot have your cake and eat it too" in the American context is readily understood as "You cannot have it both ways; you have to make a choice." That is, given your options, you have to choose one over the others. Figurative expressions convey strong imagery and feelings to set the tone of voice of the writing and are referred to as a "figures of speech." Below are some common devices authors use to emphasize a point and express strong feelings in writing.

Hyperbole—Expressions which suggest similarity between two objects deliberately exaggerating to emphasize a point. Hyperbole is a powerful tool for writers to convey a clear, vivid picture of what the author wishes to communicate. The following excerpt from *Beloved*, illustrates this.

> Past the sheds where the *dogs lay in deep depression*; past the two guard shacks, past the stable of sleeping horses, past the hens *whose bills were bolted into their feathers*, they waded. The moon did not help because it wasn't there. The field was a marsh, the track a trough. *All Georgia seemed to be sliding, melting away. Moss wiped their faces* as they fought the live-oak branches that blocked their way. (*Beloved* pp. 110–111)

Personification—Expressions that give human qualities to objects. The use of personification gives readers a "word picture," and may express strong feelings about the object that would otherwise remain inanimate, lifeless. In the following excerpt from *Beloved*, human qualities are ascribed to a house to account for strange and unexplained occurrences:

> 124 was spiteful. Full of a baby's venom. The women in the house knew it and so did the children. For years each put up with the spite in his own way, but by 1873 Sethe and her daughter Denver were its only victims…first one brother and then the next stuffed quilt packing into his hat, snatched up his shoes, and crept away from the lively spite the house felt for them. (*Beloved*, p. 3)

Metaphor—Expressions that compare two dissimilar things. Figurative language provides the reader with a vivid description in order to visualize a picture of what is being described. Metaphors appeal to our senses and therefore are key to how we respond emotionally to text.

Simile—Also expressions that compare two unlike objects but includes the words "as" or "like" in the comparison. A simile provides a striking comparison for the reader bringing to life that which is being compared. Read the excerpt below from *Beloved* that describes an account of the character Sethe, a slave, who has been beaten across her back at the instructions of her slave master. Follow the language carefully as it is a powerful illustration of metaphor that serves a number of purposes in the novel.

> "Your back? Gal, you a mess…It's a tree, Lu. A chokecherry tree. See, here's the trunk—it's red and split wide open, full of sap, and this here's the parting for the branches. You got a mighty lot of branches. Leaves, too, look like, and dern if these ain't blossoms…I had me some whippings, but I don't remember nothing like this." (*Beloved*, p. 79)

As you read this excerpt, one can easily picture the grotesque scars on the back of the character as the scars across her back have been described in vivid detail how the scars resemble a tree.

Irony—Events that are an unexpected turn of events; it contradicts our expectations. In *Beloved*, the slave plantation was called "Sweet Home Plantation"; this was ironic since it was a place where human beings were captive slave labor. The name "Sweet Home" connotes an idyllic, pleasant, serene surrounding—this of course was not the case. The following excerpt illustrates irony for this name "Sweet Home":

> It made sense for a lot of reasons because in all of Baby's life, as well as Sethe's own, men and women were moved around like checkers. Anybody Baby Suggs knew, let alone loved, who hadn't run off or been hanged, got rented out, loaned out, bought up, brought back, stored up, mortgaged, won, stolen or seized. (*Beloved*, p. 23)

Idioms—Expressions which are closely connected to a cultural group and understood within the context of that particular culture. Idioms may be colorful and humorous expressions, although this is not always the case and are referred to as idiomatic expressions. In *Beloved*, the following expressions reflect the language usage of the 1870s:

> Buffalo soldiers—Native Americans gave this name to the African soldiers for their fearlessness and bravery. The buffalo was a sacred animal to the Native Indians thus this was a name of honor and respect.

Other common American idiomatic expressions:

- I will pick your brain—to learn all one can from another person

- I put my foot in my mouth—to say the wrong thing
- Raining cats and dogs—raining very hard

Read the following excerpt from *Beloved*, illustrating the idiomatic expression, "Buffalo men," and other figurative language.

Passage 8:

1. Past the sheds where the dogs lay in deep depression; past the two guard shacks, past the stable of sleeping horses, past the hens whose bills were bolted into their feathers, they waded. The moon did not help because it wasn't there. The field was a marsh, the track a trough. All Georgia seemed to be sliding, melting away. Moss wiped their faces as they fought the live-oak branches that blocked their way. Georgia took up all of Alabama and Mississippi then, so there was no state line to cross and it wouldn't have mattered anyway. If they had known about it, they would have avoided not only Alfred and the beautiful feldspar, but Savannah too and headed for the Sea Islands on the river that slid down from the Blue Ridge Mountains. But they didn't know.

2. Daylight came and they huddled in a copse of redbud trees. Night came and they scrambled up to higher ground, praying the rain would go on shielding them and keeping folks at home. They were hoping for a shack, solitary, some distance from its big house, where a slave might be making rope or heating potatoes at the grate. What they found was a camp of sick Cherokee for whom a rose was named. . . .

3. The prisoners from Alfred, Georgia, sat down in semicircle near the encampment. No one came and still they sat. Hours passed and the rain turned soft. Finally a woman stuck her head out of her house. Night came and nothing happened. At dawn two men with barnacles covering their beautiful skin approached them. No one spoke for a moment, then Hi Man raised his hand. The Cherokee saw the chains and went away. When they returned each carried a handful of small axes. Two children followed with a pot of mush cooling and thinning in the rain.

4. *Buffalo men, they called them*, and talked slowly to prisoners scooping mush and tapping away at their chains. Nobody from a box in Alfred, Georgia cared about the illness the Cherokee warned them about, so they stayed, all forty-six, resting, planning their next move. Paul D had no idea of what to do and knew less than anybody, it seemed. He heard his co-convicts talk knowledgeably of rivers and

states, towns and territories. Heard Cherokee men describe the beginning of the world and its end. Listened to tales of other Buffalo men they knew—three of whom were in the healthy camp a few miles away. Hi Man wanted to join them; others wanted to join him. Some wanted to leave; some to stay on. Weeks later Paul D was the only Buffalo man left—without a plan. (*Beloved*, pp. 110–112)

Authors' Devices for Figures of Speech	Purpose
Hyperbole	Expressions which deliberately exaggerate to emphasize a point
Personification	Expressions which give human qualities to objects
Metaphor	Expressions comparing qualities of two objects to suggest similarity without the use of "like" or "as"
Simile	Expressions which always use "like" or "as" to compare two unlike things
Irony	Expressions which state one thing but mean something opposite
Idioms	Expressions which are unique to a particular group or culture and have meaning within the context of the group

Lesson 5: Deconstructing Paragraphs

What do we mean by deconstructing paragraphs? It is the process of determining the meaning of four basic categories of comprehension: (1) literal, (2) interpretive, (3) critical, and (4) affective responses. Under each category you look for different types of information. You may do this by taking into account general questions as you seek to interpret what you read.

Literal Comprehension

This category is concerned with what the author states. You ask questions to identify who, what, where, and when. This includes identifying the topic, main idea, supporting details, recognizing characters, vocabulary meaning as it is used in context, and facts—all are considered under literal comprehension. You begin by asking these basic questions.

Ask:
- "Who or what is this about?" → Topic
- "What does the author say about the topic?" → Main Idea
- "Is there proof?" → Supporting Details*

*Details explain, prove and support the main idea; it answers questions such as what, why, where, when, what kind, and how many?

Main Idea as a Declarative Sentence

After identifying the topic, state the main idea in a declarative sentence—a sentence in your own words. Writing the sentence in your own words assures that you understand the author's main point. Each paragraph may have a main point about the topic, or two or more paragraphs may emphasize a main idea to add illustrations or examples to make it clearer. Each paragraph builds upon the preceding one to help you interpret the overall theme or thesis of the article. Do not start your declarative sentence with "This is about…" Begin you main idea as a factual statement claimed by the author. For example, let us say that the main idea is education. Then you declarative sentence might read, "Education is necessary to get a good job."

This is what the author asserts. As a reader, we must determine if the author has provided sufficient evidence to support this main idea. The supporting details should explain and provide details that support this statement.

Thesis

The thesis is the sum total of what the author has stated to convince the reader of his or her position. In the same way you identified the main idea in paragraphs, the sum total of these major ideas identify the thesis to write a declarative sentence for the entire article. Thus, as you identify major points in an article, it will be easier to write a thesis sentence. Then you will be able to write a thesis sentence for the article. For example, let us say you have read an article on air pollution, the thesis sentence might read as follows:

> Without legislation, air pollution will continue to be a serious problem for children with asthma.

Preview and read the following abridged essay, "The Problem That Has No Name," by Betty Friedan (1983) and apply the reading strategies previously discussed. Write a thesis sentence for the essay and read the sample student thesis sentences. Compare your thesis sentence with the student samples and note the common elements between your sentence and student samples.

Passage 9:

1. The problem lay buried, unspoken, for many years in the minds of American women. It was a strange stirring, a sense of dissatisfaction, a yearning that women suffered in the middle of the twentieth century in the United States. Each suburban wife struggled with it alone. As she made the beds, shopped for groceries, matched slipcover material, ate peanut butter sandwiches with her children, chauffeured Cub Scouts and Brownies, lay beside her husband at night—she was afraid to ask even of herself the silent question—"Is this all?"

2. For over fifteen years there was no word of this yearning in the millions of words written about women, for women, in all the columns, books and articles by experts telling women their role was to seek fulfillment as wives and mothers. Over and over women heard in voices of tradition and of Freudian sophistication that they would desire no greater destiny than to glory in their own femininity.... They were taught to pity the neurotic, unfeminine, unhappy women who wanted to be poets or physicists or presidents. They learned that truly feminine women do not want careers, higher education, political rights—the independence and the opportunities that the old-fashioned feminists fought for....

3. The suburban housewife—she was the dream image of the young American women and the envy, it was said, of women all over the world. The American housewife—freed by science and labor-saving appliances from the drudgery, the dangers of childbirth and the illnesses of her grandmother. She was healthy, beautiful, educated, concerned about her husband, her children, and her home. She had found true feminine fulfillment. As a housewife and mother, she was respected as a full and equal partner to man in his world. She was free to choose automobiles, clothes, appliances, supermarkets; she had everything that women ever dreamed of....

4. If a woman had a problem in the 1950's and 1960's, she knew that something must be wrong with her marriage, or with herself. Other women were satisfied with their lives, she thought. What kind of a woman was she if she did not feel this mysterious fulfillment waxing

the kitchen floor? She was so ashamed to admit her dissatisfaction that she never knew how many other women shared it. If she tried to tell her husband, he didn't understand what she was talking about. She did not really understand it herself. For over fifteen years women in America found it harder to talk about this problem than about sex. "There's nothing wrong really," they kept telling themselves. "There isn't any problem."

5. The alternative offered was a choice that few women would contemplate. In the sympathetic words of the *New York Times:* "All admit to being deeply frustrated at times by the lack of privacy, the physical burden, the routine of family life, the confinement of it. However, none would give up her home and family if she had the choice to make again."

6. Even so, most men, and some women, still did not know that this problem was real. But those who had faced it honestly knew that all the superficial remedies, the sympathetic advice, the scolding words and the cheering words were somehow drowning the problem in unreality. A bitter laugh was beginning to be heard from American women.... Most adjusted to their role and suffered or ignored the problem that has no name. It can be less painful, for a woman, not to hear the strange, dissatisfied voice stirring within her. (Betty Friedan, "The Problem That Has No Name," in *The Feminine Mystique*, New York: W.W. Norton, 1963, pp. 15–26.)

Write a thesis sentence for Passage 9 and compare your thesis sentence with students' sample thesis sentences below.

Student sample thesis sentences:
1. Women are not happily fulfilled in their role as mothers and housewives.
2. American housewives in the twentieth century were displeased without a career.
3. The women in the twentieth century find it hard to understand their role in the society.
4. Women are not satisfied only being housewives.
5. Women who are housewives feel empty not being able to have a career.
6. Women in traditional roles of mothers and housewives is a problem.

The thesis sentences clearly identify the major points in the essay and appear in some or in all of the thesis sentences: (1) women are discontent with their roles as mothers and housewives. Two sentences give us the time element—the twentieth century and one sentence gives the identity as American women. Both these facts are important as they make it clear to the reader the time period of the essay's information. However, Friedan's essay was written over thirty years ago, identifying one segment of American women: white suburban housewives she interviewed. In Chapter Five, we return to this essay to discuss the importance of evaluating material.

Facts and Opinions

It is important to distinguish between facts and opinions to evaluate expository text. How do we determine this? Factual information can be proven based on current knowledge to assess or measure events and objects. Whereas opinions are based on our personal biases and preferences and people will differ. Although this may seem to be straight forward, writers often mix fact and opinions and it is not always easy to determine the difference. Even in academic text, opinions are freely given to support the point of view of the author. At the literal level of comprehension you also need to determine what facts are included to support the ideas.

Facts can be proven and are based on our current knowledge and ability to determine the accuracy of information. For example, someone says she is six feet tall; we have the means to measure the height of this person to determine the accuracy of the statement. The reader checks the passage for what the author states as fact.

Opinions cannot be proven true or false. Opinions involve our values, beliefs, personal preferences, and biases, i.e., you engage your Personal Matrix. For example, the statement "I think that is a beautiful portrait" is a sentiment of preference; someone else may think the portrait is unattractive. Different criteria of beauty are being applied to judge the portrait. Both opinions are valid.

Read the following passage for literal comprehension of the passage: identify the topic, write a declarative sentence stating the main idea, list the supporting details, and indicate which phrases are facts or opinions.

- Monitor your thinking and emotional responses.
- Use contextual clues to define boldfaced and unfamiliar vocabulary and phrases.
- Identify the topic for the excerpt and write a declarative sentence for each main idea for the passage.
- List details which support the main ideas.
- Thesis—write a declarative sentence.

Passage 10:

1. We've heard a great deal of talk about differences in the women's movement. I personally feel very much a part of a special constituency that is best represented by the phrase "European ethnic Catholic women." We are the people who represent a population of about 20 million women residing primarily in the urban areas of the North—from Boston to Baltimore, New York to Milwaukee—and other major industrial centers.

2. One of our problems is that many people don't understand us. We are *stereotyped* in the media as *passive* Edith Bunker types, even as *reactionary*. But if you know us, you will know this to be untrue. You'll find there are two themes that run through our public attitude. *Number one*, we are associated with the Democratic Party through the ideas of Franklin Delano Roosevelt and Jack Kennedy, and programs like Social Security. *But* when you look at our cultural lives, which stem from both our ethnic traditions and our religious heritage, you'll find that we are somewhat *conservative* in our outlook. So if you know us as *politically* and *economically progressive* but *culturally moderate*, then you will understand our attitudes in relationship to the women's movement. The women in our *constituency* have mixed feelings about the women's movement.

3. Though we hate to *categorize* people, it seems there are two groups within the movement. There are the *women's rights activists* and there are the *women's liberation activists*. The women's rights activists have been in the *forefront* of those programs dealing with concrete benefits for people in terms of child care, day care, educational opportunities, senior citizens programs, Social Security reform, changing the work place, and fighting for the minimum wage to cover more people. We feel very much a part of this group.

4. Then there are the women's *liberationists* who perhaps have had the most publicity and have presented what we would regard as *culturally provocative* ideas. These are the people who have talked about role changes, changing life-styles and *changing orientations* in the family. Many of the people in our communities find these ideas very threatening and very confusing. (Barbara Mikulski, "The White Ethnic Catholic Women," in *All American Women: Lines That Divide, Ties That Bind*, Johnnetta B. Cole, ed., New York: Macmillan, 1986, p. 330.)

Questions for Passage 10:
Main Idea: _____
    Check the following statements with "F" = fact or "O" = opinion
    _____ There are 20 million European Ethnic Catholic (EEC)
    _____ Most of these women reside in the northeast of the United States
    _____ People do not understand EEC women
    _____ EEC women are stereotyped as passive
    _____ EEC women are associated with the Democratic Party
    _____ Politically and economically progressives
    _____ Culturally moderate
    _____ Women's liberation activist
    _____ Women's rights activist

Interpretive Comprehension

This category involves thinking about the literal meaning of the text to determine what is suggested to draw inferences. For example, what can you infer based on the character's actions, what they think or said, and so on. Your interpretation is acceptable as long as it is supported by the details making it reasonable to make your inference. In many cases, readers may differ in how they interpret events since you can have a different perspective regarding the events in the story. Your prior knowledge and your Personal Matrix plays a significant role in interpreting text therefore more than one interpretation is valid.

Drawing Inferences

This is the process whereby writers suggest information to the reader without actually stating it. In a sense, we must "read between the lines," and determine what the author may be suggesting by what he or she states. Therefore, during the process of reading, we anticipate events and draw inferences based on supporting evidence provided. It is at the interpretive level of comprehension at which we draw inferences, thus enabling the reader to draw inferences and come to conclusions at the end of a reading. Literal meaning is what the author actually states; for interpretive comprehension, we deconstruct to make meaning of what the author suggests. To illustrate this, read the following passage and answer the questions regarding what the passage suggests. Identify the topic, main idea, and ideas that support the main idea; then answer the question, which focus on the inferences that can be drawn from the passage. As you read you are always asking "What does the author want me to believe?"

Basic questions and guidelines for interpretive comprehension are as follows:

- What is the author suggesting by what is stated?
- Character analysis, e.g., are actions consistent with what they say and think? If not, what seems to be their intention, etc.?
- Characters' interaction with others
- Connotation and denotation of language
- Figurative language
- Point of view/Tone of voice and intent
- What does the author want me to believe and why?
- What inferences can be drawn?
- Are the actions of the characters consistent with their thinking? If not, what seems to be their intention?
- Define the nature of the problems and solutions.
- In what ways has your Personal Matrix helped to interpret the events?

Exercise:
Preview and read Passage 11 to deconstruct it for literal and interpretive comprehension. Apply the skills of an interactive reader.

Directions:
- Identify the topic, main idea, and supporting details.
- Write a declarative sentence for the main idea.
- Use context clues to get the meaning of unfamiliar vocabulary words and those that are boldfaced in the passage. Jot down your definitions in the margin.
- Monitor your emotional response. Highlight words and phrases which reflect your emotional response to this passage.
- Monitor your thinking: what do you think the author wants you to believe? Which words or phrases helped you understand what the author wants you to believe? Write a sentence stating what you understand the author point of view is and what he wants you to believe.
- What action would you take under similar circumstances?
- What experiences have you had to suggest you would take any action?

Passage 11:

1. After arriving in the morning, we would fetch our picks, shovels, hammers, and wheelbarrows from a zinc shed at the top of the quarry. Then we would **array** ourselves along the quarry face, usually in groups of three or four. **Warders** with automatic weapons stood on

raised platforms watching us. Unarmed **warders** walked among us, urging us to work harder. "Gaan aan!" (Go on! Go on!), they would shout, as if we were oxen. By eleven, when the sun was high in the sky, we would begin to flag. By that time, I would already be drenched in sweat. The warders would then drive us even harder. "Nee, man! Kom aan! Kom aan!" (No, man! Come on! Come on!), they would shout. Just before noon, when we would break for lunch, we would pile the lime into wheelbarrows and cart it over to the truck, which would take it away.

2. At midday, a whistle would blow, and we would make our way to the bottom of the hill. We sat on makeshift seats under a simple zinc shed shielding us from the sun. The **warders** ate at a larger shed with tables and benches. Drums of boiled **mealies** were delivered to us. Hundreds of seagulls, screaming and swooping circled above us as we ate, and a well-aimed dropping could sometimes spoil a man's lunch.

3. We worked until four, when we again carted the lime to the waiting truck. By the end of the day, our faces and bodies were caked with white dust. We looked like pale ghosts except where **rivulets** of sweat had washed away the lime. When we returned to our cells, we would scrub ourselves in the cold water, which never seemed to completely rinse away the dust.

4. Worse than the heat at the **quarry** was the light. Our backs were protected from the sun by our shirts, but the sun's rays would be reflected into our eyes by the lime itself. The glare hurt our eyes and, along with the dust, made it difficult to see. Our eyes teared and our faces became fixed in a permanent **squint**. It would take a long time after each day's work for our eyes to adjust to the **diminished** light.

5. After our first few days at the quarry, we made an official request for sunglasses. The authorities refused. This was not unexpected, for we were then not even permitted reading glasses. I had previously pointed out to the commanding officer that it did not make sense to permit us to read books but not permit us glasses to read them with.

6. During the following weeks and months, we requested sunglasses again and again. But it was to take us almost three years before we were allowed to have them, and that was only after a sympathetic physician agreed that the glasses were necessary to preserve our eyesight. Even then, we had to purchase the glasses ourselves.

7. For us, such struggles—for sunglasses, long trousers, study privileges, equalized food—were **corollaries** to the struggle we waged outside prison. The campaign to improve conditions in prison was part of the **apartheid** struggle. It was, in that sense, all the same; we

fought injustice wherever we found it, no matter how large, or how small, and we fought injustice to preserve our own humanity. (Nelson Mandela, *Long Walk to Freedom*. New York: Little Brown, 1994, pp. 405–406)

Vocabulary	Meaning used in context
1. array	
2. warders	
3. mealies	
4. rivulets	
5. quarry	
6. squint	
7. diminished light	
8. corollaries	
9. apartheid	

Drawing Inferences:
1. Mandela's simile "they would shout, as if we were oxen" evokes strong imagery. What inferences can be drawn from this? List words and phrases that convey the meaning of how the warders viewed the prisoners.
2. Mandela and the other prisoners fought the injustices in the prison to maintain their humanity. Why was this crucial for their survival?

Critical Comprehension

This category involves the evaluation and analysis of the material. Your opinion, prior knowledge, and your Personal Matrix will all be of considerable help in evaluating reading material. Some basic questions and guidelines for your consideration as you evaluate text are as follows:

- Distinguish between fact and opinion.
- What is the author's tone of voice and purpose?
- What is his point of view?
- What are the biases and attitude toward the topic?
- Is there sufficient evidence/information to draw the conclusions?
- Is the information accurate?

56   READING BETWEEN THE LINES

- Compare the text contextually—how does the date affect the evidence?

Preview the following speech given in 1995 by Colin Powell, Secretary of State of the United States 2000–2005.

- Preview the article, formulate questions, read interactively.
- Deconstruct the speech: Identify the basic structure, write a declarative sentence for each main idea, identify supporting details.
- Distinguish between facts and opinions.
- Identify terms and vocabulary using context clues and dictionary.
- Use marginal notes.

Passage 12:

1. From the privacy of retirement, I watch a fundamental transformation of a world I knew so well for the thirty-five years of my career. That world was defined by a historic struggle between the Soviet Union and the West with rules that structured our political, economic, and military relations. It was a dangerous period, but relatively stable, and one in which we understood the role we had to play. With the end of the Soviet Union and the death of communism as an ideology, we face a world so far without a new structure or a new set of rules. Our strategy of **containment** died with the Soviet Union.

2. **Yet**, however different the world, the United States remains its leader. We are still the foundation on which Western security rests, and we are increasingly looked to as the foundation upon which the newly freed nations of Eastern Europe want their security to rest. America is trusted and respected as no other nation on earth. This trust comes not only out of respect for our military, economic, and political power, but from the power of the democratic values we hold dear. The Cold War was ultimately won not by armies marching, but by triumphant democratic ideals that proved superior to every competing **ideology**. Democracy, the rights of men and women, and the power of free markets are proving themselves around the world. We see it happening in Latin America, Asia, parts of Africa, and wherever else these principles have the opportunity to take root.

3. In this new world, economic strength will be more important than military strength. The new order will be defined by trade relations, by the flow of information, capital, technology, and goods, rather than by armies glaring at each other across borders. Nations seeking power through military strength, the development of nuclear weapons, ter-

rorism, or **tyrannical** governments are mining "fool's gold." They can never hope to match or challenge the military and economic power of the free world led by the United States. **Despotic regimes** will come to realize it in due course, when they find themselves left behind while free nations prosper and provide a better life for their people. One only as to look at China to see a nation slowly finding a place in the world, not through the strength of the People's Liberation Army or Mao's Little Red Book, but through the release of the creative **entrepreneurial** power of the Chinese people. In Vietnam, American businesses are being invited in to repair the economic disaster created by two decades of "victorious" communism. We should encourage and support these impulses. Only Marxist Cuba and North Korea still cling to a political and **ideological corpse**, perhaps hoping for protection under the endangered species act. But even they cannot escape the tide of history, and we must begin to adjust our policies of Cold War isolation to hasten their integration into a new world.

4. I am heartened by the **reconciliations** taking place around the globe, by a fundamental shift from **chronic** conflict to **negotiated** settlements. The IRA and Britain, the Middle East peace process, South Africa, Angola, Mozambique, Cambodia, El Salvador, Nicaragua, all offer examples of once-**intractable** conflicts resolving themselves through the exhaustion of the **protagonists** and diplomatic intervention, especially on the part of the United Nations. The way ahead for these nations will not be easy or without violence, but I believe their commitment to reconciliation will prevail in the end. (Colin L. Powell, *My American Journey*. New York Random House, 1995, pp. 604–605.)

- Write a thesis sentence for the above passage.
- List the facts and opinions.
- List the evidence the author provides to support his thesis.
- Does the date of the speech affect the facts?
- What does the author want you to believe?
- Is there sufficient evidence to convince you of the thesis?
- Write a summary and your reaction to this speech.

Affective Comprehension

This category engages your emotional response to the text. It involves the author's tone of voice and intent and your emotional response to the text. You are evaluating your emotional responses to the language of the author. In fact, the author hopes you will react in a certain way. With careful analysis at the level of critical comprehension you understand how you are being influenced at an emotional level.

Emotional Responses to Text
- What are your emotional responses to the characters?
- What are your emotional reactions to the essay or story?
- What experiences in your Personal Matrix enable you to respond in this way?

Read the following excerpt to monitor your emotional responses to the text and note how your Personal Matrix influenced your responses.

Passage 13:

1. Thus began on April 18, 1879, the now almost forgotten civil-rights case of Standing Bear v. Crook. The Poncas' lawyers, Webster and Poppleton, argued that an Indian was as much a "person" as any white man and could avail himself of the rights of freedom guaranteed by the Constitution. When the United States attorney stated that Standing Bear and his people were subject to the rules and regulations which the government had made for tribal Indians, Webster and Poppleton replied that Standing Bear and any other Indian had the right to separate themselves from their tribes and live under protection of United States laws like any other citizens.

2. The climax of the case came when Standing Bear was given permission to speak for his people: "I am now with the soldiers and officers. I want to go back to my old place north. I want to save myself and my tribe. My brothers, it seems to me as if I stood in front of a great prairie fire. I would take up my children and run to save their lives; or if I stood on the bank of an overflowing river, I would take my people and fly to higher ground. Oh, my brothers, the Almighty looks down on me, and knows what I am, and hears my words. May the Almighty send a good spirit to brood over you, my brothers, to move you to help me. If a white man had land, and someone should swindle him, that man would try to get it back, and you would not blame him. Look on me. Take pity on me, and help me to save the lives of the women and children. My brothers, a power, which I cannot resist, crowds me down to the ground. I need help. I have done."

3. Judge Dundy ruled that an Indian was a "person" within the meaning of the *habeas corpus* act, that the right of expatriation was

a natural, inherent, and inalienable right of the Indian as well as the white race, and that in time of peace no authority, civil or military, existed for transporting Indians from one section of the country to another without the consent of the Indians or to confine them to any particular reservation against their will.

4. "I have never been called upon to hear or decide a case that appealed so strongly to my sympathy," he said. "The Poncas are amongst the most peaceable and friendly of all the Indian tribes.... If they could be removed to the Indian Territory by force, and kept there in the same way, I can see no good reason why they might not be taken and kept by force in the penitentiary at Lincoln, or Leavenworth, or Jefferson City, or any other place which the commander of the forces might, in his judgment, see proper to designate. I cannot think that any such arbitrary authority exists in this country."

5. When Judge Dundy concluded the proceedings by ordering Standing Bear and his Ponca band released from custody, the audience in the courtroom rose to its feet and, according to a newspaper reporter, "such a shout went up as was never heard in a courtroom." General Crook was the first to reach Standing Bear to congratulate him. (Dee Brown, *Buried My Heart at Wounded Knee*. New York: Bantam Books, 1979, pp. 342–344).

Paragraph Patterns

Authors want readers to follow their thinking; therefore, they structure paragraphs using patterns to develop their ideas so that their discourse is presented in a logical order. There are many patterns authors may use and, at times, authors may employ more than one pattern in an essay. The purpose of identifying paragraph patterns makes it easier to deconstruct paragraphs for meaning and organize the material to write a summary. By identifying paragraph patterns and following signal words, efficient readers are able to identify consistent patterns and note when an author shifts his or her thought. For example, let us suppose you are reading an account of a historical event that may be developed in chronological order or a cause-and-effect relationship of the particular historical account. Or a science text may present information developed with a problem-solution structure to focus on a particular problem. When authors wish to persuade you about issues they may present the ideas in an opinion-reason pattern. The shift in language provides the clues as to whether the author is presenting facts and opinions, cause-and-effect relationship, simple listing, or opinion reason. Examples of paragraph patterns are discussed below.

Simple Listing

If authors present information in chronological order, the way in which events happen, simply listing events is often the format used. Signal words are used in the context to guide the reader to identify the list in this particular paragraph pattern. Signal words associated with a paragraph pattern of simple listing are presented with terms such as "first, second, third, etc." or "first, then, finally, etc." The passage below illustrates this.

Passage 14:

1. *Firstly*, as I have already observed, it would greatly lessen the number of Papists, with whom we are yearly overrun, being the principal breeders of the nation as well as our most dangerous enemies; and who stay at home on purpose to deliver the kingdom to the Pretender, hoping to take their advantage by the absence of so many good Protestants, who have chosen rather to leave their Country than to stay at home and pay tithes against their conscience to an Episcopal curate.

2. *Secondly*, the poorer tenants will have something valuable of their own, which by law may be made liable to distress, and help to pay their landlord's rent, their corn and cattle being already seized and money a think unknown.

3. *Thirdly*, whereas the maintenance of a hundred thousand children, from two years old and upwards, cannot be computed at less than ten *shillings* a piece per *annum*, the nation's stock will be thereby increased fifty thousand pounds per annum, besides the profit of a new dish introduced to the bales of all gentlemen of fortune in the kingdom who have any refinement in taste. And the money will circulate among ourselves, the goods being entirely of our own growth and manufacture.

4. *Fourthly*, the constant breeders, besides the gain of eight shillings sterling per annum by the sale of their children, will be rid of the charge for maintaining them after the first year. (Jonathan Swift, "A Modest Proposal," 1729, http://art-bin.com/art/omodest.html)

In the above passage, the signal words make it is easy to follow the authors ideas. This paragraph pattern makes it easy for the reader to follow and write a summary. What the reader will still have to determine is if the examples the author has given are valid. Here we are simply addressing the structure of the paragraphs.

Compare and Contrast

To show differences and similarities authors provide "word clues" to help the reader understand the issues under consideration. In addition, comparing and contrasting helps readers understand topics which are unfamiliar and with no point of reference. The author provides comparisons and examples, which are familiar to the reader to understand the unfamiliar. In the following passage, the author does this to compare and contrast American culture to traditional Chinese culture.

Passage 15:

1. Americans have a sense of space, not of place. Go to an American home in exurbia, and almost the first thing you do is drift toward the picture window. How curious that the first compliment you pay your host inside his house is to say how lovely it is outside his house! He is pleased that you should admire his vistas. The distant horizon is not merely a line separating earth from sky, it is a symbol of the future. The American is not rooted in his place, however lovely: his eyes are drawn by the expanding space to a point on the horizon, which is his future.

2. By *contrast*, consider the traditional Chinese home. Blank walls enclose it. Step behind the spirit wall and you are in a courtyard with perhaps a miniature garden around the corner. Once inside the private compound you are wrapped in an *ambiance* of calm beauty, an ordered world of buildings, pavement, rock, and decorative vegetation. *But* you have no distant view: nowhere does space open out before you. Raw nature in such a home is experienced only as weather, and the only open space is the sky above. The Chinese is rooted in his place. When he has to leave, it is not for the promised land on the terrestrial horizon, but for another world altogether along the vertical, religious axis of his imagination. (Tuan, Yi-Fu, "American Space, Chinese Place," *Harper's Magazine*, July, 1974, vol 249, p. 8.)

In the above passage, the author has provided the demarcation between the two cultures with his language, e.g., "By contrast" the reader simply has to list the differences between the two cultures as described by the author.

Cause and Effect

A cause-and-effect relationship suggests that one can trace an incident back to a particular event as the cause. This is a simplistic way of describing what can become a very complex endeavor when dealing with issues of cause and effect in history, politics, and societal significance or even family relationships. When authors give a "cause" for some occurrence, look for word clues which signal the "effects." For example, "consequently," "as a result," "because," and so on. The cause-effect relationship is illustrated in the expository text example given below.

Passage 16:

1. Dedicated watchers of soap operas often confuse fact with fiction. Sometimes this can be endearing, sometimes ludicrous. During the Senate Watergate hearings (which were broadcast on daytime television), viewers whose favorite soap operas were preempted simply adopted the hearings as substitute soaps. Daniel Shorr reports that the listeners began "telephoning the networks to criticize slow-moving sequences, suggesting script changes and asking for the return of favorite witnesses, like 'that nice John Dean.'"
2. Stars of soap operas tell hair-raising stories of their encounters with fans suffering from this affliction. Susan Lucci, who plays the promiscuous Erica Kane on "All My Children," tells of a time she was riding in a parade: "We were in a crowd of about 250,000, traveling in an antique open car moving ver-r-ry slowly. At that time in the series I was involved with a character named Nick. Some man broke through, came right up to the car and said to me, "Why don't you give me a little bit of what you've been giving Nick?" The man hung onto the car, menacingly, until she was rescued by the police. Another time, when she was in church, the reverent silence was broken by a woman's astonished remark. "Oh my god, Erica prays!"
3. Just as viewers come to confuse the actors with their roles, so too they see the soap opera image of life in America as real. The National Institute of Mental Health reported that a majority of Americans actually adopt what they see in soap operas to handle their own life problems. The images are not only "true to life"; they are a guide for living.
4. Under the surface of romantic complications, soap operas sell a vision of morality and American family life, of a society where marriage is the highest good, sex the greatest evil, where babies are worshiped

and abortion condemned, where motherhood is exalted and children ignored. It is a vision of a world devoid of social conflict. There are hardly any short-order cooks, bus drivers, mechanics, construction workers, or farmers on soap operas. Blue-collar problems do not enter these immaculate homes. No one suffers from flat feet or derriere spread from long hours spent at an unrewarding or frustrating job. The upwardly mobile professionals who populate soap operas love their work. Probably because they are hardly ever at it—one lawyer clocked in at his office exactly once in three months. Their problems are those of people with time on their hands to covet the neighbor's wife, track down villains, betray friends, and enjoy what one observer has called "the perils of Country Club Place."(Donna Woolfolk Cross, *Mediaspeak, Sin, Suffer and Repent*. New York: Coward-McCann, 1983, pp. 124–141.)

Questions for Passage 16

1. Write a declarative sentence stating the problem.
2. List the causes of the problem.
3. List the effects.

Persuasive Argument

The persuasive essay is a form of writing in which the author takes a position and attempts to persuade readers to take a particular position on a topic. This essay may include evidence to support the position, or the argument may take the form of an opinion-reason essay—relying heavily on the opinion citing reasons for the position taken. The reader must determine if the argument and positions have been presented in a logical manner offering sufficient evidence or information to convince the reader that the position is reasonable and logical position for the reader to consider and accept. For example, when we decide whether one painting is better than another, our Personal Matrix, will influence the choice; when we have preference for one food over another, or preference for one form of music over another, or in a contest one person is consider more beautiful, this is one's opinion. If we gather sufficient evidence and apply criteria to determine how we will judge a specific issue, it is still in the realm of opinion, as we cannot have a definite measure. However, there may be an agreed upon measure among a group of people; that is, one group may decide that everyone with brown eyes should be considered beautiful; another group may say blue eyes.

Read the following excerpt from Hillary Rodham Clinton's speech at the United Nations Fourth World Conference on Women (1995) in which the writer makes a strong appeal for the human rights of women.

Passage 17

By gathering in Beijing, we are focusing world attention on issues that matter most in the lives of women and their families: access to education, health care, jobs and credit, the chance to enjoy basic legal and human rights and participate fully in the political life of their countries....

What we are learning around the world is that if women are healthy and educated, their families will flourish. If women are free from violence, their families will flourish. If women have a chance to work and earn as full and equal partners in society, their families will flourish.

And when families flourish, communities and nations will flourish....

Women comprise more than half the world's population. Women are 70 percent of the world's poor, and two-thirds of those who are not taught to read and write.

Women are the primary caretakers for most of the world's children and elderly. Yet much of the work we do is not valued—not by economists, not by historians, not by popular culture, not by government leaders....

They are being forced into prostitution, and they are being barred from the bank lending office and banned from the ballot box....

As an American, I want to speak up for women in my own country—women who are raising children on the minimum wage, women who can't afford health care or child care, women whose lives are threatened by violence, including violence in their own homes.

I want to speak up for mothers who are fighting for good schools, safe neighborhoods, clean air and clean airwaves; for older women, some of them widows, who have raised their families and now find that their skills and life experiences are not valued in the workplace; for women who are working all night as nurses, hotel clerks, and fast food cooks so that they can be at home during the day with their kids; and for women everywhere who simply don't have time to do everything they are called upon to do each day....

We also must recognize that women will never gain full dignity until their human rights are respected and protected....

No one should be forced to remain silent for fear of religious or political persecution, arrest, abuse, or torture....

Tragically, women are most often the ones whose human rights are violated.

Even in the late 20th century, the rape of women continues to be used as an instrument of armed conflict. Women and children make up a large majority of the world's refugees. When women are excluded from the political process, they become even more vulnerable to abuse.

I believe that, on the eve of a new millennium, it is time to break our silence. It is time for us to say here in Beijing, and the world to hear, that it is no longer acceptable to discuss women's rights as separate from human rights....

It is a violation of human rights when women and girls are sold into the slavery of prostitution.

It is a violation of human rights when women are doused with gasoline, set on fire, and burned to death because their marriage dowries are deemed too small.

It is a violation of human rights when individual women are raped in their own communities and when thousands of women are subjected to rape as a tactic or prize of war.

It is a violation of human rights when a leading cause of death worldwide among women ages 14 to 44 is the violence they are subjected to in their own homes.

It is a violation of human rights when young girls are brutalized by the painful and degrading practice of genital mutilation.

It is a violation of human rights when women are denied the right to plan their own families, and that includes being forced to have abortions or being sterilized against their will....

Women must enjoy the right to participate fully in the social and political lives of their countries if we want freedom and democracy to thrive and endure....

Let me be clear. Freedom means the right of people to assemble, organize, and debate openly. It means respecting the views of those who may disagree with the views of their governments. It means not taking citizens away from their loved ones and jailing them, mistreating them, or denying them their freedom or dignity because of the peaceful expression of their ideas and opinions.

In my country, we recently celebrated the 75th anniversary of women's suffrage. It took 150 years after the signing of our Declaration of Independence for women to win the right to vote.

It took 72 years of organized struggle on the part of many courageous women and men. It was one of America's most divisive philosophical wars. But it was also a bloodless war. Suffrage was achieved without a shot being fired.

As long as discrimination and inequities remain so commonplace around the world—as long as girls and women are valued less, fed less, fed last, overworked, underpaid, not schooled, and subjected to violence in and out of their homes—the potential of the human family to create a peaceful, prosperous world will not be realized. (Hillary Rodham Clinton, "Women's Rights Are Human Rights," September 5, 1995, Gifts of Speech: http://gos.sbc.edu/c/clinton.html)

Questions for Passage 17

1. What is the basic problem the writer has identified which plague women?
2. Identify the evidence the writer presents to support her argument: list evidence of opinion and fact.
3. Write a paragraph stating why the evidence presented thus far is convincing and or the kind of information you still need to convince you of this argument.

Summarizing Authors' Language

An important point to remember in summarizing the language of the author is to write what the author states—your opinions or emotional responses are not included in a summary. As you read, determine what the author is stating—a main idea may appear in each paragraph or one main idea may recur in a number of paragraphs. Your task is to write a summary that is true to the author's writing. Summarizing is an important skill that is discussed in detail in Chapters Three and Five.

Chapter Three

Alternative Ways of Thinking About Reading

Thinking in a new way always necessitates personal transformation.
—Joe L. Kincheloe

Lesson 6: Thinking Outside of the Box

As we discussed, literal thinking, from point A to point B, gives you the stated meaning of the text, and is the first and necessary step in constructing meaning. In Chapter Two, we addressed those literal questions, who? what? when? where? how? why? to get answers for the stated meaning of text and focus on the order in which things happen. Your Personal Matrix plays an important role, validating what you know, alerting you to what seems puzzling for lack of experience, knowledge, etc. In this Chapter we discuss alternative ways of thinking to critically examine what you read and go beyond linear thinking questions to provide you with tools to do an in-depth analysis of what you read. Alternative ways of thinking will help you understand the author's point of view, make connections, see relationships from a perspective in ways you have not done so before. For critical analysis, we exam the following alternative ways of thinking to construct meaning: (1) lateral thinking, (2) concept webbing, (3) semantic mapping, and (4) character analysis. In each process, your Personal Matrix serves as the starting point.

What Is Lateral Thinking?

Lateral thinking is used in many organizations to help people find creative ways to solve complex problems. However, I have found it particularly useful for readers. Over the past 20 years, students in my classes have applied lateral thinking to their reading strategies and have shown significant improvement in their critical thinking skills. Utilizing lateral thinking, their interpretations of complex issues indicated an in-depth analysis that was lacking prior to applying lateral thinking strategies. In addition, they write crisper, stronger analysis about their readings.

Lateral thinking gives readers an opportunity to change your perceptions, find alternative ways of viewing issues, explanations, and interpretations. Thus, applied to reading, lateral thinking encourages you to try new approaches, come up with new ideas, and view a topic from a fresh angle so that your interpretations are focused and clearer. Thus, you experience issues, events, characters, etc., from a broader perspective.

Lateral Thinking and Reading Strategies

The reading strategies in Table 2 explain how to apply lateral thinking to your reading. As you do so, you will see an immediate improvement in your writing about text, as it will dramatically improve. In Lessons 7 and 8, student examples are presented to show you how to apply lateral thinking to reading strategies.

TABLE 2

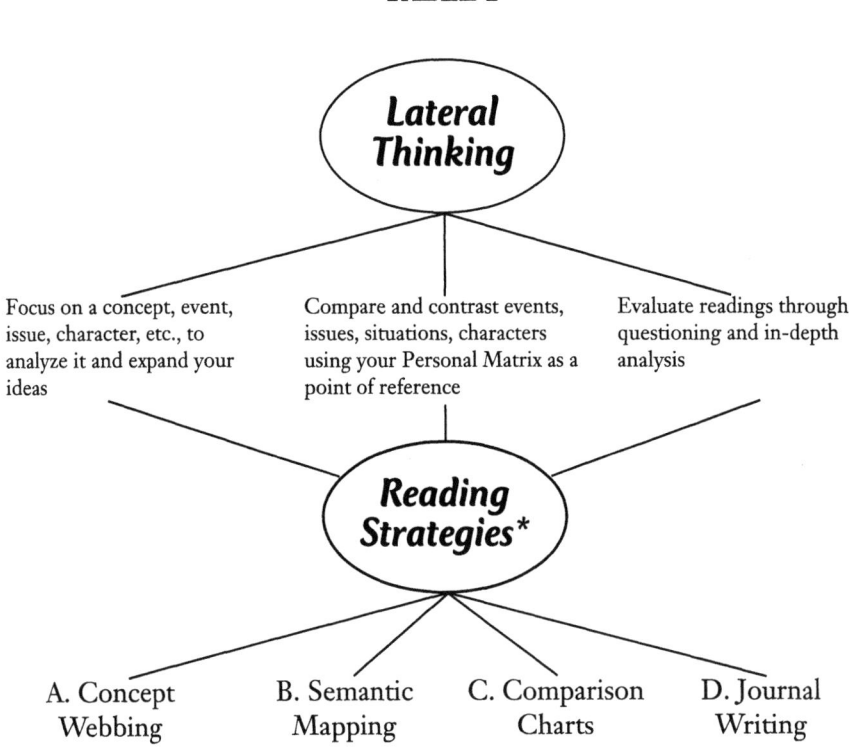

*Use reading strategies in a combination or as a single application.

Ask the right questions—that is, think creatively and ask questions which will expand your ideas. As you apply these strategies, always ask critical questions, for example:

- Who? What? Where? How? When? Why?
- How does this reflect my Personal Matrix? What is different?
- What other situations, ideas, concepts, etc., are like this?
- What does the author suggest by what he or she states?
- What does the author want me to believe?
- Why does the author want me to believe this?
- Who benefits?
- Additionally, what action would I take or what posture would I assume if I believe this?

Lesson 7: The Concept Web

A concept web is a nonlinear process that encourages lateral thinking. It enables you to recall information, monitor your thinking, clarify issues, and gain a broader view of the topic. When you create a concept web, you generate a visual diagram to view a topic from a fresh perspective. A concept web is an individualized web meaningful to you, the reader; it becomes a visual representation of your expanded ideas. In addition, your web will help you to write improved, comprehensive essays.

Creating a Concept Web

A web begins with a topic which is placed in a circle in the middle of the page. You begin by adding words or phrases around the topic, whatever comes to mind, e.g.,

Let us say that you have read an article on "family"; the concept web might develop as follows:

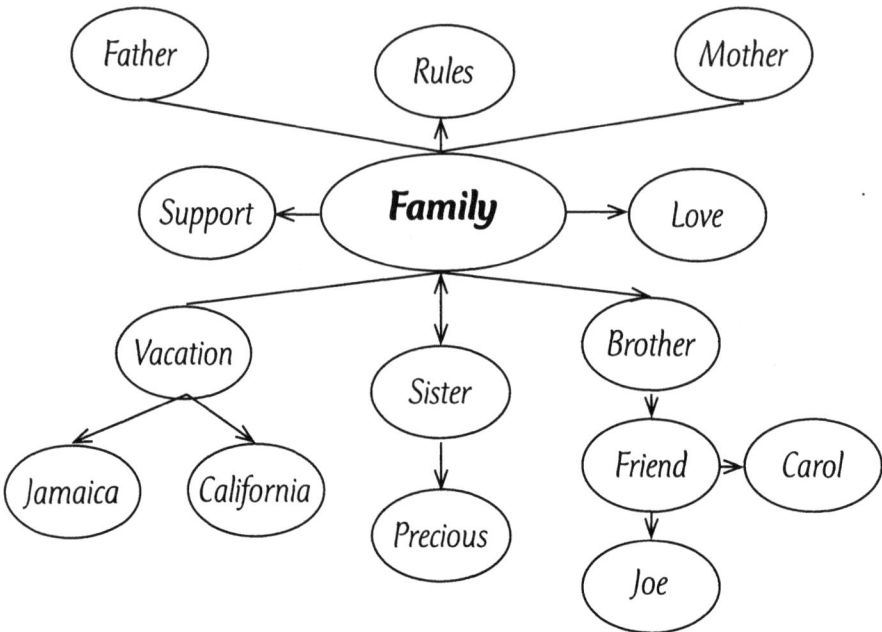

As this concept web illustrates, the reader can generate ideas to write an essay about the family. The ideas are organized as (1) the introduction, (2) body of the essay, and (3) ending or conclusions. You may wish to use these numbers to label each category. For example,

- Introduction ideas labeled as "1"—family, love, support, rules, mother, and father
- Body of essay labeled as "2"—which might include other members of the family, sisters with supporting details—precious—and brother which would also include the other supporting details listed under brother; additional information would include the family vacation examples of places; and family friends with specific names, and so on.
- Conclusion would be labeled as "3."

By continuing this web, addition ideas can be generated which would give you the foundation for beginning your essay. The following are examples of using the concept web—as an alternative way of thinking—to expand thinking about reading and writing.

The Writing-Web-Rewriting Process

Students used a writing-web-rewriting process to monitor their thinking about reading and expand their writing about text. Student concept webs, which appear here, read books on "autonomy." One book was *Dibs in Search of Self* by Virginia Axline. After reading several chapters, students prepared concept webs to explore issues of autonomy and write a character sketch on the main character.

First students wrote a character sketch on the main character without referring to the book. They wanted to determine how well they could recall information, make connections to draw inferences. When they completed this paragraph, they created a web on the character. Then using their web as a guide, students added the additional information from the web to expand their paragraphs.

The following examples illustrate the writing-web-writing process. The difference in the students' thinking is clearly demonstrated in writing the second paragraph.

Step 1: Student "A" Paragraph Before Concept Web

> A little boy named Dibs would behave very differently from the other kids of his age and because of this was a subject of great interest to two of his teachers. He was 6 years old, being in one of the best schools and yet he wasn't performing, as he should have. He wouldn't take something from you when asked. Instead of sitting on a chair, Dibs would be on the floor crawling. The trouble was to get him to take his hat and coat off in the morning and as it appears, he didn't even want to come to school. After school, all the kids would leave, for him it was different. The teachers would have to fight with him to get him to put his coat and hat back on. And at times, the chauffeur had to carry him to take him to the car and get him back home.

Step 2: Student "A" Web After Writing the First Paragraph

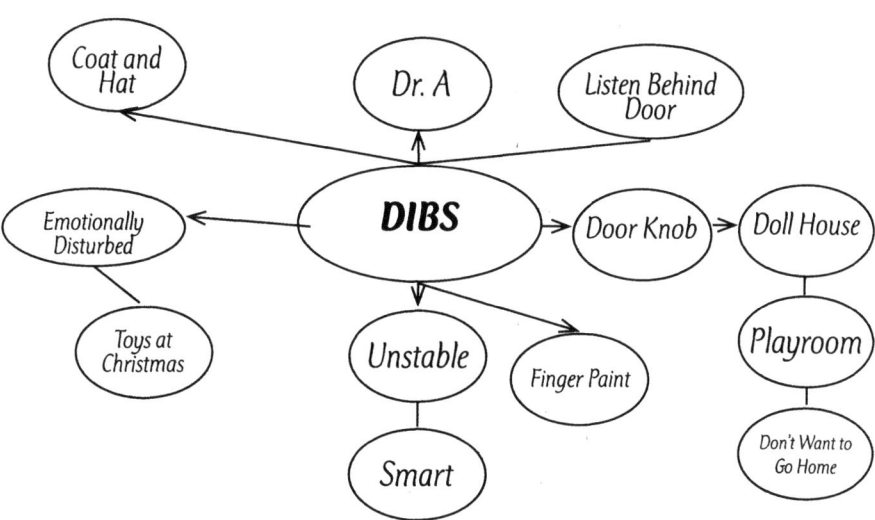

Step 3: Student "A" Paragraph Using the Web

> Once upon a time, there was a little boy named Dibs. He was 6 years old and he had been in a private school for two years. The two teachers in charge knew that he was emotionally disturbed because he was not behaving as his peers. He would not take his coat and hat off and when he was handed something he would categorically refuse. So they thought a specialist should see him just to give a definite opinion. So Dr. Axline was called in and she agreed to see Dibs. They scheduled a session for the following Thursday for the two of them. After Dr. Axline saw the parents, she was particularly interested in seeing the mother. Dibs got to know Dr. Axline and he started to enjoy the sessions since he could play and had a chance to be "Dibs." He enjoyed the sandbox, and all the soldiers he got for Christmas and played with them in the dollhouse. Dr. Axline was surprised to learn that Dibs had a vast vocabulary and wondered how he acquired it. She found out that Dibs listened behind doors when people talked. He wasn't crazy about the finger painting because he thought it was messy. So each time he touched it he would wipe his hands off. The worst time was when he had to leave because he would rather stay at school.

Compare the two paragraphs, what do you notice right away? In the first paragraph, basic information about Dibs is given, but the sentences are short and lack transitions from one idea to the next. The paragraph does not have many details nor does it give a very interesting picture of the character. In the second paragraph, we get a better understanding of this character. It is immediately apparent how concept webbing helped this student expand her ideas, present more details which resulted in a more expressive passage. The second paragraph also provides a reader with additional information to support assertions about Dibs. The two paragraphs were then combined, and the following passage was included in the student's essay.

Student "A" Combined Paragraphs 1 and 2

> A little boy named Dibs was a subject of great interest of two teachers because he would behave very differently from the other kids of his age. Dibs was a little boy 6 years old and for two years attended one of the best private schools in the city. Yet, he was not performing as he should. The two teachers in charge knew that he was emotionally disturbed because he was not behaving as his peers. It was trouble just trying to get him to take his hat and coat off in the morning. And it appeared that he did not even want to come to school. When he was handed something, he categorically refused to accept it. Instead of sitting on a chair, Dibs would crawl around on the floor. The worst time came for Dibs when it was time to leave the school. At the end of the day when all the kids would leave, for Dibs it was different. The teachers had to fight with him to get him to put on his coat and hat. At times, the chauffeur had to carry him to get him to the car and take him back home. So the teachers thought that a specialist should see him to get a definite opinion. Dr. Axline was called in and she agreed to see the kid. They scheduled a session for the following Thursday for Dr. Axline and Dibs. Dr. Axline also saw the parents; she was particularly interested in talking with the mother. Dibs got to know Dr. Axline and he started to enjoy later sessions because he could play and

had a chance just to be "Dibs." He enjoyed the sandbox, and all the toy soldiers he got for Christmas and played with them in the dollhouse. He was not crazy about the finger painting because he thought it was messy. Each time he touched it, he would wipe his hands off. Dr. Axline was surprised to learn that Dibs had a vast vocabulary and wondered how he acquired it. She found out that Dibs listened behind doors when people talked.

From the combined paragraphs, it is clear that lateral thinking applied to concept webbing encouraged an expanded interpretation of the reading material giving the character more depth. With lateral thinking and the web connections, relationships make sense.

Below is another example of a student's initial writing sample and concept web with rewriting. In this case, the reader's initial writing indicates difficulty in recalling information and writing the paragraph.

Step 1: Student "B" Initial Paragraph

Dibs is a very young child who was afraid of locked doors. He did not communicate with anyone, and was completely withdrawn from the world around him. He was later found to possess a level of intelligence and knowledge far beyond his age. How he attained this could only be told by himself, "sitting on the edge of things close enough to hear what is happening." Dibs showed tremendous inner strength in coping with his parents. He was also a very keen observer, and expressed himself very well.

Step 2: Student "B" Concept Web

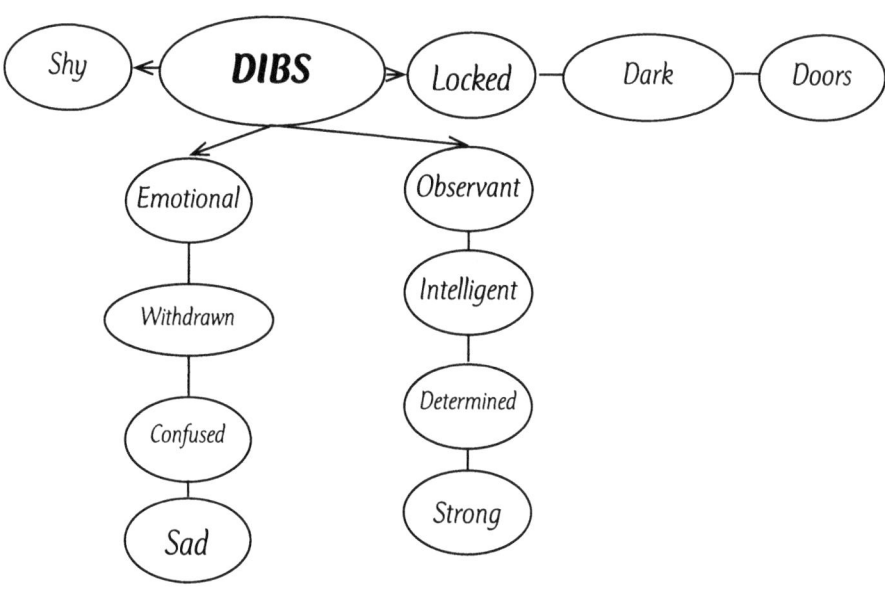

74   Reading Between the Lines

Step 3: Student "B" Combined Paragraphs 1 and 2

> Dibs was a shy five year old boy withdrawn from his parents, sister and those at school. He did not communicate with anyone, and was completely withdrawn from the world around him. This, however, was only the opinion of those who did not know him. He always seemed sad, frightened and upset over almost anything. It was hard to communicate with him. He bore a bitter hatred for his family—and he expressed unhappiness in going home. He seemed to be constantly locked in his room surrounded by his toys and other material things. Perhaps even in the dark basement for punishment. This caused him to develop a fear of locked doors and dark rooms. Dibs showed tremendous inner strength in coping with his parents. In his therapy play sessions he was found to be very intelligent, observant and intellectually advanced for a child of his age. He was also a very keen observer, and expressed himself very well. He was always determined to try and solve his problems at the therapy play sessions where he showed keen observation and inner strength. He was later found to possess a level of intelligence and knowledge far beyond his age. How he attained this could only be told by him, "sitting on the edge of things close enough to hear what is happening."

Student "B's" second paragraph shows a remarkable improvement as the reader had time to reflect and use lateral thinking with the concept web to expand his writing. The web provides the format to make connections, see relationships to draw inferences for a more comprehensive and interesting character sketch of Dibs. What we can also observe are the additional thoughts and ideas generated in the web to develop a more expressive writing.

The next student's example also illustrates how lateral thinking helps the writer expand ideas and write a significantly better character sketch.

Step 1: Student "C" Initial Paragraph

> Dibs is a boy who is very withdrawn, he did not speak or play with the other children in the private school that he attended. He started to show signs of his intelligence by reading books at his school, or at least acting as though he was reading by concentrating on the pages. There was a therapy session set up for him where he went once every week and after two or three weeks he began to show great signs of normal intelligent behavior.

This paragraph is straightforward, to the point with little depth in the description of the character. The student then generated an elaborate concept, monitoring his thinking, applying linear thinking to the concept web recording his thinking. This process enabled the student to write a more expressive, interesting description on the character Dibs.

Step 2: Student "C" Web After Initial Paragraph

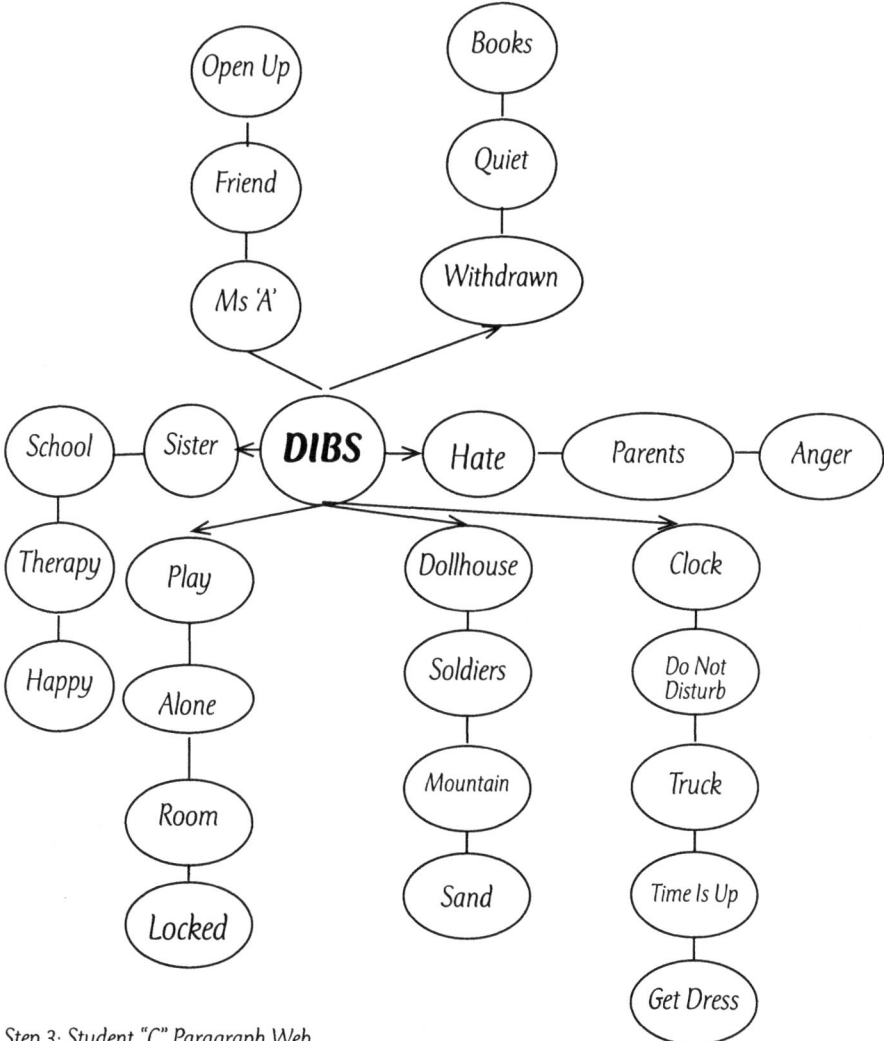

Step 3: Student "C" Paragraph Web

Dibs was a little boy who was very withdrawn, he did not speak or play with the other children in the private school that he attended. He was very quiet when he was at home and even at the private school he attended. It seems although he was most happy when he was at therapy sessions that took place every Thursday. He named his therapist "Ms. A." After a few weeks, he began to start conversations and even ask questions. He was very alert; he read, matched colors and told time perfectly. Dibs started to show signs of intelligence by reading books at his school, or at least acting as though he was reading by concentrating on the pages. He was very aware of what was going on around him, He even noticed the observers behind the screen who were taping his sessions. Dibs was never very happy when it came time for him to go home. One time his father came to pick him up after his therapy session and Dibs tried to tell him something but his father would not take time to listen. Dibs became very angry and he shouted at the father that he hated him.

Therapy sessions were set up for him where he went once a week. After two or three weeks, he began to show great signs of normal intelligent behavior. Dibs loved going to therapy, there he could be himself or anyone he wanted to be. Whereas when he was at home, he spent most of his time in his room where he had everything money could buy, but he was still lonely. He needed love and attention; he needed someone to share things with.

Student "C's" initial paragraph was limited and not a great deal of information was given. After an elaborate web was created, student "C" recalled much more information to expand his original paragraph; applying lateral thinking to the concept web enabled this student to compose an excellent expanded character description of Dibs. It is cohesive, expressive, and characterizes Dibs in a way which makes it clear to the reader that the character Dibs is unusual. It is also evident that student "C" was able to draw inferences based on the connections made in the web, e.g., "Dibs needed love, attention and someone to share things with."

Through reflecting and monitoring thinking, the reader applied lateral thinking to write a dramatically different passage. For the last character sketch on Dibs we can once again see the dramatic effects of lateral thinking on a student's writing.

Step 1: Student "D": Initial Paragraph

> Dibs is a child who showed all the symptoms of mental retardation or autism at the school and in the kindergarten class he attended for the first time in his life. Among several examples is one when someone ask him to take off his coat and gloves he would not answer and would stand in the classroom in the same spot where his mother dropped him off in the morning. At times he would go limp, showing no interest at all for anything. Still he did not open up enough to be judged by anybody.

The opening sentence of this paragraph is a good one as it tells the reader the focus of the story—whether the main character has problems. The writer also cites examples to indicate why he has drawn these conclusions. But, the writing is without much expression or detail to gain the reader's attention and convey a strong sense of Dibs. The student then created the following web applying lateral thinking to rewrite the paragraph and added details that give a stronger picture of the character.

Step 2: Student "D" Concept Web

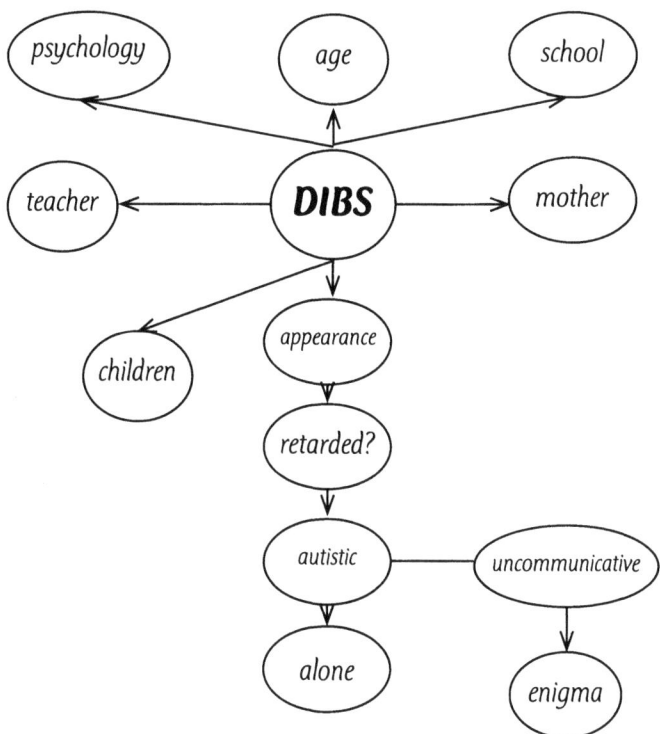

Step 3: Student "D" Second Paragraph After Web

This is a true story about a young child, Dibs, which at first glance, is a sad story, but evolves and ends into a wonderful victory—one of psychology over prejudice. At the age of three, Dibs started his kindergarten class and showed all the symptoms of mental retardation or autism. He was uncommunicative, lonely and unhappy. When a teacher talked to him, he would not answer. His natural tendency was to stand crouched against the wall. He would not play with his classmates either. So he became the object of curiosity for all the teachers. His teachers discussed the possibility that he might be retarded or autistic. The teachers began to watch him surreptitiously. Why? The child would not open up to anyone. Among several examples of this was when a teacher would ask him to take off his coat and gloves he would not answer and would stand in the classroom in the same spot where his mother dropped him off in the morning. At times he would go limp, showing no interest at all in anything. Still he did not open up enough to be judged by anybody. Like the moonlight trying to illuminate a closed room, the good intentions of the teachers to observe him to understand him fully, only projected some light on this poor child. For lack of sufficient information, they could not reach an honest decision.

Review these student concept webs again. All of the webs are different and clearly reflect information about the same character, but each web reflects the individual's thinking in a format that encouraged lateral thinking—applying one's thinking in a random manner unconcerned with order or sequence. In addition, the influence of one's Personal Matrix is apparent as one engages in metacognition—monitoring your thinking—to record information. After creating the webs, all of these students not only improved their understanding of the reading but they also improved the quality of their writing. Their thinking became more involved and the analysis more complex. Thus, there is a compound effect: as students use alternative ways to think more critically, the analysis of the story becomes more multifaceted.

The final example of lateral thinking is included to illustrate the ease with which a student uses language to express his ideas after following the process of the concept web.

Step 1: Student "E" Initial Paragraph

> Dibs is a five year old little boy born of very affluent parents. His mother is a famous doctor and his father a well-known scientist. The family lives in a brownstone on the upper Eastside of Manhattan. When Dibs' mother found out that she was pregnant, she thought her career was ended. Throughout her whole pregnancy she was upset that Dibs was impeding her social life. When Dibs was born, his mother gave him all the toys, clothing food, and shelter, but there was no love or warmth or affection from his parents.

Step 2: Student "E" Concept Web

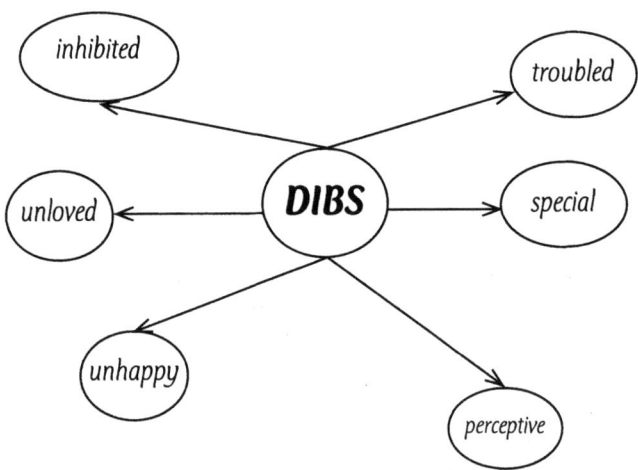

Step 3: Student "E" Combined Paragraph After Concept Web

> Before conception, Dibs was an unwanted child. Dibs was born of wealthy parents and had enough food, clothing and shelter but he was lacking the warm, love, attention and affection that his neglectful mother overlooked and that he needed. His selfish mother treated Dibs as if he were an obstacle in her life. Having Dibs changed her social status. The fact that Dibs turned out to be an emotionally disturbed child made her bitter towards him. When all of this built up inside of her, poor Dibs was left to school teachers' interest. They took time out to see what Dibs' real problems were. For example, there was a teacher who took time out to button his coat when it was time to go home and even though he refused her, she insisted on helping him in the midst of his tantrums. Dibs was not a stupid child. When he was in school, he would creep around on the floor, stay in the corners and pretend to be strange. He was afraid to open up his feelings. His perceptions around the classroom were really great—even though he did not communicate with the rest of the class, he noticed his surroundings, e.g. the paint pans, the colors, the signs and various other things. But Dibs was lacking attention, cuddling, affection, love and warmth denied by his cold mother. He hated to go home whenever it was time to go home, he would go into tantrums and cry. I think that Dibs was happier in school than he was at home.

As we read these examples, it is understandable that lateral thinking engages the reader to view situations from various points of view, expanding ideas to construct better interpretations of the text. To make connections to other characters involved in the text, creating webs on other characters will enable the reader to understand the complexities between characters. In the case of the character Dibs, students wanted to understand Dibs' connection to his parents and generated concept webs on the parents.

Step 1: Student "F" Parent Profile

> Dibs' parents are very wealthy, intelligent and educated. The mother is a surgeon and the father is a scientist. They are very rich. But, they are two frightened, lonely, unhappy people that cannot admit that they have failed. His mother is an elegant woman but arrogant. She feels very lonely and insecure and so does the father.

Step 2: Student "F" Parent Profile Web

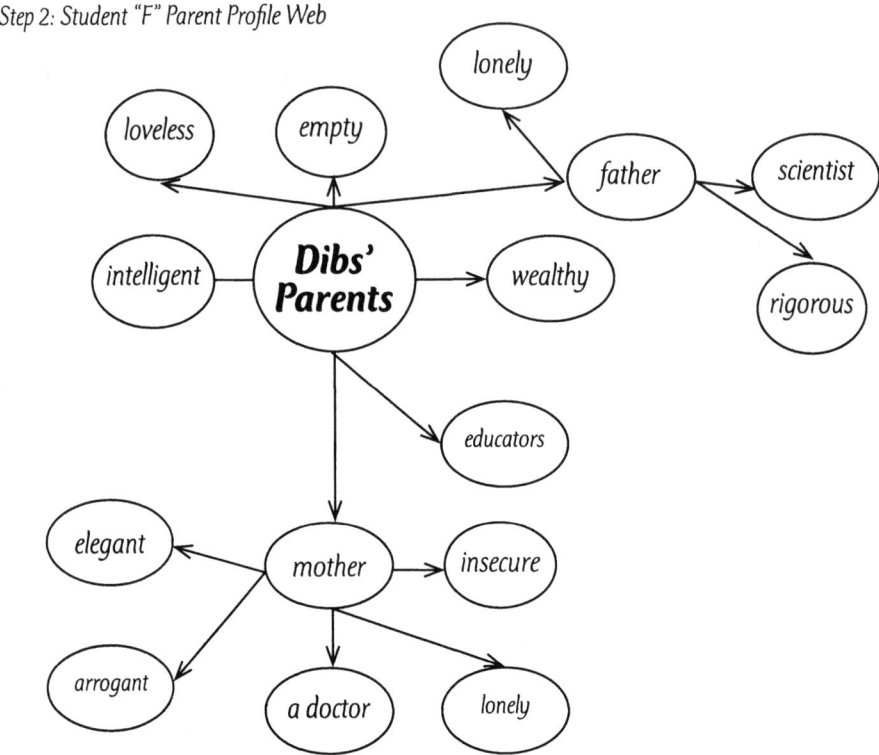

Step 3: Student "F" Parent Profile Combined Paragraph

> Dibs' parents are very wealthy, intelligent and educated. The mother is a surgeon and the father is a scientist. But, they are two frightened, lonely, unhappy people and they cannot admit that they have failed as parents. His mother is elegant but she is arrogant, cold woman. She is very sophisticated and likes to see everything perfectly and properly done. Both the father and mother is very lonely and insecure. The father is also very strict.

After creating the web, the student's combined paragraphs are better organized, with some additional information creating a better profile of the parents. The next parent profile gives us a broader description of Dibs' parents.

Step 1: Student "G" Parents Profile

> Dibs' mother is a successful medical doctor with great intellectual abilities, but lacking the patience and warmth necessary to raise children. Dibs' father possesses the same intellectual abilities, but he has very little patience with Dibs. He never seems to have time or patience to listen or try to understand the emotional needs of his son. Parents such as these should not be blessed with children.

Step 2: Student "G" Parents Profile Web

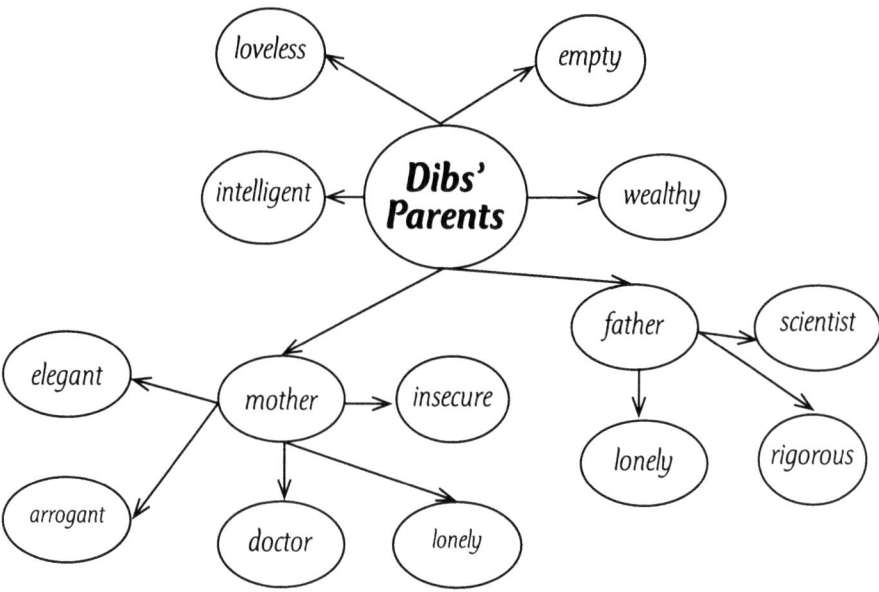

Step 3: Student "G" Parents Profile Combined Paragraph

> Dibs' parents are lonely people trapped in their own selfish worlds; lacking warmth, understanding and patience. Dibs' mother is a successful medical doctor with great intellectual abilities, but lacking the warmth necessary to raise children. She is a very scared woman, embarrassed by a son she believes is retarded. Dibs' father possesses the same kind of intellectual abilities as the mother but has very little patience with Dibs. He never seems to have time or patience to listen or try to understand the emotional needs of his son. The father felt that everything Dibs said was meaningless and stupid. These parents felt tied down socially and burdened by their child. They both seemed to be perfectionist and their lives seemed cold. Parents such as these should not be blessed with children.

The above examples are extraordinary illustrations of how lateral thinking applied to concept webs enables readers to broaden their interpretations, analyze the events in the story, and articulate these ideas in an expanded form.

Create Your Concept Web

Now that you have seen student samples of concept webbing, follow the instructions below to create your own web employing lateral thinking.

Exercise/Directions:
Try the following exercise to combine your thinking and writing.

- Choose a topic for your web, for example, an emotion, an idea, a character from a book you are currently reading or have read.
- Next, begin writing on this topic for five or ten minutes.
- When you have finish writing, create your concept web.
- Use your web to write a new paragraph and combine your two paragraphs.

Compare your paragraphs. Your combined paragraph should be clearer with more precise language and more details and should be much more interesting to convey exactly what you intended. This helps demonstrate why authors must choose precise language to get their meaning across to readers. Get feedback from a friend. Let him or her read the first paragraph and your combined paragraphs. Practice and apply the process to your current reading material.

Lesson 8: Semantic Maps

A semantic map is an alternative thinking strategy that also gives you a visual representation for expository text and imaginative literature. However, semantic mapping differs from a concept web. When you create a semantic map you are making a conscious effort to connect ideas in a way that gives you a clear representation of complex events, issues, or character relationships. For example, you may want to use a semantic map to trace events and dates, or to show linkages between complex issues or concepts. Or you may wish to understand the complex relationships between characters. What emerges from semantic mapping is a clear visual representation for you to follow.

Expository Text

Semantic maps are very helpful in clarifying terminology and technical concepts in expository text and to keep track of ideas and how they are connected. To illustrate this further, following are passages and students' semantic maps as examples of how these students used semantic maps with expository text.

Passage 18

Everyone talks about the "five" senses of man. And it's true that we get our information about the outside world from our sense of sight, hearing, smell, touch and taste. Researchers tell us that the sense of sight—our visual sense—gives us up to 80% of what we know about the world outside our bodies; while the other senses, the auditory (hearing), the olfactory (smell), the tactile (touch), and the gustatory (taste), bring into our brains information about the other 20% of what is happening. But there are two other senses that we cannot get along without, though they are very seldom given any credit for helping us to survive in this difficult world. These are the sense of balance and the kinesthetic sense.

The sense of balance, without which we would act like a drunk after a heavy bout with the bottle, is located in the inner ear. The inner ear contains three curved tubes (the semicircular canals) filled with liquids. The shifting of these liquids activates nerve endings in the linings of the canals, and nerve impulses from these nerve endings help our brains to keep us upright.

The kinesthetic sense is actually made up of nerve impulses that arise from nerves planted in close contact with our muscles. These nerve messages are constantly telling us what position our limbs, trunk and head are in. They serve as a continuous "feedback" system to help us know how to move our various parts, and when to hold them still. Otherwise, we would lack the coordination to run, jump, dance the twist, or even sit still. Incidentally, the word "kinesthetic" comes from two Greek words meaning "motion" and "feeling." The kinesthetic sense gives us our ideas about our own motion. (M. Gilmore, A. Sack and J Yourman, eds. *88 Passages to Develop Reading Comprehension*, 3rd Edition, Baltimore, MD: Media Materials, 1984, passage 61.)

Student Semantic Map

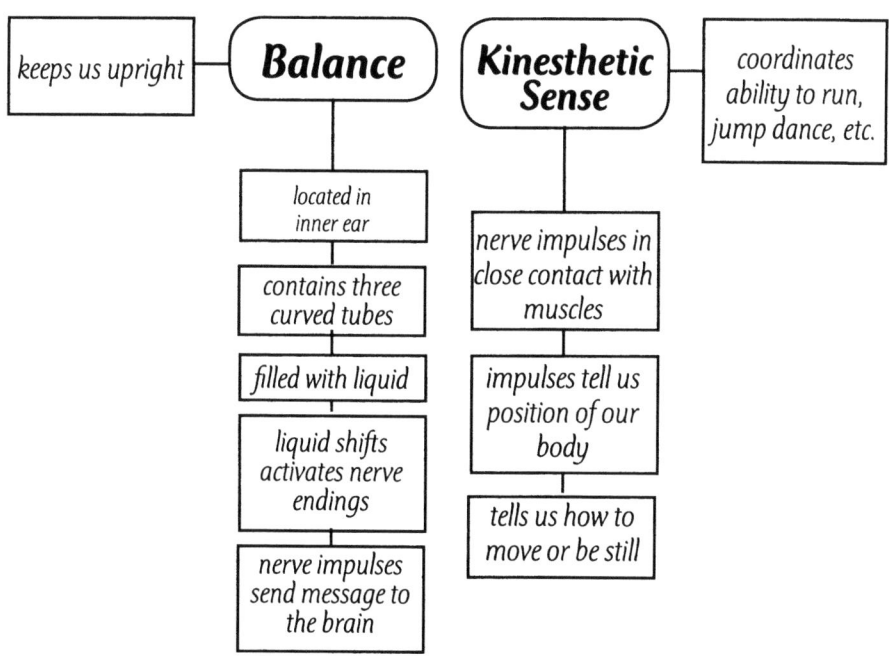

These semantic maps provided the student with a diagram to indicate the function of the sense of balance and kinesthetic sense. It also served as a study guide or outline for an essay; this student was able to see connections clearly and made the following inferences.

Examples of Student Inferences:
- Signals from the inner ear stops us from falling.
- Without nerve impulses, we would not know which way our body is going.
- We need the inner ear and nerve impulses to keep our balance.

In addition, many students find semantic maps helpful to create a traditional outline that is often required for papers.

I. Sense of Balance
    A. Description
        1. Inner ear
        2. Curved tubes filled with liquid
        3. Activates nerve endings in canals
        4. Nerve impulses gives us balance
    B. Keeps us upright
II. Kinesthetic Sense
    A. Description
        1. Nerve impulses
        2. Close connection to our muscles
        3. Impulses let us know our body position
        4. Impulses tell us when to move or be still
    B. Coordination
        1. Ability to run.
        2. Jump, dance.

In the next expository passage, the student again used a semantic map to clarify points in the passage and draw inferences.

Passage 19:

Inventors like Thomas A. Edison were called crazy. Their inventions were ridiculed. John Fitch, who invented the steamboat, became so discouraged that he took his own life. Charles Goodyear's family lived in poverty while he conducted his experiments. When Charles Newbold's cast-iron plow first appeared, farmers refused to use it. They said it would poison the soil. In both England and America, the car companies objected to railroads because they feared the competition. Horse breeders fought the introduction of the automobile. In France, tailors destroyed sewing machines that were being used to make uniforms for the army. Weavers wrecked the home of Richard Arkwright, the inventor of the power loom. Everywhere resistance to invention was strong. (M. Gilmore, A. Sack and J Yourman, eds. *88 Passages to Develop Reading Comprehension*, 3rd Edition, Baltimore, MD: Media Materials, 1984, passage 63.)

INVENTORS	INVENTIONS	OBSTACLES
John Fitch	Steamboat	ridiculed/commited suicide
Charles Goodyear	experiments	family in poverty
Charles Newbold	cast-iron plow	farmers reject it/say it poisons soil
Richard Arkwright	power loom	weavers destroyed his home
——	Railroads	Americans and English feared competition
——	automobiles	horse breeders objected
——	sewing machines	tailors destroyed machines

Student Inferences:
1. People were not open to change and did not accept new ideas that would change their lives.
2. Resistance to invention was strong, because people feared their jobs were in danger by new inventions.
3. People feared new inventions because they did not want the competition to share the money.
4. Inventors believed in their ideas even though they were ridiculed and suffered.

Imaginative Literature

The following student examples are given to illustrate how semantic maps may be used with imaginative literature to keep track of characters, make connections, and trace the intricate relationships between characters. A student on characters did the first illustration from the book *Beloved* by Toni Morrison. The student found it difficult to follow the connections between the many characters who did not always appear in each chapter but were nonetheless essential to the understanding of the complexities and long-range effects of slavery. She created this initial semantic character map and added additional names as the novel unfolded.

Student 1: Semantic Map—Part One: Beloved

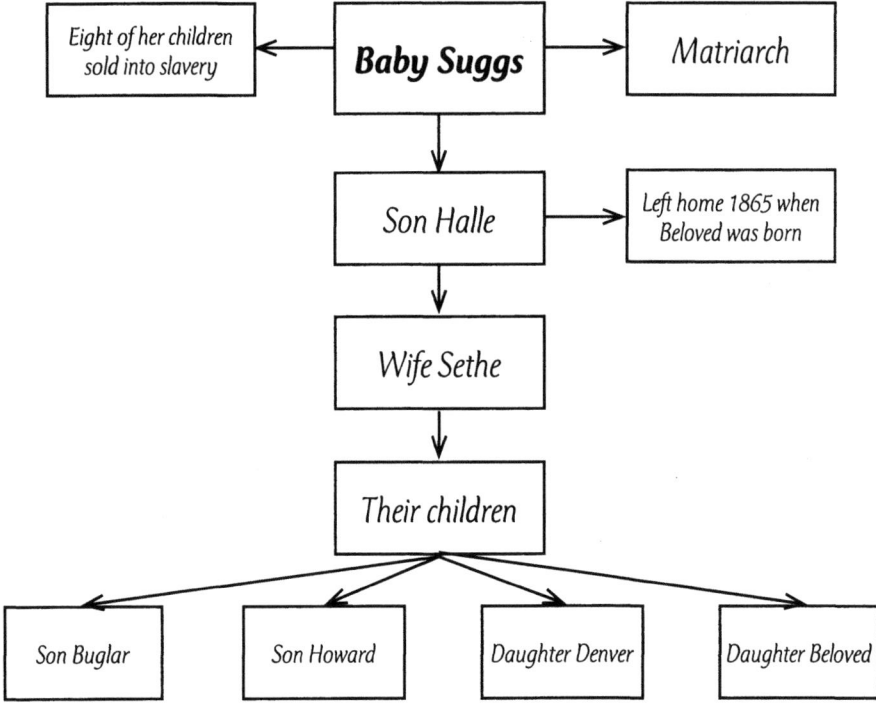

As the story unfolds there are other characters, who were intricately involved in the interactions of characters' relationships. Additional names were added to the original map and helped the student keep track of the characters and their relationships.

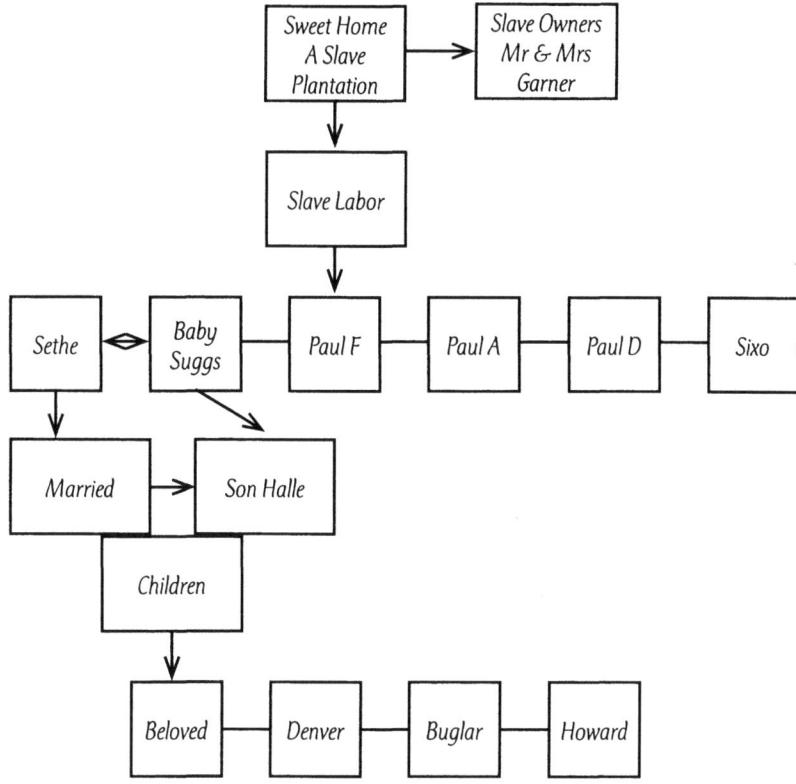

As this semantic map illustrates, maps can be a particularly useful strategy to sort out complex relationships between characters.

Character Analysis

During your readings, as you employ reading strategies suggested in *Reading Between the Lines*, you will automatically consider what characters are thinking, how this relates to their actions, and their interactions and reactions to other characters and events. Using semantic maps will help you write an analysis of the characters. In *The Joy Luck Club* students used semantic maps to delineate and sort out the many characters and complex relationships between mothers and daughters and make connections across time. In the two diagrams that follow, notice how the character maps changed across chapters.

88 READING BETWEEN THE LINES

Student 2: Semantic Map – Chapter: An-Mei Hsu: Scar

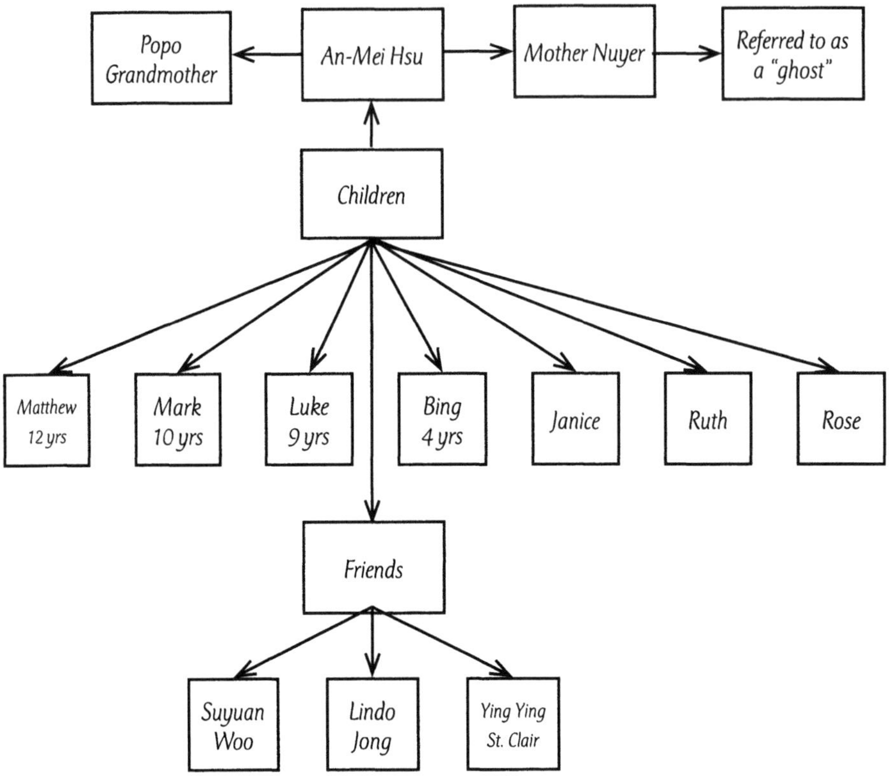

```
Popo           An-Mei Hsu        Mother Nuyer      Referred to as
Grandmother  ←              →                  →   a "ghost"
                    ↑
                Children
       ↙  ↙  ↓  ↓  ↓  ↘  ↘
  Matthew  Mark  Luke  Bing  Janice  Ruth  Rose
  12 yrs   10 yrs 9 yrs 4 yrs
                     ↓
                  Friends
              ↙    ↓    ↘
         Suyuan  Lindo   Ying Ying
         Woo     Jong    St. Clair
```

In the next map, the student continued to trace the relationships of An-Mei Hsu's daughter Rose Hsu Jordan.

Student 3: Chapter: Rose Hsu Jordan: Half and Half

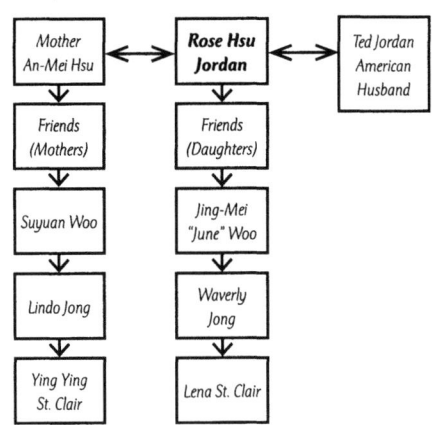

Below are student examples of semantic maps and the character analysis based on the novel *Sula* by Toni Morrison.

Student Character Maps:

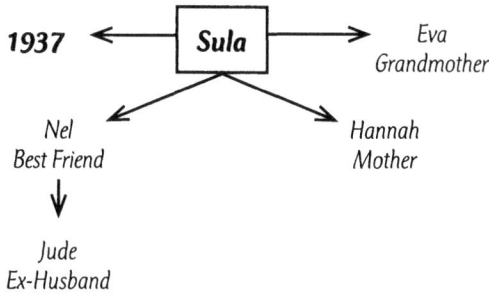

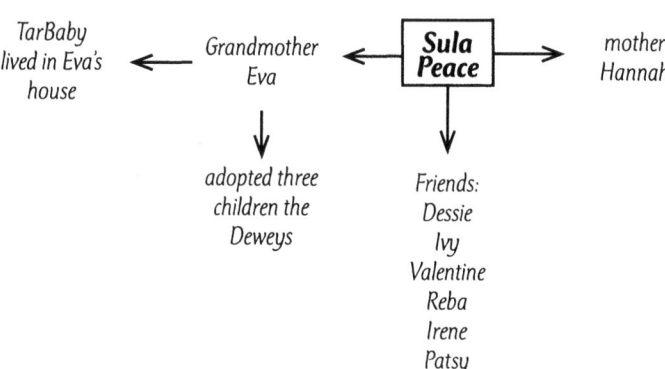

Character Analysis

Student Example:

> When Sula returned to Medallion, it was such a surprise to everyone especially Eva. Eva was upset because Sula just showed up without any warning or notice. They had a lot of arguments between them, about things that happened in the past among them and the family. They argued about Eva burning Plum and they argued about Sula standing and watching her mother burning. This part of the book was pretty amazing when the people at the bottom found out about Sula putting Eva in a home they hated her. In my opinion Sula did a lot of things that made the people in the town talk about her. They said things about her that they did not know about whether it was true or not. But I think it was Sula's nature to sleep with all of the men because it was her way of trying to find some security.

She was missing something in her life and tried to find it in men without loving them.
    When Sula was ill, Nel went to see her and asked why she slept with her husband. Sula's explanation was that she wanted to fill up the space inside of her and Jude was there to fill it. Nel was pretty upset because Sula did not love Jude and just wanted to use him. Nel felt that Sula had ruined her life just because she wanted to "fill up space." Nel was finally seeing the kind of person Sula was—she didn't care about other people and their feelings and the things that mattered to them.
    Nel left because she could not take the pain she felt and told Sula that she did not know if she would ever be back. I think what Sula did to Nel was wrong and immoral because they were suppose to be best friends. Sula dies and the people felt that it was the best thing that happened at the bottom—they were happy, joyful that she was gone. They felt that life would go back as usual. They would not have to keep an eye on their husbands keeping their children and husbands close. They felt free to let go of the things they were holding close in their hearts. But strange things started to happen. The harvest was poor, things turned to ice, fowl died, people became ill—people suffered. The people were dancing and singing and fell into an unfinished tunnel that was being built. Many died. Even though the people felt that Sula was the cause of their problems and were happy when she died, their actions after her death were destructive to themselves. When she was alive, Sula's actions made people look after each other, even though it was because they feared her. But when she died, they slacked off and did not take care of each other.

From the above student analysis, we can see how semantic maps help the reader write extended character analysis. Reading and writing are companions; writing about your readings expands your thinking and ideas to make connections and see relationships.

Lesson 9: Reading Aloud

Everyone enjoys hearing a good story. Generally we associate reading aloud to children of a young age. However, in many cultures storytelling is an art that continues throughout one's life. In some cultures everyone gathers around to hear elders tell stories of the group's past—to teach, pass on traditions and values of the culture. This is particularly true in oral cultural traditions.

In American culture in addition to hearing stories read aloud in the home and in schools, the format in which we hear stories are also conveyed through the media, radio, television, our attendance at plays, and other gatherings. Not only do we hear these stories, we see them acted out. As adults, picture books we read as children become "moving images" before our eyes in movies, videos, plays, and other dramatizations. We recognize the gestures, nuances, and other cultural subtleties to make meaning of the play, movie, or video. I am suggesting that when you are reading silently and you find it difficult to connect to tone of voice try reading the passage aloud; you may then "hear" differences in the story that escaped you when you read silently. Reading aloud with someone or by oneself is another way to help you construct meaning. As one student stated when assessing her reading habits, "When reading out loud, I understand what I read better."

Reading aloud is one method I use to help students "hear" inflections, nuances, and emphasis of a text. In my college reading classes, reading aloud to the students has been an excellent strategy to help make difficult passages accessible. When readers have difficulty with an ethnic dialect, class members read passages aloud to each other and were able to get the tone of voice, thus making the dialect easier to understand. Once the inflection and rhythm was clear, students continued to read the book silently without difficulty. Thus, when it seems hard to get the tone of the article, try reading the difficult paragraphs aloud. Reading aloud is effective with both expository text as well as imaginative literature.

The following passage from *How the Garcia Girls Lost Their Accents* by Julia Alvarez is a description of the character Manuel and his relationship with one of the sisters. Read the passage silently; identify story elements noting your emotional responses. Reread the passage aloud and record your emotional responses. Determine if tone of voice has changed or expanded significantly for you.

Passage 20:

1. He looks like a handsome young double for Papi, and a lot like us, the family eyebrows, the same high cheek bones, the full, generous mouth. In short, he could be the brother we never had. When he roars into the compound in his pickup, all four of us run down the driveway to greet him with kisses and hugs.
2. "Girls," Tia Carmen says, frowning, "that's no way to greet a man."
3. "Yeah, you guys," Fifi agrees. "Get off him, he's mine!"
4. We laugh, but we keep fussing over him, waiting on him as if we've never been to the States or read Simone de Beauvoir or planned lives of our own.
5. But, as the days go by, Fifi grows withdrawn and watchful. Daily, there are little standoffs and puts and cold shoulders because one of us has put her arm around Manuel or has gotten involved in a too-lengthy conversation with him about the production of sugar cane.
6. To reassure her, we tone ourselves down and become more reserved with Manuel. From this new distance, we begin to get the long view, and it's not so pretty. Lovable Manuel is quite the tyrant, a mini

Papi and Mami rolled into one. Fifi can't leave the house without his permission. And what's more disturbing is that Fifi, feisty, lively Fifi, is letting this man tell her what she can and cannot do.

7. One day Fifi, who rarely reads anymore, becomes absorbed in one of the novels we brought along, and not a trashy one for once. Manuel Gustavo arrives, and when no one answers the door, comes in the back way. In the patio, all four of us are draped over lawn chairs reading. Fifi sees him and her face lights up. She is about to put aside her book, when Manuel Gustavo reaches down and lifts it out of her hands.

8. "This," Manuel Gustavo says, holding the book up like a dirty diaper, "is junk in your head. You have better things to do." He tosses the book on the coffee table.

9. Fifi pales, though her two blushed-on cheeks blush on. She stands quickly, hands on her hips, eyes narrowing, the Fifi we know and love. "You have no right to tell me what I can and can't do!" "Que no?" Manuel challenges. "No!" Fifi asserts.

10. One by one we three sisters exit, cheering Fifi on under our breaths. A few minutes later we hear the pickup roar down the driveway, and Fifi comes sobbing into the bedroom.

11. "Fifi, he asked for it," we say. "Don't let him push you around. You're a free spirit," we remind her.

12. But within the hour, Fifi is on the phone with Manuelito, pleading for forgiveness. (Julia Alvarez, *How the Garcia Girls Lost Their Accents*, pp. 119–122)

Excercise—Reading Aloud

- Write a paragraph to describe your emotional reaction to the passage when reading aloud.
- When you read the passage aloud, which words and phrases seem to change the meaning of the text?
- In your reading aloud what seemed to make the difference?

Reading aloud helps focus our attention on how the language makes us feel. When you are having difficulty with text, whether reading expository text or imaginative literature, try reading the passage aloud to hear the language orally and to give "sound" to the text. This is a strategy which may be particularly helpful for students who have a positive response to text read aloud.

Chapter Four

Journal Writing

> Writing and performance should deepen the meaning of words, should illuminate, transfix and transform.
> —bell hooks

Lesson 10: Recalling, Reflecting, Rethinking Context

Journal Formats

The following journal format is suggested for recording your entries. Include the title of the article, chapter, section, page numbers, etc., and any other identifying notations in the margin for easy reference to review your entries. The following entries should be placed in the center. If you are including the thesis or theme of the selection this should be recorded at the beginning of your entry. If you are creating character maps, you may wish to place them right before the annotations. As you write the summary annotations, the character maps can be used as a reference. Commentary and questions are entered to the right of the annotations. You may prefer to write your comments and questions combined directly under each annotation. This format is useful for both expository text and imaginative literature to comment on specific issues, events, or characters. The point is to keep your journal entries accessible, i.e., to accommodate your learning style. Thus, flexibility is important in choosing which notations to use. The following journal format is suggested and each component is discussed below.

SAMPLE JOURNAL FORMAT

On the Margin	Center	Right Side
Date Title Chapter Issue Event Themes Etc.	Thesis or Themes Character Maps Annotation Commentary and Questions or →	Commentary and Questions

Remember to be flexible when choosing a journal format: combine your comments and questions, or keep them separate; add additional components to your journal as needed, e.g., identify themes, rewrite titles, vocabulary to define technical terms, and so on.

There are many ways in which to record journal entries, but whatever journal format you choose, keep it simple and accessible for easy reference. In *Reading Between the Lines*, we focus on five areas for journal entries: (1) themes and thesis, (2) summary annotations, (3) commentary, and (4) questions. You may also wish to include additional notations on specialized vocabulary and technical terms. An alternative to these forms, a narrative format, is also included.

Lesson 11: Journal Entries

Journal writing is a reflective practice to analyze your readings, react to complex material, and record your responses to text. You reflect to rethink your interpretations, sharpen your analytical skills, and integrate your responses and interpretations. Journal writing helps to summarize material, actively interact with the text, design questions to follow the author's point of view, and write commentary on events. It is also an appropriate strategy to improve fluency with language to express ideas with greater facility.

In your journal entries, summary annotations are written to cite specific events, aspects, record your opinions and responses to text, and pose questions about characters and events for which you need further clarification. Questions posed assist to make predictions and anticipate events in the ensuing reading. To unravel complex character relationships you may also include character maps that are discussed in detail in Chapter Three. In addition, journal writing encourages the reader to take time to reflect and work at your own pace, make connections, see relationships as characters develop and events unfold.

Use your journal in combination with other reading strategies suggested in this Handbook.

As an interactive reader, journal writing gives you another opportunity to continue your dialogue with the text, rethink events, issues, and ideas in your readings that seem unclear. Your journal entries may be brief or as long as you wish; it will depend on what you need to clarify and the nature of the text. The emphasis in journal entries is to evaluate your readings for a better understanding of the text in a broader context. In addition, the journal gives you an added opportunity to include your opinions, feelings, and responses—an important aspect to consider as you interpret text. Thus, journal entries are a personal account of what you wish to comment on or have questions about.

Themes and Thesis

The theme is the focal point in an essay or there may be more than one theme in chapter books. Themes may be written as a phrase or sentence. The thesis, on the other hand, is the overall position or focus of an entire selection, essay, or article. The thesis is written as a declarative sentence. For both the theme and the thesis, focus on who or what is this article, chapter about? What does the author want me to believe? You may find it helpful to include themes or thesis in your journal entries to help identify issues you write about in the annotation. Examples of themes from the Annotated Bibliography in Chapter One are given below.

In *The Joy Luck Club*, titles of each chapter provide a literal way in which to interpret the chapter, but the title also provides a metaphor for connotative subtext in the chapter. Students reading the *The Joy Luck Club* found it helpful to expand chapter titles by identifying these subtext themes as each chapter developed. These themes were recorded in their journal entries before writing their annotations. Doing so, helped students focus on major points to write their annotations and a broader description of what one could expect in each chapter. The following examples are themes for different chapters from the four sections in the *Joy Luck Club*. The themes are a representative composite of some key themes students identified.

Amy Tan, The Joy Luck Club

Section: *Feathers From a Thousand Li Away*
Chapter: " Jing-Mei Woo: The Joy Luck Club"
Themes: From China to San Francisco
           Members of the Joy Luck Club
           Death of Jing-Mei Woo's mother

	Jing-Mei's trip to China to find her sisters
Chapter:	"Ying-Ying St. Clair: The Moon Lady"
Themes:	Preparation for the Moon Festival
	A secret wish
	Ying-Ying's disaster in the water
	Ying-Ying finds her family

Section: The Twenty-Six Malignant Gates

Chapter:	Rules of the Game
Themes:	An important Christmas party
	A fine gift
	Rules for life
	Dissension between mother and daughter
Chapter:	The Voice From the Wall
Themes:	Things out of balance
	Caught in between
	Yearning for a mother–daughter relationship
	Death of a baby

Section: American Translation

Chapter:	Without Wood
Themes:	Without strength
	Fear and confusion
	Unable to make decisions
	Divorce
Chapter:	Best Quality
Themes:	Making choices
	A mother's wish

Section: Queen Mother of the Western Skies

Chapter:	An-Mei Hsu: Magpies
Themes:	Sorrow in a new home
	Trying to find happiness
	Suicide
Chapter:	Ying Ying St. Clair: Waiting Between the Trees
Themes:	Mother waiting to tell the daughter her past
	Waiting for the right time to speak
	Shame about the past

In *Sula*, Toni Morrison simply uses the year of the events as the title for each chapter. The themes are layered in the lives of the characters as they unfold during the particular time period. The following examples are some themes students identified for different chapters in Part I.

Sula, Part I

Chapter: 1919
Themes: The Bottom
          Private Shadrack's war
          National Suicide Day

Chapter: 1921
Themes: Eva's struggle to survive
          Eva and her children
          Plum's death

Chapter: 1922
Themes: Sula and Nel
          Best friends
          A coldhearted secret

Chapter: 1923
Themes: Strange signs of disaster to come
          Hannah confronts her mother
          Disaster and death by fire again

Chapter: 1927
Themes: Nel's wedding
          Sula's suspicious leave taking
          Growing pains

By writing themes for these chapters, students have identified major points in each chapter making it easier to recall information relevant to the time frame of the events. In addition, identifying these themes helped students anticipate events and unravel complex issues affecting the characters and the community. Continuing with Part II of *Sula,* indicate how the choices characters made in their early lives had an impact during their mature years.

Sula Part II
Chapter: 1937
Themes: Sula's return to Medallion
          Sula'a return brings evil
          The change of Sula's and Nel's relationship

Chapter: 1939
Themes: Sula and Ajax
          Sula discovers passion
          Sula's obsession
          A lost friendship
          Townspeople's hatred of Sula

Chapter: 1940
Themes: Sula's death
Nel's and Sula's last meeting
Chapter: 1941
Themes: Reactions to Sula's death
Turning point in Medallion
Sula's death changes the town for the worse
National Suicide Day
Chapter: 1965
Themes: A different world
The emptiness of the Bottom
Eva reveals a secret
Nel's regret
Nel's realization of her friendship

Summary Annotations

A summary annotation is a synopsis in your own words conveying the essence of a selection, focusing on characters, issues, conditions, or events. When you write your annotation, write a concise factual statement of the selected material. You condense the information in a form that will enable you to recall details, clarify points, and\or ask questions. In some instances, you may also want to record quotes that are particularly powerful and which you wish to make comments to construct meaning or to question.

In the summary annotation given below, the student wrote a summary annotation of the chapter, "Jing-Mei Woo: The Joy Luck Club," from *The Joy Luck Club*. In the second annotation, the student focused on particular events.

Student #1—Summary Annotation

"Jing-Mei Woo: The Joy Luck Club"

> Suyuan tells Jing-Mei how she ran away from Kweilin, China. The Japanese had invaded and it was not safe. Suyuan took her two babies and two bags with food and clothing. By the time she got to Chungking, she did not have anything. Not even her babies! She was very tired on her way and she had to drop her bags and her two babies. Jing-Mei Woo hears many versions of this story from her mother, Suyuan Woo. In Chungking Suyuan Woo gets married. She then goes to America and settles in San Francisco where she gives birth to another daughter, Jing-Mei, and creates the Joy Luck Club. The Joy Luck Club was a social club at which she and three other ladies gathered each week, served special food, played mahjongg and talked about different matters. Suyuan Woo dies and her

daughter, Jing-Mei Woo takes her place at the Joy Luck Club. Once at the Joy Luck table she was told by one of the ladies that she has two sisters in China and she should go there and tell her sisters everything about their mother. They were the babies that her mother Suyuan left on the side of the road and it is Jing-Mei's responsibility now to tell them their mother's story.

Student #2—Summary Annotation

"Jing-Mei Woo: The Joy Luck Club"

Suyuan Woo came to America from China in 1949. When she was in China she had a Joy Luck Club and decided to form one in San Francisco with three other women. It was a way for the immigrant mothers to come together and support each other. When Suyuan died, her daugher Jing-Mei Woo was invited to take her place. This is when she found out that she has two sisters in China and one of the ladies encourages her to go see them.

The above annotations have some of the same factual information but student #1 chose to go into detail and write more. Since your journal entries are your personal accounts to interact with the text, both these annotations serve the purpose for the reader to recall information, clarify points, and personalize how one responds to text.

Commentary Annotations

The commentary in the journal is your critical analysis of the reading; you evaluate the logic, truthfulness, facts, and opinions and record your reactions and opinions. Since your entries will reflect your personal responses the length will vary according to what you wish to comment about. Again, we shall cite examples of comments from the journal entries of the students' annotations which appear above on the chapter "Jing-Mei Woo: The Joy Luck Club."

Student #1 Commentary: "Jing-Mei Woo: The Joy Luck Club"

I wonder how Suyuan Woo felt when she left her two babies and ran to Chungking. How did the three ladies feel when Suyuan Woo died and her daughter took her place at the Joy Luck Club?

Student #2 Commentary: "Jing-Mei Woo: The Joy Luck Club"

I felt sorry for Suyuan because of the loss of her two daughters. When I was reading it, I felt like I was watching some kind of war movie. I wonder if Jing-Mei will find her sisters?

In these commentaries, which also include questions, both students are concerned with the revelation that Suyuan Woo had to leave her babies as she escaped from China. These comments and pondering questions to reflect on the reading helps to anticipate events and to focus on discovering the answers to questions. Efficient readers always pose questions as they read: it keeps the reader focused and helps follow the events as they unfold making it easy to change direction as events change.

Question Annotations

As noted under previewing text, asking questions is an important element to read critically. In the journal, it is a way to have a continuing "dialogue" as you interact with the text. You may simply pose questions or write annotations about what is confusing. If you are attending a class, these are the questions to present during your class sessions. Below are a few examples of student questions posed as they read *Sula*.

1921:
- How did Eva a woman with nothing to her name, come back home with enough money to pay Mrs. Suggs, plus build a house for her family?
- How did Eva really lose her leg? Why did she let Boyboy in the house? He did not even ask about the children!

1923:
- Why did Hannah ask her mom if she loved them? Couldn't she remember the love and tenderness of her mother's touch?
- Why did Hannah react this way to her mother instead of trying to help her?

1927:
- I do not understand why Sula left town without saying good-bye to Nel and did not congratulate Nel on her marriage to Jude. Sula and Nel were very good friends.
- Why was Sula amused by Nel's marriage to Jude?

1939:
- What does Sula mean when she said, "Soon I would have torn the flesh from his face…. And nobody would have understand that kind of curiosity" (p. 136, last para.) ?

These examples give you an idea of the range of questions students asked as they read interactively. As students continued to read, these questions were answered and note were made in the margins of the journals.

Character Maps and Analysis

Character maps are used as the pivotal point from which to understand the particular character or to gain an understanding of the story in general. Character maps may be used with autobiographies, biographies, and imaginative literature. When there are many characters, you may wish to create character maps to keep track of relationships. These maps will prove to be particularly helpful to trace character relationships and when reading across cultures, it helps to remember names unfamiliar to you. After reading "Best Quality" in *The Joy Luck Club*, a student created the following character map and annotation.

Student Semantic Map—Best Quality

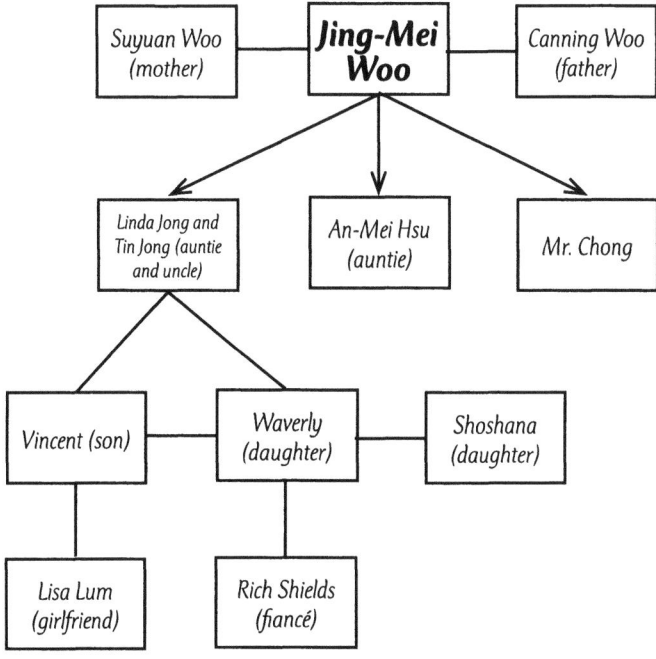

Student Character Analysis Using the Semantic Map:

> After a crab dinner in a New Year's celebration Suyuan gave Jing-Mei a jade pendant on a gold chain. For the New Year's celebration, Suyuan invited her close friend and relatives and friends from the Joy Luck Club. At this dinner, Jing-Mei

observed everybody at the table and she saw how Waverly and her whole family picked up the best crab. Jing-Mei chose what was left which was not a good crab. Her mother asked her why she picked the worse crab when nobody else wanted it—they wanted the best one. Even though Jing-Mei's mother was annoyed, I think that sometimes we pick up what is left because we don't have another choice. I am sure that everybody wants the best for their life. At least Jing-Mei was strong enough to ask for her money that Waverly owed her. Since they were little, Waverly has always tried to embarrass Jing-Mei.

A character analysis is included in your journal entries to rethink and understand characters' behavior in the context of what is happening at a particular point in the story. That is, what is this character doing? Saying? What is he or she thinking? Does the behavior of the character follow what he or she is thinking? Why or why not? What is the character trying to achieve by saying one thing and doing another? How does this affect the behavior of other characters and the nature of events? Add any questions you have about a character that is unclear. Character analysis will help you with predictions and to anticipate outcomes. Consider the setting as well to understand behavior of characters.

The following is an analysis of Jing-Mei Woo, the main character included in the character map above.

Student's Character Analysis of Jing-Mei Woo

Jing-Mei Woo was a good daughter to her mother. She didn't show any disrespect towards her family and friends. In the Joy Luck Club she honored her mother's memory after she died, she took her mother's place in the club and tried to do what her mother would have done if she were alive. In doing this, she showed courage, bravery and discipline. Jing Mei always tried to please her mother. Her mother thought she could grow up to be a super star if she put her mind to it. Her mother pushed her and took over her life, turning her into two different people.

For example, in Best Quality, Jing-Mei stood by her mother, even though it was a dishonorable situation. She loved her with all her heart. She was an obedient daughter and understanding child. She befriended her mother when nobody else would. She forgave her mother for her past mistakes, giving her chances to prove herself.

In this analysis, the reader is left with the impression that the daughter, Jing-Mei Woo, is obedient to the point of not exerting much of her personality. Since this is the first chapter, this is an initial analysis of this character. Other dimensions of the character are yet to be revealed and the student's analysis may be adjusted as the character is further developed in subsequent chapters.

Let's examine examples of extended journal entries from students' journals.

Extended Journal Entries

For complex issues in essays, articles, or imaginative literature you may wish to write extended annotations and commentary. The following extended journal entries illustrated here were written by students to clarify issues in reading *Sula* by Toni Morrison. The journal entries include themes, annotations, and commentary. Notice how students' commentary reflects their Personal Matrix to help them with content and characters. Two students' journal entries have been included to illustrate how personal preferences and interpretations are reflected in the entries.

Annotations	**Student #1/Sula**
Sula-1919	Shadrack Returns Home
Themes:	National Suicide Day
	Annotation
	Shadrack was a twenty year old young man but he did not have much experience before he went to war to fight in France. During the war, Shadrack experienced an explosion and a shock that left him with a mental illness and body injuries. He saw a soldier's head fly off and the headless body kept on going without any direction. After this shock, it took him a year to recover. After his release from the hospital, he was weak, unable to walk straight and suffered from blinding headaches. He struggled a great deal because he had seen death and was terrified. It seems that it was not death that terrified him; it was that he had witnessed the unexpected occurrence of death. That's when he decided to institute National Suicide Day.
	Commentary
	I think that Shadrack was a young man who was shell shocked after he went to war. It made him crazy and pretty much like those veterans that were in the Vietnam War. I saw him as a scared, weak person trying to gain some kind of recognition. He was crazy, BUT NOT IN A WAY TO HARM ANYONE. War is very gruesome; Shadrack's life was destroyed because of it. He was affected physically and mentally. His hands were abnormal, he became crazy and declared a National Suicide Day to set aside a day for the people to think of their fears, or their hard lives, so that they could go on with their lives without being fear-

ful every day. He cared for those people. Although the people of the bottom did not join in his parade, it became a part of their life.

In the above commentary, the student added themes for the chapter title "1919" to identify major events. Notice, too, that she was able to use her prior knowledge and make a comparison about the "Vietnam War," to help explain the behavior and actions of the character, who had been affected by the war. And although Shadrack's war (World War I) was far removed from this student's reality, she compared her *Sula* prior knowledge about war to this character's actions to gain insight into the character's actions. Read the following student journal entries on "1919" and compare how these students interpreted events in this chapter.

Annotations	**Student # 2/Sula**
1919 Theme:	Shadrack's Solitary Parade
	Annotation
	In December 1917, Shadrack was sent to war in France. After his time in the war, not knowing when death would come, the idea of death and dying frightened him. He was injured and dwelled in a hospital for a long while after the war. When he was released from the hospital he was too weak to walk steadily on the road. A policeman thought he was drunk and he had to spend some time in jail. When he returned to Medallion he instituted National Suicide Day to devote one day to sort out your fears and troubles and go on with your life the rest of the year. In the town where he lived, in the bottom of Medallion, Ohio, National Suicide Day became a part of the life of the people.
	Commentary
	The aftermath of war left Shadrack bewildered. People in Medallion wondered what Shadrack was like before he went into the war (p. 7). The hospital Shadrack was in wasn't a very nice place. The male nurse was dressed in a green cotton jacket (p. 9). Shadrack's notion of National Suicide Day was called a yearly solitary parade (p. 15). He was the only one who marched. But Suicide Day became a part of the people's lives.

In the above journal entries, both students identified the same theme and recognized the importance of the character introducing a "National Suicide Day" and implications for the townspeople. In addition, both annotations defined events which shaped this character but different examples are cited. It is the commentary, the analysis, which suggests the depth of understanding of one reader over the other. Student #1's commentary is a clear indication of how a reader may interact with the text to develop a critical analysis of characters and events. This student was also able to rely on her Personal Matrix, specifically her prior knowledge, to make sense of the character's behavior, and place it in the context of her experience. Student #2's commentary cited specific points raised in the story and page numbers but does not go beyond the meaning stated. Thus, not producing a critical analysis of these events may prove problematic for this student as he continues reading. What student #2 needs to do is to expand the ideas and interact with the text to create an in-depth analysis of the particular event.

In the following journal entries, we view the comments students made on *Sula*, chapter "1920." Compare these students' interpretations and note how each has a slightly different emphasis which indicates how their Personal Matrix influenced their interpretations.

Annotations	Student #1/Sula
1920	
Theme:	Helene and Her Daughter Nel
	Annotation
	Helene Sabat was the daughter of a Creole whore who worked in a whore hourse called the Sundown House. Helene grew up with her grandmother and her grandmother was constantly on guard for any sign of Helene's mother's wild blood. Helene was a very beautiful lady and married Wiley Wright and moved to Medallion with him. Her husband was a lake-man away from home most of the time so she devoted her life to her daughter, Nel. Helene disliked her daughter's physical appearance and was constantly trying to change her looks. When Helene learned her grandmother was dying she returned to New Orleans with her daughter. The trip took three days and they experienced horrible, racist treatment from the conductor on the train.
	Commentary
	I kind of dislike Helene's attitude toward people in Medallion and toward her daughter Nel. Helene likes to

manipulate her daughter Nel because she wanted things her own way. Helene disliked Nel's nose and told her to put things on her nose to get it well formed. I think that this was not smart to tell a young kid this as it sends the wrong message. I think this is why Nel looked outside of her home for love and friendship. She wanted to experience a different life than she was living. That is why she became friends with Sula whose life was so different than her own.

Questions
Why didn't Helene want to go to see her grandmother in New Orleans?

Now read student #2's journal entries on the same chapter, "1920," to compare these journal entries and note the difference in interpretations and emphases.

Annotations	Student #2 Journal Entries "1920" in *Sula*
Theme	Helene Wright Returns Home
	Annotation
	Helene Wright was born in New Orleans to a Creole whore. She was raised by her strict grandmother. Helene married Wiley Wright and moved to Medallion. She has one daughter Nel and is constantly telling her to "straighten" her nose. Nel was very obedient and polite but her enthusiasm to do anything was suppressed by her mother. Helene had to go back home to New Orleans to see her dying grandmother and it is on the journey back to New Orleans that she is painfully reminded of the suffering of black people. When they arrive in New Orleans, Helene's grandmother is dead, and Helene is shamed by her mother. Nel sees her mother in these situations and realizes that her mother is not perfect after all.
	Commentary
	I believe there is a tension between Helene and her mother, but I am not sure why. I liked that Nel became friends with Sula against her mother's wishes. It gives me the idea that there is something special about Sula.

Questions
Why doesn't Helene speak Creole? I believe she is denying her culture. Helene does not want Nel to be anything like her mother. I think Helene's mother's profession was the reason Helene disliked herself.

In these journal entries, the focus of the themes are somewhat different. However, in both annotations two events stand out in both annotations: Helene's relationship with her daughter and the horrific experience on the trip back to New Orleans. When we compare the commentary, both students agree that the relationship between the Helene and her daughter Nel is problematic and will affect Nel adversely. In these journal entries both students ask important questions which concentrate on wanting to understand the behavior and actions of Helene. Again, questions such as these help the reader gain a better understanding of the character and the reasons why he or she take the actions. These readers obviously care about the character Nel and wonder if the mother's actions will have deleterious effects on Nel. Further, the reader is trying to determine why the mother does these things to the daughter. These commentaries are very good examples of readers interacting with text, responding to the events, and asking questions in anticipation of what will happen. These journal entries are good examples of how efficient readers use journals to interact with text as they construct meaning.

Comparing Journal Commentaries

The above journal entries—themes, annotations, and commentary, give a good example of how our Personal Matrix will influence our interpretations. We use our Personal Matrix to begin our interaction with the text, but we need not be limited by our prior knowledge and experience. That is why questioning as we read is an important aspect of interpreting text. Compare the student journal commentaries on the events described in the annotation to note how the Personal Matrix of each of the students leads to a different interpretation and emphasis.

Annotations	Students' Journal Entries / Sula
1921	
Theme:	Eva's Past and Present
	Summary Annotation # 1
	Eva Peace took care of her family under very harsh conditions. She married a man named Boyboy and they had three children, Hannah, Eva-Pearl and a son Ralph who

they called Plum. After five years of marriage, Boyboy abandoned her and left her poor. Neighbors tried to help by giving her food, but it was not enough. One day she asked a neighbor to take care of the children and she would be back in two days. But she returned in eighteen months. She came back with plenty of money but only one leg. There were rumors that she deliberately had her leg cut off by the train for insurance money. She buys a house, takes in boarders and adopts three boys and calls all of them Dewey. We can say she was a caring woman. The men would call on her because they enjoyed her company. Hannah, her daughter, on the other hand enjoyed men's company in a different way. She made love with them, not for love, but for fun. Hannah's husband died and she had a daughter, Sula. She moved back with her mother Eva to take care of her. Plum comes back home after going to the war and then living in the states. When he gets back to Medallion he has nothing and is on drugs. Eva thought he was an alcoholic. When she goes into his room and realizes he is a drug addict, she does not want to see him suffer. She thinks it is best to put him out of his misery and sets him on fire.

Commentary
Eva did everything to the extreme, for example, getting her leg cut off for insurance and burning her son. Eva felt she had to relieve Plum from his suffering again; she had done it before when the baby was constipated and now as a man she relieved him from his drug addiction.

Student #2 also wrote a summary annotation and an extensive commentary on "1921."

1921
Themes: Eva and Her Family Life Story
Plum's Death
Summary Annotation #2
Eva Peace was a lady that somehow lost her leg and nobody knew the real story of how she lost her leg. Eva married a man named Boyboy who was a womanizer, liked to drink and abuse Eva. Eva had three children with Boyboy.

Hannah, who was the oldest, Pearl, and Plum who was the only boy. After five years of sadness and a discontented marriage, Boyboy left Eva with the three children. Eva had no source of income to support the children. She was pushed to leave her children with a neighbor to find work. After eighteen months, Eva returned and reclaimed her children and built a house where she rented out rooms. Her only son goes to war and returns home looking strange like a homeless person. He started to steal and spent a great deal of time in his room. When his mother discovered that he was taking drugs, it was too much to bear. She remembered how hard it was to raise him and could not stand to see him suffer. She made a heart wrenching decision and while he was sleeping, soaked Plum with kerosene, rolled up a newspaper and lit it and threw it onto the bed as he slept. Eva burned her child Plum, her only son.

Commentary
I certainly disliked the idea that Eva killed her son Plum because he became a drug addict. I feel that she should have used another alternative to deal with that problem. But I also understand that she probably killed him because she loved him and she did not want to see her son looking like a junkie after she went through many difficult life situations to raise him. I think that Eva felt she had the right to take his life. I strongly disagree; Eva should have found another alternative.

Students had a profound reaction to the provocative events in "1921" and the additional students' commentary are worth noting to understand how one's Personal Matrix helps construct meaning.

Student #3 Commentary
Since Eva saw Plum killing himself slowly with drugs and saw all that suffering in him, she decided to stop it. I would say her mistake was that she did it in front of Hannah.

Student #4 Commentary
Eva saw it was necessary to release Plum from his misery. She chose the fire as the means. It took a lot of guts to set her son on fire. This love for a child reminds me of *The Joy Luck Club* when Nuyer sacrifices her life to make her

children's lives better and when Suyuan Woo left her children by the roadside in hope that someone would find them. These are women who have gone to extremes to make the best decisions in favor of their children's welfare. Eva knew that Plum was better off dead.

Student # 5 Commentary
So far we don't know how Eva lost her leg. There are a lot of rumors. In my opinion she did it in order to get money for her family. I think she is a very strong person and cares about children.

In each of these commentaries, students all agree that Eva was a strong person, had a great love for her children, and would go to extremes to save them from harm. They seem to understand her extreme behavior, e.g., burning her son to save him from drugs, but are conflicted about whether Eva is justified in taking the action. Student #3 goes further in her analysis, making connections to her prior knowledge from another novel, comparing how a character in *The Joy Luck Club* took extreme measures to help her children. All of these of journal entries, writing themes, annotations, and commentary help to interpret text. These commentaries illustrate how writing about your reading will help expand your interpretations for an in-depth analysis of what you read.

The following journal entries give examples of how writing questions as you read helps you continue a dialogue with the text thereby making predictions and anticipating outcomes to go beyond your prior knowledge and expand your knowledge. The combination of commentary with questions actually places you in a position to interpret complex relationships and events. We shall examine journal entries based on the chapter "1923" from *Sula*. One summary annotation is given as the basis for the commentaries and questions which follow.

Annotations	Student Journal Entries/*Sula*
1923	
Themes:	Hannah Confronts Her Mother
	Signs of Disasters
	Disasters Strike the Peace Home
	Summary Annotation
	Hannah confronts her mother Eva and asks if she ever loved them (Hannah, Pearl, and Plum) and if she did love them, why did she kill Plum. Eva becomes furious to hear this. She told Hannah of all the sacrifices she made, her nursing them back to perfect health not knowing whether

they would live or die after her husband abandoned her. All the years she provided for them. Eva also tells Hannah the reason she burned Plum was he wanted to "return to her womb" and this could not be. He was suffering and she wanted to stop the pain. Strange things were happening at this time. The night before there were strong winds and everyone waited for the rain which usually follows, but it never came. Eva's comb was missing, Sula was acting strange wanted to bathe the Dewey boys who never liked water. The same day Hannah caught fire in the yard. Eva smashed the window and dove out in order to save Hannah's life. Eva only succeeded in injuring herself. Hannah died on the way to the hospital. While Eva was recovering she remembered that she saw Sula watch her mother burn and made no attempt to help her.

Students' journal comments and questions reflect the very strong reactions and opinions regarding these events. Several student commentaries are given below to indicate how interpreting text has much to do with what we bring to the text.

Notations	Student Comments/*Sula*
1923	Commentary #1
	Hannah confronted her mother, Eva, and wanted an explanation about what she did and why she did it. I could understand Eva. Plum was destroying his life and Eva could not see her son deteriorating.
	Question Annotation
	Is there significance in the fact that both Hannah and Plum die in fire? What is the significance in the fact that Sula watched Chicken Little drown and watched her mother burn?
	Commentary #2
	I think it was ironic and bizarre that Eva Peace lost two of her children to fire under such different circumstances. I felt a great deal of empathy for her because two of her children were gone whom she loved so much and made a lot of sacrifices for. Also it's funny how children whether young or old mix up how a mother feels about them. I

think Eva Peace loved her children more than she loved her own life. I feel Eva had been trying so hard to make ends meet, she couldn't be the affectionate, sensitive mother her children wanted. She had to work so hard and working hard made her tough and strong. As she said, "There was no time to play."

Commentary #3
Sula is a sneaky weird girl. I believe she did not care that her mother was burning.

Question Annotation
What did Eva mean when she said Plum wanted to crawl back into her womb (p. 71, para. 2)? What was the gray ball, which Nel saw over her shoulder (p. 109, line 1)?

In other entries, students combined questions with their commentary.

Commentary and Question #4
This part was very sad because Hannah was acting strange and she was burned to death by the yard fire. Also why did Eva respond to her daughter in a way that Hannah felt she was not wanted? Their relationship was not that close. I realize mothers can show their love in a different way not in words but the things they do.

Commentary and Question #5
This chapter clearly brings out a cultural side of the African American. That is, the belief in dream and strange signs. All these things lead up to the death of Hannah. It was like writing on the wall. I can't imagine why Sula would watch her mother die and not do anything. There must be something that I've missed that indicated or justifies this behavior.

A different approach is illustrated in the following journal entries; instead of writing a single theme, explanations are given to relate events to the chapter title. This clarified meanings for which they may not have had a point of reference in their personal matrix. Characters were listed as well to keep track of relationships between characters.

The journal entries are based on chapters of *The Joy Luck Club*, with character analysis, annotations, commentary, and questions.

Chapter	Student #1 Journal Entries
The Joy Luck Club Themes:	The Joy Luck Club was formed in China when the Japanese invaded China. In San Franciso, it was formed to keep the Chinese traditions.
Characters:	Jing-Mei – daughter; Suyuan Woo – mother; Auntie Lin, Ying, Uncle George, and Jack – friends
	Annotations It was time for Jing-Mei to take the place of her mother after she died. Suyuan wanted her daughter to find her twin babies that she lost when Japan invaded China. Suyuan used to tell her daughter different stories about Kweilin and how she lost the babies.
	Comments Why does Suyuan always change the end of the story about the war and her two lost daughters?
Scar Themes:	"Scar," referred to the literal wound An-Mei had on her neck, and the internal wound she had because her mother was the concubine of a married man. She was forced to hate her mother.
Characters:	Popo – grandmother; Nuyer – daughter; An-Mei – granddaughter; An-Mei's uncles, aunts, and little brother
	Annotations An-Mei and her little brother lived with their uncle, aunt, and grandmother (Popo). An-Mei was told by her grandmother to hate her mother and never mention her name. Nuyer returned to see her mother, Popo, when she was dying to honor her. Nuyer cut her arm to put the flesh in the soup, a tradition, to save Popo.
	Comments I do not agree with Popo's actions. I do not think she should encourage An-Mei to hate her mother.

Red Candle:	"The Red Candle" was a symbol for marriage. It had to be lit at both ends and had to continuously burn without going out. This means that the marriage would never break up.
Characters:	Huang Taitai – mother; Tyan-yu – son; Lindo Jong – promised wife for Tyan-yu

Annotation
Lindo Jong has to obey her family and marry Tyan. Her husband's mother Huang treated her as a slave. When they got married Huang wanted grandchildren. However, the marriage never consummated and Lindo wanted her freedom back. Lindo made believe that she had a dream in which the ancestors told her to leave her husband or he would die.

Comments
I think Lindo is very smart because she got her freedom back and she did not break her promise to her family. So she did not dishonor them.

The Moon Lady Themes:	"The Moon Lady" was the incident Ying-Ying St. Clair remembered of her childhood. When she was a little girl, she went to a festival where she thought she was making a wish to a lady but it turned out to be a man. It was an appearance which did not turn out as it seemed. Now Ying and her daughter do not know each other.
Characters:	Ying-Ying St. Clair; Ying's parents, sister, brothers, and her amah (nurse); Lena – Ying-Ying's daughter

Summary Annotation
Ying-Ying St. Clair remembers she got lost at the festival and fell into the water. She could not make the wish she wanted to because the moon turned out to be a man. Her wish was to be found as today, she wanted to be found by her daughter. Ying did not understand her daughter. Ying-Ying married an English-Irish individual and they had a daughter, Lena. Because of the language problem, Ying-Ying and her husband hardly talked. So Lena was

the translator between them. Sometimes Lena lied about what her mother was saying because she wanted to avoid problems between her parents.

Commentary
Ying-Ying lost her position and lost her accurate birth date. Then she married an English man and lost her name and she could not communicate with her husband. I think all of these things are important to a Chinese woman. If Ying-Ying and her husband can't communicate, why get married? This story showed me that things are not always as they seem in life. I think Ying made a mistake in not telling her daughter her true feelings.

Alternative Journal Entries

Journal formats and entries should remain flexible to accommodate your learning style and what you wish to record and reflect upon. The above format has been suggested as one way to record your responses. There are many variations. Below are other examples for journal entries in which students chose to write annotations embedding questions in their commentary. These student annotations were responses to a play *Antiogne* by Jean Anouilh. Antigone's brother has violated the law and upon his death is subject to the law that he is not allowed a decent burial.

Commentary 1: The main idea behind this fascinating story is power and determination. It clearly shows a life-threatening conversation between uncle and niece. Antigone, being as determined as she could to bury her brother even though she was aware of the consequence—her death. Creon, her uncle, and the king of Thebes passed a law stating that anyone attempting to bury Polynices (Antigone's brother) is to be punished by death. Hence, the alternative she had was to marry Creon's son and bear him a son. Nevertheless, Antigone chose to be her own individual.

My bias is against her uncle Creon. He was chosen to be king of Thebes, of course to rule and protect his people. Instead he ruled his kingdom on a very personal basis. He only accepted the throne because he knew he would have power over Thebes and could do whatever he wanted to. He does not deserve respect. On the other hand, Antigone has all my respect due to the fact she was a determined, self-respected, and faithful character. She stood up to her uncle, the King, for what she believed and knew what she had to do which was burying her brother to ensure the peace of his soul.

Commentary 2: In the play *Antigone by* Jean Anouilh, Antigone tries to put her brother's body to peace. Creon, Antigone's uncle who is also king, made a decree and passed a law never to bury Antigone's brother and decreed that anyone buries him, that person would be put to death. Antigone is very stubborn and would rather die knowing her brother has a proper burial and is at peace. Even though Creon doe not want Antigone to bury her brother, when she does, Creon tries everything in his power not to kill her.

I believe that Creon had a good heart and you could see deep in his heart family meant something to him. I agree with how he gave Antigone chances to keep quiet in order that no one would know that she was still alive. I would do the same if I was in her place. Putting a body to rest at peace would be my first priority especially if it's my family. I also believe that towards the end, Creon felt bad and wanted his nephew buried.

Commentary 3: I definitely agree with Antigone. Polynices is her brother, and she owes him the respect of taking care of his burial. After all, if the king is her uncle an exception should be made. So, Antigone followed her feelings and did whatever she thought was right. When the king said that he was going to kill her if she disobeys him, she decided to go for it. The king was just threatening her and she knew it.

Commentary 4: I agree with what Antigone did to stick up for her dead brother Polynices. He died from attacking the city of Thebes. Creon, the king of Thebes, is also Antigone's uncle. The law states that anyone who is a rebel against Thebes, his body must rot in the sun and anyone that violates the law and tries to bury Polynices deserves to die. Creon does not want Antigone to die and is willing to let her go without a word to anyone. Antigone refuses and would rather die and bury her brother to let him rest in peace. If Antigone did not say anything about the absurd law, then she would never bury her brother and he would rot in the sun. Antigone had the intention of doing the right thing and stopping others from not being buried. Antigone's actions show how much she loves her brother and is willing to die so that he can rest in peace. Nobody is perfect in the world and people should be forgiven. The people in Thebes should forgive Polynices and bury him and let him rest in peace.

Commentary 5: In Jean Anouilh's play *Antigone*, Creon and Antigone both are adamant about their own decision and unsuccessfully try to persuade the other to change each other's mind. I believe Creon when he says it is easier to say "no" than to say "yes." On the other hand, I wonder how Creon would feel that if he refused to be king he would die. But I disagree with Antigone; if she lets herself be killed under a government she does not believe in, she gives into the government. Or if she gives in to the government and marries, she may live long enough to see a change or she could be the one to change the government someday. Either way, she gives in to Creon but at least she lives. If Antigone chooses to die, there will always be two souls who are going to be lost and will never be in a place of peace.

Similar to the other formats, this narrative also provides the necessary information to review at a later date. The important point is to use a journal format which will accommodate your learning style. Be flexible, alter and adapt formats to suit your needs. In the above commentaries, students are clearly engaged in a dialogue to determine if the actions of the characters make sense in the context in which events are happening. For some students these types of journal entries reflect more of their learning style making it more accessible for review.

Chapter Five

Reading and Writing Analytically

Read and revise, reread and revise, keep reading and revising until your text seems adequate to your thought.
—Jacques Barzun

Lesson 12: The Summary

As we have emphasized throughout *Reading Between the Lines*, reading and writing are "two sides of the same coin." The reading and writing strategies you have put into practice and become skilled at will all be part of your personal assessments to determine if you have internalized the art of efficient reading. In this section, evaluating reading by writing critiques and synthesis will be helpful in making your assessments. Therefore, longer passages of expository text and imaginative literature are included along with corresponding extended examples of student summaries, critiques, and synthesis. The summary, critique, and synthesis are interconnected: an accurate summary is essential to write a critique and both are integral to the synthesis.

In addition, scoring guides are included to help you assess the summaries, critiques, and synthesis which you may write. These scoring guides are inherently flexible guides to help you determine if you have included basic requirements for these kinds of writings. Therefore, if you are enrolled in a course, be sure to check with your instructor for additional criteria that may be required.

At the end of this Chapter, we will address test-taking issues. There are specific methods you can employ to prepare for taking tests and to write exams. As you read this Chapter, apply the strategies to your reading and writing and to tests you may take.

The summary is one way of taking "ownership" of what you read. It is a concise factual statement, in your own words, of the author's main points.

Writing the summary will help you determine if you understand the author's stated meaning. Your interpretations, opinions, emotional reactions, or conclusions should not be included. At this point, you suspend judgment and simply write a factual statement of what the author intends. The summary is not always easy to write because you must reduce the material to a comprehensible paragraph. In addition, if the material is long, reducing the material can sometimes seem to be a formidable task. However, concept webs and reading annotations will be helpful in the process. The summary does not have to include minor details, but it should include major details as examples to clarify concepts and these major details will help when you have to review the summary for other purposes. For example, to write a critique or synthesis, an accurate summary is an important part of the process. In essence, the summary must be accurate and only reflect what the author intended. Guidelines for writing a summary are presented below, followed by extended text and student examples of summaries.

Guidelines for Writing the Summary

- When summarizing a chapter include the title of the chapter and themes. Include the main ideas, specific terms and concepts, and provide examples to clarify key ideas.
- Summarize sections of expository text as you read.
- When summarizing an entire article or book, in the opening sentence include the title, author, and central idea, and then write a concise, clear statement in your own words.
- Follow the paragraph structure of the article, i.e., cause/effect, listing, etc.
- Write a sentence to express the main idea for each paragraph. In some instances you will be able to combine ideas from two or more paragraphs and write one sentence.
- In some instances, there may be a sentence that expresses the main idea, sometimes referred to as the topic sentence; restate this sentence in your own words.
- If the main idea is not stated, look at the supporting details and examples and write the main idea.
- End your summary with the author's conclusions.
- Do not include your opinion, emotional responses, or conclusions.

Summary Scoring Guide

SUMMARY	THOROUGH	GOOD	NEEDS IMPROVEMENT (Rewrite)
Opening Sentence	Include: Title of article, author, thesis (i.e., controlling or central idea, theme, etc.), and purpose of the article. For chapters, include title of chapter and theme(s).	Title, author, thesis (i.e., the controlling or central idea, theme, etc.). Purpose not stated. Introduction to chapter does not include theme(s).	Title and author identified but the thesis (controlling or central idea, theme, etc.) not clearly stated.
Restatement of Author's Ideas	A concise restatement in your own words stating the author's position. Do not include your opinions, responses, etc.	A good restatement in your own words, but may need to cut unnecessary examples or details	Long and confusing: seems to be having difficulty restating the author's position in your own words. (Review Chapter Two.)
Major Points	All major points are included	Major points included	Focused on supporting details/ Major points omitted
Examples	Important and accurate examples to explain major points	Examples included to explain major points	Examples included as major points
Conclusions	Conclusion of the author included	Conclusions of the author included	Conclusions not clearly stated
Spelling and Grammar	Free of spelling errors, minor grammatical errors	Free of spelling errors, a few minor or major grammatical errors	Spelling errors, a number of minor and major grammatical errors—difficult to follow ideas

Expository Text With Concept Webs

The first student summaries illustrate how to summarize sections of an expository text to clarify key terms and ideas as you read. The three student summaries were written based on a section of an article on organisms and space. To be sure that they understood key points, they created a concept web and wrote their summary statement directly from the web, restating the major points in their own words.

Student A – Expository text concept web and summary

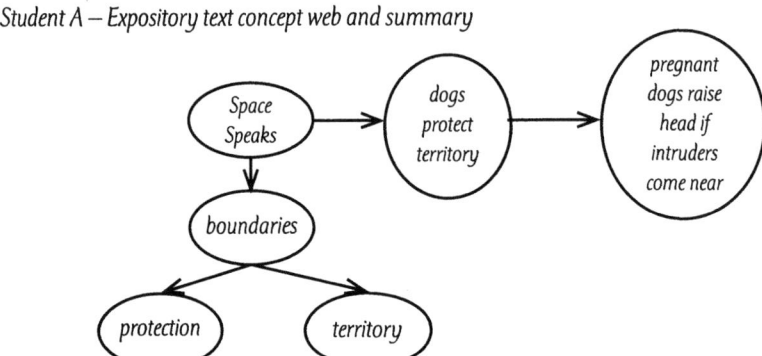

Space Speaks discusses how human beings and animals protect their property from intruders. There are certain boundaries that they place around themselves. The first of these is physical boundaries; this is when a human being puts up a fence around his or her property. An animal, for instance a dog, has a sense of where he or she belongs and sleeps in a certain place. When a dog is pregnant she raises her head if any intruder gets too close to the litter.

Student B – Expository text concept web and summary

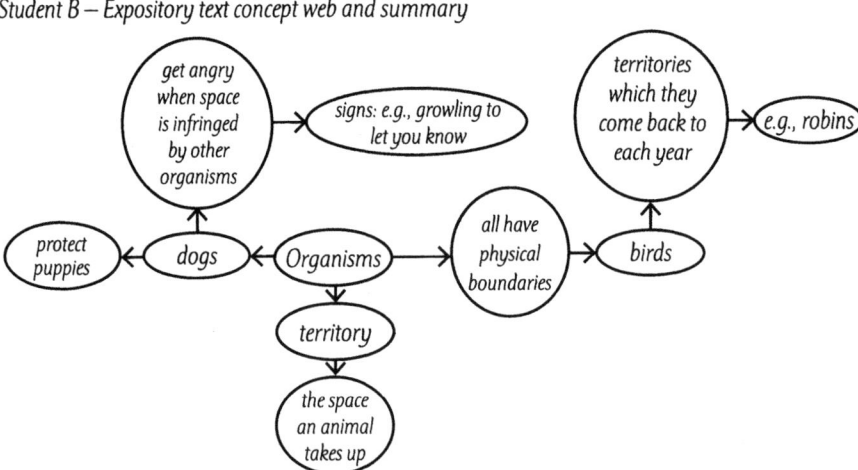

Space Speaks talks about the reaction of different organisms in an environment when another person or organism infringes upon their space. Every organism has physical boundaries and will react when another organism intrudes on that space. Animals occupy certain territories that they always return to no matter where they go. For example, birds leave their territories but return to them each year. Dogs also have territories that they consider to be their own. They get angry when someone comes near their territory. They also show signs like looking at the person or growling.

Student C – Expository text concept web and summary

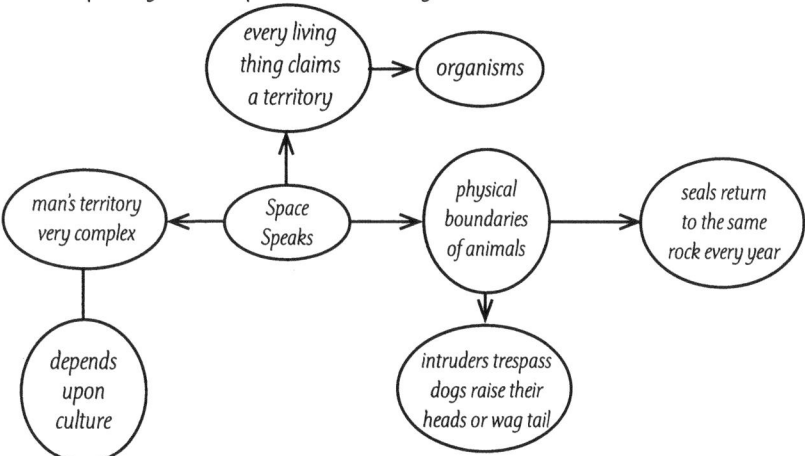

Every living organism has a physical boundary, but man's boundary is very complex depending upon his culture. With animals, boundaries are just as important. For example, dogs have physical boundaries, such as sleeping near the stove in the kitchen or sleeping in the dining room. These spaces are called "physical boundaries" because the animals lay claim to their territory.

These three summaries, written independent of each other, include the same key ideas and points of information. It is clear that these students restated the main points in their own words and have given an accurate account—each included the same major points: (1) man and animals set physical boundaries and (2) both man and animals protect their space from intruders. The points of difference are the examples given, and this is to be expected. The examples included in any summary will reflect what a writer will choose to help remember the main points under consideration. What is important are that the main points have been accurately restated in a concise, clear statement in the reader's own words. We can also see this in summaries of longer articles.

To write a summary for longer text, i.e., chapters or articles, you may wish to create concept webs and annotations and refer to any notes you have written during your reading. The following summaries are based on a textbook, on human sexuality, on a chapter on gender roles. After reading these summaries, compare the two summaries to determine if the thesis is similar and if major points to support the thesis and conclusion. Use the scoring guide to evaluate these summaries.

Student Summary #1 on "Gender Roles"

> According to William H. Masters, Virginia E. Johnson and Robert C. Kolodny in *Human Sexuality* (1988) change in gender roles and sex differences have extremely influenced social, political and economic systems and recent trends have threatened age-old distinctions. They state that masculinity and femininity is not enough to distinguish the characteristics of a male and female. However, scientists have longed viewed masculinity and feminity as separate characteristics that "coexist to some degree in every individual." Cultural expectations of parents influence their earliest relationship with their newborn child in that it makes possible gender differentiation. In early childhood, the personal sense of being one of either sex is assisted by verbal skills, object playing activities, picture books, television are all sources which can be used for difference in gender-role socialization—e.g., it is accepted that boys tend to be more active than girls. During school age of a child, an activity either athletic or entertaining is most noticeable. Moreover, the male is engaged in more vigorous activities. In the adolescence stage, the male views masculinity and femininity as completely opposite and they become interested in girls and sex, are achievement-oriented, competitive, independent, self-confident and so on. During adulthood, men continue showing proof of strength, physical competence and occupational achievement becomes important. For women, marriage and motherhood is their cultural expectation. But roles for women and men are changing and making little difference.

Compare the following "Gender Roles" summary with the preceding summary. Note the differences between the two.

Student Summary #2 on "Gender Roles"

> "Gender roles" by William H. Masters, Virginia E. Johnson and Robert C. Kolodny (1988) conducted research to understand sex-appropriate behavior for men and women. The authors were the first to observe physiological and anatomical human sexual behavior. They give many examples describing typical stereotypes Americans have in judging the behavior of men and woman. The traditional stereotyped gender roles for American men and women have been that males are to be masculine and females are to be feminine. Parents often have a preconceived attitude about the sex of an unborn child. Boys are usu-

ally wanted by expecting parents because of the belief that men are stronger, smarter, braver and more productive. The researchers discussed the traditional approach of masculinity and femininity by studying early patterns of gender-role socialization of an unborn child and by looking at the behavior of parents. For example, parents preparing for an unborn boy's room or a girl's room would choose colors that are considered "feminine" or "masculine." Children learn of gender roles through parents, teachers, and society, i.e., books, television and magazines. Different patterns of generalized roles continue during school. It is during the teenage years that boys are expected to show masculinity by demonstrating physical competence and a competitive spirit. Differences in culture and attitudes in upbringing affect gender roles also. Boys, when they become adults are expected to be physically and mentally healthier than woman. Psychological tests for gender role characteristics have changed in recent years. Scientists now look at masculinity and femininity as separate characteristics that coexist to some degree in every individual. The authors believe that roles are changing as men and women take jobs that have traditionally been considered male or female jobs.

Summary #1, begins with a strong thesis statement which describes the authors' major point. We are given a clear understanding of how the authors supports their thesis. In summary #2, the thesis statement is stated somewhat differently, but conveys the same information. Both summaries provide the reader with supporting evidence to support the thesis: gender roles are influenced by societal, cultural, and parental expectations. The second summary provides a number of examples and minor details. Examples may be helpful to explain major concepts, but minor details are not necessary. Both summaries provide the conclusions of the authors.

Imaginative Literature With Concept Webs

To summarize imaginative literature, the guidelines outlined for expository text can also be applied to imaginative literature. However, when reading narratives, novels, short stories, etc., many characters may be involved in complex relationships and it is sometimes difficult to determine what events should be included. Therefore, it is desirable to create character maps as described in Chapter Three to help unravel the relationships. Student examples below illustrate how character maps help to write clear, focused summaries. As you view the character maps and accompanying summary, note how students incorporated the information from the character maps to write their summaries.

The following character map and summary is based on chapter "1920" from *Sula* by Toni Morrison.

"1920" – Student # 1 Character Map and Summary

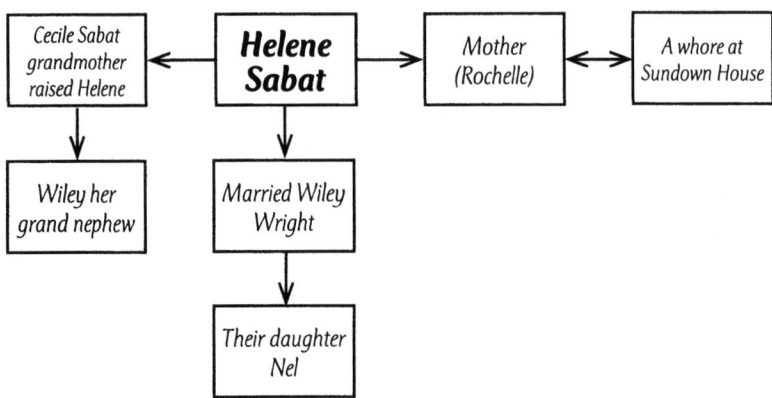

Helene Sabat was born in New Orleans behind a whorehouse where her mother worked. Her grandmother did not want her to live under these conditions so she took Helene to New Orleans to live with her. Helene eventually marries Wiley Wright who is a seaman and her grandmother's great nephew. Helene and Wiley leave New Orleans and settled in the town of Medallion. After nine years she finally gives birth to a girl, Nel. Helene is a church-going woman who is very active in her community. She tries to bring culture to the community or how she defines it. For example, Helene places flowers on the church altar and welcomes Negro veterans back to Medallion. One day she received a letter informing her that her grandmother has a serious illness and she must to go back to New Orleans. Very significant things happen to her on her trip that have to do with racism. For example, when she walks through the "whites only" train coach, the white conductor stops her and tells her to get her "butt" in the other coach. In 1920, colored people were not permitted to use restrooms on the train. Helene and her daughter have to get off at certain stops and go to the bathroom in a field full of weeds. Helene was completely humiliated by these incidents. And to make matters worse, when she arrives in New Orleans, her grandmother had already died. Another important event was when she meets her mother. Her mother tries to show her affection but Helene is completely shocked by the fact that her mother wore a yellow dress to her grandmother's funeral. All of these events lets Nel realize that her mother is not perfect and this realization gives her courage to be herself and become friends with Sula who she knew her mother did not like.

"1920" – Student # 2 Character Map and Summary

The themes in "1920" were about Helene Sabat's background, how she raises her daughter and how she deals with the death of her grandmother and an encounter with her mother. Helene Sabat was born in New Orleans to a Creole prostitute in a place called Sundown House. She was raised by her grandmother and lived with her for sixteen years. Eventually she married Wiley Wright, a seaman and distant relative of her grandmother. They moved to the town of Medallion. After nine years she had a daughter, Nel, and Helene was a very strict mother. Nel became very obedient under Helene. Helene's husband earned a good living so she lived a

READING AND WRITING ANALYTICALLY   127

very comfortable life with her daughter and husband. Helene was very influential in the town with the people. One day she received a letter from a man in New Orleans saying that her grandmother was very ill. At first, she did not want to go back because of the racial hatred she experienced while growing up. But she felt she had to go because her grandmother had rescued her. Helene decides to make the trip with her daughter, Nel. On the trip back to New Orleans, she experiences what she feared. By mistake she goes into a coach on the train where Blacks were not allowed. The conductor insults her, makes her leave and she is totally humiliated. She is also humiliated because bathrooms on the train are for whites only and she has to get off the train and go to the bathroom in a field. When they arrive in New Orleans, Helene's grandmother has already died. Helene meets her mother and has an instant dislike for her. In the meantime, Nel sees all the problems her mother is having and she realizes that she can be herself and is no longer afraid of her mother.

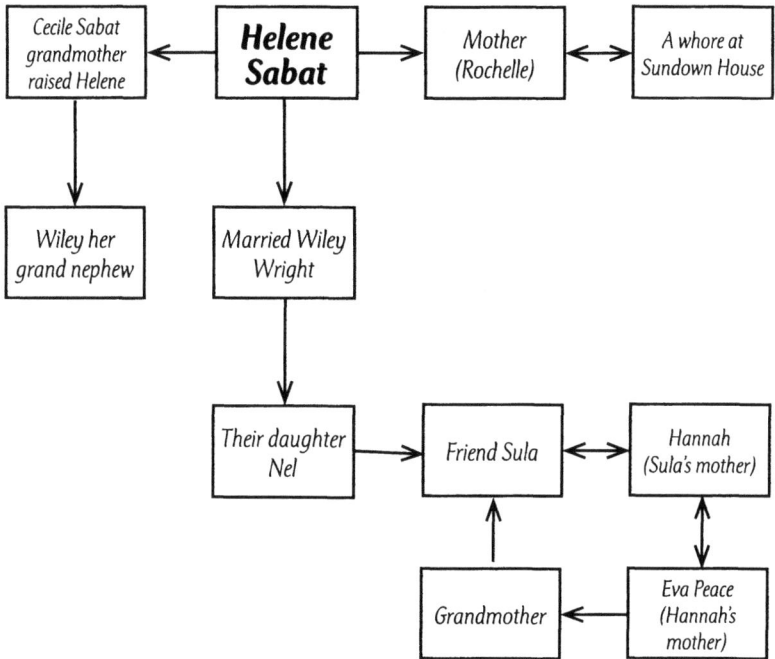

Both these summaries focus on major themes addressed in "1920": (1) incidents on the train, (2) Helene's encounter with her mother and (3) the transformation of her daughter, Nel. Both summaries give us a clear picture of the background of Helene Sabat and each cite similar examples. The author has unmistakably made it clear that these events were pivotal in the development of the characters. Both these students understood this. Reflecting on your readings via character maps helps you make connections and recognize important interrelationships. In the following concept web, additional characters are introduced.

Student # 3: "1921" – Student Character Map and Summary

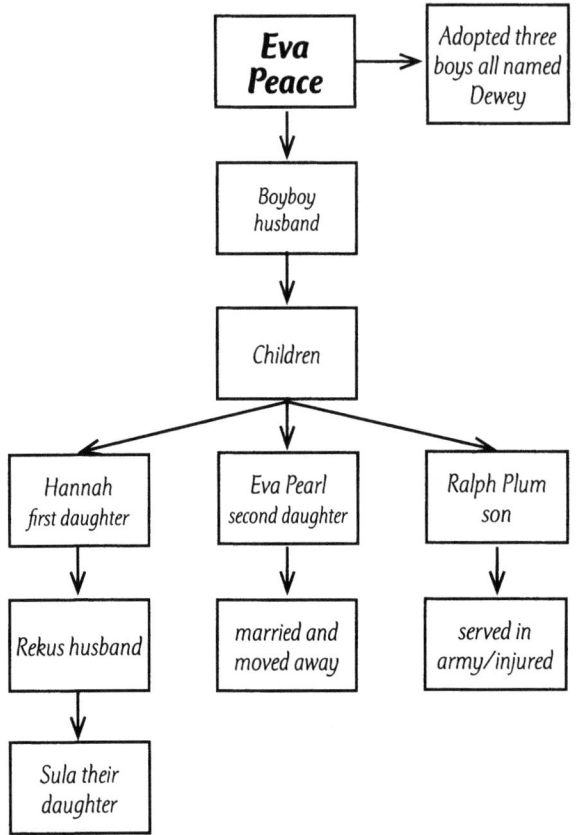

Student Summary:

In 1921, we learn about important experiences of Eva Peace. Eva has a big house and a big family and rents rooms to people. She married a man named Boyboy, and gave birth to three children: Hannah, Eva was called Pearl, and a son Ralph called Plum. Eva also adopted three children and called all of them "Dewey." She loved children. When her husband leaves her, she does not have a job or any money. Neighbors were very kind to her and gave her food. Eva knew that she had to do something to feed her children. When the children got a little older, she leaves them with a friend, Mrs. Suggs, and tells her that she will be back in two days. She does not comes back until eighteen months later without a leg and buys a house. Nobody knew how she lost her leg but there were rumors that she deliberately had it run over by a train to collect insurance money. Eva's daughter Pearl married at age fourteen and moved to Michigan. Hannah marries a man named Rekus and when their daughter, Sula, is three years old he dies. Hannah moves back with her mother and loved to flirt around with married men she liked. Eva's son Plum went to war in 1917 and comes back in 1920. He has become addicted to drugs. Eva did not like that. Once she was in his room and saw how he suffered and it made her very sad. She throws a rolled up newspaper soaked with kerosene into the bed where he is lying and everything starts burning. Eva could not bear to see her son get worse and worse as he used drugs.

Apply the guidelines in the Summary Scoring Guide to evaluate these summaries.

Lesson 13: Evaluating Text

To evaluate readings, the literal level of comprehension as well as the interpretive level of comprehension are considered to complete an analysis and evaluate text. It is in this phase that you employ all the techniques outlined in *Reading Between the Lines* to construct your evaluation of the text. Remember, the author has framed the text, the problem, the persuasive argument, personal narrative, or other form of writing from his or her Personal Matrix. The benefit is, you gain knowledge, but you must be comprehensive to achieve a critical analysis. During the evaluation phase the context of the material must be considered, e.g., sources of the information, date when the article is written. As stated earlier, these will be important to understand who is affected and the context of any political, historical, religious, cultural, or other societal influences which existed when the article was written. For expository text, it is particularly important to place events, issues, and problems in context and a time frame. When and where are these events happening? What are the historical events, social, political, economic, or religious implications? When we evaluate readings from a broad perspective, we are in a better position to produce an accurate analysis and draw reasonable conclusions. Therefore, considering context of any issue gives us a meaningful evaluation for expository text.

As stated in previous chapters, as you read, questions will naturally occur and you formulate questions before reading which helps you evaluate the text. To evaluate your reading material, consider the following points as general guidelines but do not be limited by these.

- Place the discussion in context: What is the current social milieu—political, economic, religious implications?
- What sources have been used to prove the point? Are they accurate?
- What information seems to be missing?
- Why is this issue important and/or significant?
- What does the author want me to believe?
- Who is the target audience and who does the author wish to influence?
- Who stands to gain?
- Do you agree or disagree with the ideas and conclusions?
- Why or why not?

The following student summaries illustrate the importance of considering context when evaluating. Read the following student summaries of the essay, "The Problem That Has No Name" by Betty Friedan in which she comments on the ill-fated destiny for middle-class housewives in America (see Chapter Two for this essay).

Student Summary #1: "The Problem That Has No Name"

> According to Betty Friedan (1963), in the article "The Problem That Has No Name," women were affected by one major problem in the United States of America society: they were questioning their role as housewives. For many years the roles of women were defined as mothers and wives that required certain obligations from them: housekeeper, childcare, and other activities concerning their children's education. The role of the women was understood so well that young girls did not think about careers; the only thing that mattered for them was finding a husband and having babies. By the middle of the twentieth century women started to feel the effects of their "problem," but they still were unable to state it clearly. They visited psychiatrists but could not express their frustrations. They could not even talk about the "problem" among themselves fearing that their problem was only personal, and not shared by others in general. Women, although they fulfilled their tasks as wife and mothers, were in despair. They tended to ask themselves this question: "Is this all there is?!" By talking to different mothers, the author realized that many mothers were having similar problems that implies that the problem was common in society, and countless of women in America share it.

Student Summary #2: "Problem That Has No Name"

> In the article, "The Problem That Has No Name," Betty Friedan (1963) interviews young mothers and wives who were not happy or content with their lives. Even though they had husbands, children and money they still felt empty and unsatisfied with their lives. According to Friedan, they all had the same problem but they were not able to identify it. Nobody, not even doctors, could give a name to this problem. The problem according to the writer was that these women were not satisfied with themselves. They felt empty inside and did not have anything else to look forward to. Even though they were busy all day long, the women Friedan interviewed felt unfulfilled and not alive. She used a lot of quotes from her interviews to strengthen her article and to put together common problems of the mothers and wives. Without putting together these quotes the author would not have a strong article to argue her case. Basically, these women were not fulfilled as housewives.

These summaries are concise restatements of the author's main points citing examples for the reader to understand the problem of the women. The second summary clearly defines the thesis of the essay. Thus, the reader is given a clear understanding of what the dissatisfaction is without including all the minor details and examples. However, since this article was written over forty years ago (1963), to evaluate this essay, one needs additional information to place it in context. You would also need to read what others were reporting at the time of this article and additional information on an author's current views would also be helpful.

The Critique

A critique is your critical analysis of the author's central theme and supporting ideas, evaluating facts and opinions to determine the accuracy of the presentation. The critique may be an analysis of an entire article or focus on aspects of the material. It is your analysis to determine whether it is a convincing presentation. Are the facts accurate? Does the date of the article affect the information? What are the advantages and disadvantages? Limitations? Is there sufficient information to come to a conclusion? Unlike a summary, the critique should include your informed opinion, conclusions, and general reactions to the writing. There are various formats to organize your critique. However, although formats may vary, if you are unaccustomed to writing critiques, use the basic guidelines in the Critique Scoring Guide to evaluate critiques.

Critique Scoring Guide

FORMAT	POINTS TO INCLUDE
Thesis	First sentence should include the title, author's thesis, and purpose
Major Points	Summarize the main points and follow the pattern of the article. Inform the reader which points, events, or issues you intend to address in your essay.
Analysis	Cite examples to support your points of agreement and disagreement, advantages and disadvantages, strengths and weaknesses, limitations, and so on.
Opinion and Other Sources	Include your opinion and reasons for the position you take. When necessary, add additional sources to support your point of view.
Conclusions	State the author's conclusions and determine whether there is sufficient evidence or information to accept the conclusions; state whether you agree or disagree and give your reasons.

*If you are enrolled in a course, check with your instructor to determine if additional criteria are needed to meet the standards for your class.

Expository Text

In the following student critique, it begins with the thesis and then critiques the article by citing examples, giving reasons for agreement or disagreement with the author's point of view. Review this critique and use the Critique Scoring Guide to evaluate it. Consider the following questions and formulate ones of your own.

- In this essay, what does the title, "Sin, Suffer and Repent" suggest to you?
- How does your Personal Matrix inform you of what you might expect from the title?
- Has the student writer clearly stated the thesis of the article?
- Has the student writer given clear examples to support the theme?
- Has the student stated his position logically and clearly to indicate whether he agrees or disagrees?
- Are the conclusions of the author included?
- Review the language. Has the student clearly distinguished his views from the author's? Can you agree with the student's position?

In the essay "Sin, Suffer and Repent," Donna Woolfolk Cross (in *Media Speak: How Television Makes Up Your Mind.* New York: Putnam, 1983) discusses how characters on soap operas affect American people's lives and how soap operas occasionally distort reality. The student's critique of this essay is given below.

Student Critique #1

On the whole, I believe soap operas do provide an accurate picture of America. Most people today are so addicted to soap operas that they find it difficult to cope with situations whenever they miss certain shows. Many Americans confuse soap operas' lifestyles with their real life. They believe what they see on the shows, and think they can apply the same behavior to their lives. Many of the women watching soap operas are so taken up with their special shows that they tend to neglect their housework, just to look at their shows. For instance, Cross (1983) describes a woman from Wisconsin, on hearing about the postponement of her soap opera show, called the station and cursed the operator at the television station.

People today condition themselves in such a way that they have to watch these shows. As Cross states, the characters on the soap operas portray sinful actions, which most Americans put into practice. Why is it a woman has to sleep with another man or a man cheats on his wife? Donna Cross considers cheating sinful. I agree; these are all sinful actions done by these soap opera people. Cross explains how some of the soaps have the people suffer for their behavior, and how they later try to repent. For instance, when a man insults his pregnant wife about the mashed potatoes she made, the wife suffers a miscarriage. The man repented.

He felt sorry for doing this to his wife and as such he suffers the consequence of losing his child.

Soap operas influence people very much. After seeing the behavior and actions of the characters in the shows many people try to live the same way these characters live in soaps. Many divorce their partners because of their careers. The men prefer their wives to be around, preparing their food and satisfying them in every possible way. The women are taken up so much with their careers that they find little time to spend at home. This type of attitude makes a person sad and lonely and as such he or she turns to a friend who is always ready to help.

In today's society, men and women behave like typical soap characters. One could hear men discussing soap operas characters on their jobs and in restaurants. They all wait patiently for the time when they could watch their shows. They imitate whatever they see these characters doing and they put it into practice. Young women watching soap operas tend to live a typical lifestyle. Some of them flirt with their bosses and at the same time treat their husbands nice. The society today is so taken up with soap operas shows that people do not find time for their children.

In the essay, actions portrayed by these soap opera actors are the same behaviors being seen by people in society. For example, some women dress like the characters and copy the lifestyles of the soap opera actors. Even young children are seen these days looking at these soap opera shows. So we can see from this essay how some people react to soap operas. On the whole, soap opera shows do influence Americans a lot. It is as if people are conditioning themselves to make these shows part of their lifestyle. They confuse their life with the lifestyle of soap operas. I agree with Cross that these shows help to make up your life and the way you live.

In the next critiques, students read an article, "Swimming in Cross-Cultural Currents," by C. P. Kottak (*Natural History*, May 1985) which highlights the differences between American and Brazilian swimmers.

Student Critique #1

In the essay, "Swimming in Cross-Cultural Currents," Kottak states that athletes from some countries excel in particular sports. Also that certain nations pile up dozens of Olympic medals while others win only a handful or none at all. Kottak states that in one particular sport, swimming, he cites many reasons for the success of the swimmers in the United States and the reasons for the failures of swimmers in Brazil. One such reason was the importance placed on time. In Brazil no one emphasizes the need to be punctual for any event, no record of swimmers' times are kept. Parents of swimmers cannot compare their children's previous time, or for swimmers they cannot measure their own success or failure in one meet against another meet, because they do not possess time records. In the United States, swimmers' times are better monitored. Parents or coaches time their children or athletes with stopwatches which give precise time to the hundredth of a second. Previous time recording of swimming are posted publicly for all to see; swimmers can compare time and try to better someone else's time. In the United States, swimmers get practice by swimming in a meet; the more meets a swimmer does the better his or her chances of improvement. Parents encourage their children to go to meets as often as possible and sometimes parents take their children to the meets because they know that this is important to their children's swimming. In Brazil, swimmers are not so fortunate, because the coach limits swimmers to two or three meets. This limited practice cannot determine whether one particular swimmer is a good swimmer or not. This does not give the child enough practice and motivation to do his or her best. Parents in Brazil should be more involved in their children's swimming. They should be present at the meets and protest against the limited meets given to their children. Parents should also time their children's swimming, this way they will be able to have an accurate recording of their children's performance. Kottak's reasons for the success of some countries in sports are valid. Proper preparation and dedication of both the athletes and coaches, parents and team will bring about success.

Student #2 Critique

In "Swimming in Cross Currents," Kottak felt that some countries excel in particular sports and some do not; also some pile up dozens of Olympic medals while others only a handful because of their cultures, the way they are used to doing things. He discusses time as one factor tied to their culture, organization another and the social and economic factor also contributes to their excelling in sports.

In his essay, Kottak tries to convince us that swimming competition is better in America than in Brazil. On the factor of timing, Americans take time more seriously than in Brazil. Time is collated more accurately. In Brazil, nobody makes an appointment, no one is expected to be on time.

In swimming competition the Americans have stopwatches and watch the minute quarter of a second while Brazilians chatted while their swimmers are competing. So because of the way the two countries look at time, he feels that it contributes to America excelling in swimming.

Organization he pointed out is also an important factor for bringing home the gold medal. Sports meets should be planned way ahead of time. The American swim meets are planned a year in advance. Brazilians on the other hand, do not know where their meets will be held until two days before. Most of the time the location changes and swimmers miss their meet. Thus, Kottak feels that they miss practice time and practice time is how they would acquire experience. These meets are the stepping stone towards the gold medal.

Social and economic factors also, he discusses as a factor for people to excel and bring home the gold medal. In America parents are very involved in the particular sports that their children are interested in. He feels that money, a certain social status, parents time are all important factors. He feels that because of no parental involvement, no social status is also the reason for not doing well in sports.

I think that Kottak is right as to the reasons he gave for doing well. If one is to do well in sports or anything for that matter, there must be some respect to being punctual, and take time seriously. Especially in the sport swimming that he discussed. Timing is the basis for the swimmers. Timing is vital to them. Winning is for the person who does the best times. When the coach sees the progress of a swimmer who betters his or her time each time they meet, obviously he will think of entering him or her in state then national and eventually the Olympics.

Everything that we do has to be organized. Organization ensures that everything will go all right and as planned. Being blind going into something, does not make sense. So organization is important.

Parents' involvement is also important. They need to be there to cheer on their kids, make them feel confident. Take them to their meets and encourage hard work and reward them with respect even if they do not win. Money is important also, taking part in sports competition does cost money. Special clothes, transportation to and from meets, so one has to be of a certain social status to participate in sports.

It is not fair that only people who can afford it have their children compete. There may be talented, gifted children who excel in sports but because their parents cannot afford to have them compete, they are deprived of their talents.

Imaginative Literature

The following critiques are examples of an analysis of different aspects of complex relationships. The first critique focuses on problems of obedience to one's cultural traditions when one wishes to consider alternative available choices. Students critiqued events in novels citing examples and giving their analysis.

The first critique is based on the novel *The Joy Luck Club*. In this critique, the student identifies the conflicts experienced between mother and daughter, citing examples and giving an analysis as to why the conflicts occurred.

Critique Student #1 – The Joy Luck Club

> In this chapter, "Rules of the Game," Waverly Jong is in conflict with her mother, Lindo Jong. Rules of the game really meant what Waverly needed to learn the rules of life to live a good life. Her mother is a very tough woman and made a lot of demands on Waverly. Waverly felt that nothing she did seemed to please her mother. Except chess. Waverly Jong was a champion chess player and her mother supported her participation in chess tournaments. Her mother would go around the neighborhood bragging about how well Waverly played. Waverly resented her mother for showing off to the neighbors. But this chapter is really more about her relationship and the conflicts she has with her mother rather than about playing chess. Chess represents the struggles between mother and daughter and how they try to get the better of each other. Her mother is old, a traditional Chinese and her daughter, Waverly, is American born with those values and these cultural differences cause conflicts between mother and daughter. Even though Waverly was a successful accountant, she could never seem to please her mother. Waverly could not solve her problems with her mother because although she was born in America, Waverly understood Chinese tradition and it was unthinkable for her not to be obedient. She did try sometimes.
>
> I believe Waverly had an ego problem. Her mother would brag about her ability to play chess because she was proud of Waverly. When Waverly complained about the noise her brothers were making, her mother made them move into the living room. Waverly could not see that her mother had given her every opportunity to play chess and succeed. Waverly's mother was trying to show her that she was worth a lot more than Waverly thought of herself. Once when Waverly was very excited about a fur coat that was given to her, her mother made a comment that the coat was not worth anything. I think her mother was trying to let her daughter know that she deserved better and was trying to tell her daughter that she was worth more.

In this critique, the student has clearly articulated the difficulty Waverly had interacting with her mother as she was clearly American but at the same time did not wish to dishonor her Chinese traditions; the daughter was seemingly caught between American values and traditional Chinese values.

The next critique, is based on a chapter from *Sula* by Toni Morrison. The student gives a summary and then her analysis.

Critique Student #2 – Sula

In 1939 Sula places Eva, her grandmother, in a nursing home. The townspeople were angry and called Sula a "roach." People began talking about how Hannah, Sula's mother, was burned to death. They were always suspicious that Sula burned her own mother. Sula's behavior was viewed as evil and people began to blame her for everything bad that was happening to them. For example, Teapot [a child in the story] went to see Sula to get bottles from her and he fainted and fell down the steps. His mother saw him and told everyone that Sula knocked Teapot down the steps. When Mr. Finley looked at Sula while he was sucking on chicken bones, he choked and died. And, when Mr. Shadrack tipped his hat to Sula, the women were sure she was a devil; Shadrack never acknowledged anyone. The last straw was when the men found out Sula slept with white men; then there was no excuse, and no compassion for her actions, they insisted that all such unions were literally unthinkable. Sula soon began sleeping with everyone's husband. Sula thought men could be her friend, listen to her and make her feel better; instead all they wanted was sex. It took Sula a while to realize that a lover was not a comrade. Sula loved sex because for her sex was wicked and sad and she thought she deserved those feelings. And, when they find out that Sula slept with Nel's husband, Jude, and then dumped him for other men they called her a "bitch." Nel was the first person that was real to her, and knew her best and the only person who did not scorn Sula. Yet, Sula slept with Nel's husband. Later she wanted to have sex with another man, Ajax, and she accomplished that. Sula loved Ajax because he would talk to her not talk down to her. She found out Ajax leaves her and she is very hurt.

In this chapter, it is clear to me that Sula is selfish and views everything from her point of view. I feel for Sula because to me it sounds like she has a heavy burden but doesn't know how to get rid of it. Her actions reflect her perspectives on things and how she feels about herself—not good. Sula's intention when she slept with Jude was not to hurt Nel's feelings, but she never realized how she hurt Nel. Sula thought that it wasn't a big deal for her to sleep with Jude, since she and Nel had always shared everything. So sharing Jude wasn't any big deal to Sula. Evidently Nel didn't feel the same way. Sula's self-portrayal of a friend was not of a friend. She wasn't aware of what mistakes she made. Sula thought that it was all right for her to sleep with Jude since Nel and her shared everything else. Sula was so self-absorbed she disregarded everything and everybody. She locked up her true feelings to satisfy her immediate feelings and desires and disregarded Nels feelings and everybody else. Sula definitely has problems if she is sleeping with her best friend's husband. Since Sula slept with so many men, the townspeople couldn't think that Sula was looking for someone to share her feelings. But I think that she wanted someone to talk to her someone that would actually care about her and her feelings and to listen to her. She thought that by sleeping with men they would find her inner self and they would know about her and her feelings about life itself. But she couldn't find that in men. All these men wanted was sex, and all they called her were names. In the end, the only person that really cared for her was Nel; she was the one person that listened to her, paid attention to her feelings and emotions. Sula may not have wanted anything—money, property, or desire for compliments. But, she did not know how to accept friendship or know how to be a friend. Ajax also loved her but I guess not enough because he ended up leaving her and left her with a broken heart.

In this critique, the student uses the summary to focus attention on the events she will critique. She does this very well, citing incidents and giving her analysis. Throughout her critique, she informs the reader why she agrees with the behavior or the inevitability of the consequences.

Synthesis

When you wish to research a topic, you will need to refer to more than one article, book, etc., to get a broad understanding of your topic. A synthesis focuses on a topic and incorporates more than one source of information to enlarge the scope of the topic, reinforcing the interpretation and broadening the range of the discussion. For example, you may read several articles, technical sources, newspaper, books, and other media sources to research a topic. After summarizing each of the sources you have read, you will need to make connections, see relationships, compare and contrast information, and draw conclusions to write a comprehensive document citing the various sources. When you write your synthesis it will also include a critique of the material you have documented. A synthesis takes time and careful rereading, accurate notes, and reflection. Are all of your sources reliable? Have you considered various points of view? You need to be able to compare and contrast opposing views to evaluate the readings. In addition, you must be able to determine the reliability of the facts and distinguish between the reported facts and the author's opinion. Are the author's assertions based on established facts or on the author's beliefs? And with all reading be guided by questions such as:

- What does the author want me to believe?
- What other resources support or take an opposite point of view?
- Is the source reliable?
- Is there enough information to reach a conclusion or form an opinion?

Synthesis Scoring Guide

Format	Points to Include
Introduction	A focused statement to introduce the topic and explain the issues under discussion
Major Points/Issues	Discuss the major points or issues from various points of view
Analysis Cite Sources Include your opinion based on the evidence	Cite examples to support the point of view you present; consolidate ideas and points of agreement and disagreement among sources cited. Where applicable, included advantages and disadvantages, strengths and weaknesses. Use directional words to compare and contrast issues, e.g., however, but, on the other hand
Conclusions	State the conclusions and cite which sources agree or disagree. State your conclusions

A synthesis for imaginative literature will be tied together by a theme that runs through the novels or short stories under consideration. The best way to grasp this is to review how students approached the synthesis. Students considered two ideas: (1) goodness and (2) traditions in a society. Throughout the semester, there was a continuing dialogue on these topics that were central themes throughout the novels, short stories, and articles students read. Upon completion of their reading assignments, students wrote essays on how tradition influenced their definitions of "goodness." Students addressed this assignment by writing a synthesis taking examples from three of their readings: *The Lottery* (1947) by Shirley Jackson, *Sula* (1973) by Toni Morrison, and *The Joy Luck Club* (1989) by Amy Tan. Students determined the role tradition played in influencing the actions of characters. Examples were cited from these works to support their position. Read the following student syntheses and use the Synthesis Scoring Guide to evaluate the essays.

Synthesis Student #1

> Many people think that you "have" to be good. These same people go by the rule of "If you are not good, then God will punish you." You were taught to be good therefore you remain that way. Some believe that being good during your life will allow the doors to heaven to open to you, and if you are bad you will go to hell. This is not true because the way I see it is—earth is heaven and hell. If you do

something evil you will pay for it when you are alive, and if you have good intentions, then you will be rewarded here on earth.

For example, in *Sula* (1973), she was viewed as an evil person, but in actuality she was "good." She made the people from the bottom feel love once again. People perceived Sula as an evil person and often called her names like "roach," "bitch," etc. So people were guarded and took good care of their family members because they were afraid of Sula's evilness. Even though Sula did not pay attention to "tradition," her behavior had a "good" effect. Her behavior brought families together, made women care and love their kids and take care of their husbands. People who followed tradition and what was expected of them did not have the same effect as Sula's actions did to make people behave better. Another book that reflected goodness was *The Joy Luck Club* (1989). Nuyer was called names because when her husband died she went with a rich man and became his concubine. Nuyer was not suppose to marry again. In Chinese tradition once you are married and if your husband dies then you are a widow until death. She became a man's concubine not because she wanted to but because she got raped. People thought she was a whore because she got raped and remarried. Her new husband, Wu-Tsing, told everyone that she slept with him. No one really knows what happened. She was a good person because she loved her kids so much that she ended her former life for them so that they could have a better one when she became a concubine with Wu-Tsing. Even though the Chinese tradition looked down on Nuyer for her decision, she really was a good person who only tried to make good of her situation and status. In the "Lottery" (1947), like *The Joy Luck Club* (1989) and *Sula* (1973), tradition plays an important role in how people behave. It was ridiculous. The "Lottery" (1947) takes place in a village where the people go through the tradition of a lottery to see who has to be killed. People had to pick out a paper and if the paper had a black spot on it, you were stoned to death. The kids were reluctant to go through this ritual and tried to avoid it by not listening to their parents when they were called to participate. Even the adults hesitate, but they still go through with it. For example, the men did not want to help Mrs. Summer bring the black box to the center of the town to begin the ritual. Old man Warner was always anxious to go through the ritual; this was his seventy-seventh time going through this ritual and he is still alive. People blindly followed "tradition" without questioning. The lottery always existed and no one knew why or how it started.

I believe that being good comes from within. Therefore being good pays off because it is for oneself and comes from within one's soul, it is not taught nor learned. So, tradition is not always the best way for one's life.

Synthesis Student #2

Being good is a question of values. Different people from different cultures have different values. Being good will have different definitions according to each individual. In the book *Sula* (1973) by Toni Morrison, the character Sula had different definitions of being good than the society she lived in. *The Joy Luck Club* (1989) daughters and mothers had different definition of being good and tradition was very important. And, finally in the "Lottery" (1947), the town's people also had their own definitions of "goodness" and traditions.

The character Sula did not believe in being good or bad. She only does what pleases her. Everyone else did not matter to Sula. The people in Medallion thought of her as being a bad person, no one saw anything good in her. What people in Medallion didn't realize was that the bad things she did to them made them good. Teapot's mother, for example, she never took care of her son but as soon as she thought Sula would do something bad to her son she starting acting as a good mother. And wives in Medallion protected their husbands and kids from Sula. This proved when people see someone is bad they try to be good. People fear being bad. They are afraid of society saying bad things about them so fear helps people be good. After Sula died, the townspeople went back to their trifling ways.

In *The Joy Luck Club* (1989) characters had little differences in being good and bad. The mothers in this book were originally from China where being good meant keeping tradition. Being good in this tradition sometimes came with sacrifice. A man raped a woman, a shameful act but her family rejects her. Being pregnant without a husband was bad in this society. No one questioned; no one cared whether it was an accident; the only thing that mattered was tradition. In "The Lottery" (1947), this community's definition of tradition is shocking. In that little town they have a tradition of killing people by stoning them to death. People did not think about what was good or bad, they just did it because that is what they always did.

I have come to realize that people are good only for society. Or, people do what they do because of the way parents raise them. When they are not "good" society simply rejects or punishes them.

Synthesis Student # 3

What is good? Who is to judge what is good and what is bad in society? What is society? What good advice has society brought upon us as a people—stereotypes, values, customs, and religion? Most of what society tells us to do often has a negative connotation or can mess with a person's ego or subconscious. What's the opposite of Good?—Bad? So what is bad? What is Evil? Evil is supposed to be some taboo and something that everyone is to stay away from. (This is what society tells us.) Everyone has to strive to be "good," because good is the right way to live. Those are the guidelines in every religion with the exception of satanic worship.

In class my professor asked a question, "Why are you good?" One of my colleagues replied, "I'm good because that's the right way to live. I will have an eternal life in heaven if I am good." Who is to know? Do you know anyone that came from the dead and told you that if you are good you will have eternal life? I don't think so. Am I good? Well by society's definition no, I'm not. Actually, I cannot answer that question. I don't know what is good. The word is irrelevant to me. I disregard it in everyday life. The only time I use the word "good" is when I'm referring to a good performance or when I say I did good on my test. Other than that when the question arises, "Am I good?" I answer it with silence.

In *The Joy Luck Club* (1989), tradition was their society; tradition was the thing that truly dictated what was "good" and what was "bad." In this society they had to do what was "good" or they would be looked upon as outcasts. When An-Mei's mother Nuyer was found out to have had sex with another man after her husband's death it was looked upon as "bad." Without any question, with no exception, she is an outcast. They let the society, tradition, control them. They did not question their customs. Although it might hurt them or might be immoral, they did not think twice about what they did they were like robots acting on command. With tradition people seldom question it. Tradition is something that is practiced over a long period of time and is not questioned. People automatically assume that tradition is correct and that there is a reason for what they are doing (they just may not know it). Just as in the "Lottery" (1947), people did not question their actions. They just went along with the action because it was a custom of tradition. They were committing a terrible act, but because it was something they did for many years—it was a tradition—and was automatically not questioned. I wonder if I were to ask one of those town's people if they were good, I wonder how they would respond. I think in most cases they would say that they were "good." Why? They would see no harm in what you or I might regard as being evil or bad. To them their actions were traditions; there could not be any wrong to a tradition. In their society who was to view what they did as being wrong or bad?

In *Sula* (1973), the town's people viewed Sula as evil because she did things they could not explain or understand. But what is bad? By Sula doing all of those "evil" and "bad" things, she in fact made it better for everyone else. When Sula was accused of pushing "Teapot" down the stairs, she caused his mother to take him to the hospital and there they found out that he had a fracture. Then his drunken mother finally got sober, clean and devoted. Something she never was. So, in fact, Sula's "evil" or shall we say "bad" actions caused "good" to be the result.

The question, why are we good? It is irrelevant to me. To me the question is, "What is good and who is the judge?" I don't think anyone is in the position to judge someone else's values and decide whether they are "good" or "bad." And no one can claim the position of God. Therefore, no one can dictate what is "good" and what is "bad."

Lesson 14: Test Taking

If you are to prepare for exams, this section of *Reading Between the Lines* is for you. For some students, taking tests bring on a great deal of anxiety and frustration. Very often you may take a course and feel as if you do not know what to expect on the test and believe you have to "second-guess" the teacher. As you apply what you have learned in this Handbook, you are far better prepared to take exams. Taking a test is a matter of organizing your notes and study material for review and understanding a particular test format to avoid pitfalls. This means that everything you have learned in *Reading Between the Lines* will assist you in preparing for exams. You learned what an efficient reader does, e.g., use journal notes, concept webs, summary annotations, and commentary on the readings, and the ability to write summaries, evaluations, and synthesis. In this section we discuss test strategies and how to prepare to take tests for (1) essay exams and (2) objective exams.

Essay Exams

Many students experience a great deal of anxiety when taking exams. But your practice writing in the exercises throughout *Reading Between the Lines* with commentaries, summaries, and essays all of which have prepared you for writing in your own words and this skill can be transferred to writing your essay exams. Taking essay exams actually has many advantages because you may have an opportunity to choose which questions you will answer. Thus you have the opportunity to answer the questions for which you are best prepared. Essay exams may be on a general topic (as in standardized tests such as GED and SAT), and your required answers is an opinion/reason essay. However, in cases where you will be tested on specific information and questions have not been given to you, there are study techniques and strategies to help you prepare for the test.

Directive Verbs in Essay Exams

When taking an essay exam, it is important to be clear what the question requires. One way to do this is to pay attention to the directive verbs in the question. There are a number of directive verbs which are frequently used in essay questions. When you write practice essays, pay close attention to how directive verbs have been used in your course in past exams and use the same directive verbs to develop your practice essay questions. Below is a chart with a number of directive verbs used in essay questions and suggestions to focus your essay. In the third column are practice essay questions based on topics outlined in this Handbook. Answer some of these questions: create a web, make an outline, and write an essay to answer the questions.

Directive Verbs in Essay Exams

Directive Verbs Frequently Used in Essay Questions	How to Focus Your Question	Practice Essay Questions
Explain	Make the topic clear to the reader	Explain how one's Personal Matrix relates to reading
Describe	Give the reader a "word picture so that the reader can clearly visualize what you have described	Describe how a concept web looks and its purpose
Compare and Contrast	Clearly state the characteristics of the objects or topic under discussion and explain the similarities and differences	Compare and contrast concept webs and semantic character maps

Define Terms	Give definitions of terms as used in the context of the topic and prepare to elaborate and explain how it relates to other terms with the context of the discussion	Define the elements of an efficient reader
Critical Analysis; Critique	Write a clear statement of the thesis; central idea and the purpose or reason the author has taken the position; cite the advantages and disadvantages; state if you agree or disagree citing your reasons; and state if you believe the author has met his or her purpose	Critique author's language usage for connotation and denotation
Justify	Cite causes, reasons, and conditions why the topic under discussion is supported. Cover as many reasons as possible which will explain why this position is correct	Justify the inclusion of one's Personal Matrix to become an efficient reader. Justify the inclusion of relaxation techniques before exams
Evaluate	Discuss from many points of view limitations, advantages, disadvantages, etc.	Evaluate the process of monitoring your thinking and emotional responses to text

Preparation for Essay Exams

In preparing to take essay exams, you write practice essay answers for questions on topics you have discussed in class, reviewing previous exams, and on questions you create. Now you organize the material around the exam topic and write practice essays. You have learned how efficient readers read, so at this point you will have a number of sources to begin studying for the essay exam. You will need to develop an outline to write your practice essay exams. First, organize your notes around topics, and review past exams, summary annotations, commentaries, notes, and answers to questions. Review the character analysis and maps, and in the case of literature, review your character maps and clusters. Organize your previous exams around topics. Now you are ready to formulate questions. Begin with the topics and main ideas discussion in class; then formulate questions. Most of these will be questions you addressed in your class, journals, and notes and ones which have be addressed in your textbook. Review specific vocabulary terms used in class and the text so that you can use the vocabulary in your essay. Review your concept webs and generate one to develop an outline. This outline is memorized. You are now prepared to write a well-organized opening statement and write the essay. If the question is not precisely what you formulated, it will be relevant to the topics you have studied. Your practice essay answer should open with a strong opening sentence and a well-organized body ending with a concluding statement. For example, "in conclusion," "in summary," "overall," and so on.

At the exam site:

- If you practice a relaxation technique, do so before arriving. Arrive at the test site early enough to get a comfortable seat and do not engage in conversations which will create anxiety and jar you confidence.
- Read all of the directions carefully before writing anything and be sure that you understand what is being asked. If you do not understand the directions, ask for clarification.
- Before answering any of the questions, read all of the essay questions and check off the ones you feel most confident about.
- Sample Essay Questions: If you are given the opportunity to choose which essays to write, write the most challenging ones first. If the essay questions are weighted, answer the question with the most percentage points. For example, if one essay is worth 50 points and three others are worth 25 points, be sure to give yourself enough time to do justice to the answer for 50 points.
- Begin with the opening statement you prepared.
- If the questions are general, take a minute or two to generate a concept web and use this as an outline to formulate your opinion/reason essay. Number each "bubble" of your web to organize the essay.
- If you have a poor handwriting, skip a line so that it will be easier for the instructor to read.
- Leave time to proofread your paper to make sure it is well organized, clear, and includes all that the question required. Check spelling, grammar, and punctuation. There are a number of directive verbs that you will find in essay exams and you should know exactly what these terms are expecting you to include in the essay. A few examples with definitions are given below.

Writing a Practice Essay Exam

Essay exams may include all of the material studied during the course or specific aspects of the course material. Read the two sample essay answers to determine which answers have interpreted the essay question correctly and developed a clear focused essay.

Consider the following points to evaluate each essay:

- How many parts are involved in this essay question?
- Does the examinee respond to "compare" and "contrast"?
- Is the Homestead Act of 1862 and the Chinese Exclusion Act of 1882 clearly defined?
- Is there a conclusion?

Background information: After studying nineteenth century emigration to the United States, students responded to the following essay question: Compare and contrast the immigrant experience of European immigrants with the Chinese immigrant experience. Discuss how the following acts affected each group: (1) Homestead Act of 1862 for Europeans and (2) the Chinese Exclusion Act of 1882.

Answer #1 – Emigration

> First, European immigrants came to America between 1820 and 1860 because of the social, economical and political conditions in Europe. After 1880, many Catholics from Europe and Jews from Eastern Europe came here in order to escape religious persecution. Most of them expected to start their lives over and start from the beginning. Instead, they found some difficulties in their new country. New immigrants from Europe had to undergo degrading questioning, medical examinations; changes of their names and many of them were not admitted to America. Those who stayed found little help from organized labor unions, so they had to work long hours for little money. Some of them took advantage of the Homestead Act of 1862, which gave them land for free. Others lived in urban areas under very poor living conditions but still opened small businesses.
>
> On the other hand, Chinese immigrants, many males, came to America because of the poverty in China and stories of the gold rush in California, 1849–1870. They saw America as a "Gold Mountain" with lots of opportunities. They came here hoping that they would make money and after spending some time here, return to China to their families. Instead, they found prejudice. In the 1860s Chinese immigrants were unable to attend schools, or open any kind of business. In spite of this, Americans found Chinese immigrants helpful in building the railroads, working in mines and creating a rich cultural history. Later, the Chinese Exclusion Act of 1882 made it difficult for Chinese to enter the country. The act prohibited Chinese from entering America. Some tried to enter through Mexico or Canada.

Compare student #2's essay with the answer above to determine if the issues were addressed in each essay.

Answer #2 – Emigration

> There are many differences when we compare and contrast the European immigrants under the Homestead Act of 1862 and the Chinese immigrants under the Chinese Exclusion Act of 1882. The Homestead Act promoted free ownership of land by people willing to settle on and cultivate it, under certain circumstances. The first one being, you were provided 160 acres of public land free of charge to anyone either 21 years of age or head of a household and had to live on it for five years to take complete ownership. The second statement specified that if a citizen or person who had filed for citizenship, who had lived on and cultivated the land for at least five years. The Chinese Exclusion Acts made it hard for Chinese Immigrants to be allowed into the United States. It stated in several sections of the act, the hardships the Chinese immigrants had to go through. Examples would be, if a captain of any ship had Chinese laborers on their vessel they would be found guilty, fined at least $500 and be put in prison for approximately one year. Both these acts had drawbacks. At least in the Homestead Act, if you were lucky enough you could live on the land for five years and it would then be yours. In contrast, the Chinese Exclusion Act made it impossible for Chinese immigrants to come into the United States and become a citizen.

Write a Practice Essay Exam:

- Organize all of your notes, journal commentaries, text, etc., around a question, which you will answer.
- Create a concept web and develop an outline to memorize.
- Be aware of the time—but leave your watch and cell alarms off. Time yourself when writing estimating the time for each section of the exam.
- Include examples to clarify points.
- Write your practice essay and time yourself.

Objective Exams

Objective exams are designed to have one best answer; and the test taker is usually given a specific time to complete the test. Because of these constraints students may find objective tests more difficult than essay exams. On the other hand, objective test are sometimes preferred to eliminate the possibility of a subjective evaluation of your test. Examples of objective exams include multiple choice, true/false, matching, fill in sentences, and other questions requiring a single answer.

Studying for Objective Exams

Facts, details, formulas, dates, etc., will be important to study for objective exams. Therefore, look over all pass tests you have taken. You will have to determine which of these questions may appear again and the kinds of questions that may appear. Review the following in preparation for objective exams:

- Determine the kind of questions which may be asked: details (names, dates, places, etc.).
- Definitions (past quizzes, definition of terms; vocabulary instructor has emphasized over the semester).
- Organize all of your materials and review over a period of time.
- Schedule study period specifically for exam; studying with a partner may be helpful.
- Practice your relaxing techniques.

Multiple Choice Tests

Multiple choice tests are generally the preferred format for standardized tests which must be given to large groups. These standardized tests include tests such as the SAT, GED, GRE, and others. Multiple choice tests are designed to be mechanically scored and answers are consistent—that is, the goal is one best answer eliminates the prospects of error on the part of an examiner even if the test is hand scored. When taking the multiple choice test for reading, there are three parts you need to consider: (1) short paragraphs you read for understanding, (2) the question, and (3) choices from which you are expected to choose the one best answer. There are some practical steps you should follow to help you with the process for multiple choice tests:

1. Skim the passage for a quick preview of the passage to get a general idea of the topic. As you do so, you will pick up key terms and the language to get an idea of the tone of the selection.
2. Read all the questions to determine what you are expected to know. Do not read the choices yet; reading the choices at this point may distract you from the meaning of the passage.
3. Read the passage carefully and keep one of the questions in mind as you read to find the answer for this particular question. The question in mind will help keep you focused. Students often complain that it is difficult to keep focused during standardized tests.
4. When you have completed reading the passage, mentally state the main idea and what the author wants you to believe.

5. Read the question, then read all the choices.
6. Eliminate the obviously wrong answer first.
7. If wording in the answer is inclusive, using such words as "all," "every," "always," and "only" or exclusive, with such words as "never" and "none," be sure the same wording is clearly stated in the passage.

Chapter Six

Reading Selections: Freedom and Choice

In the first five chapters of this Handbook, the passages and books focused on ideas of freedom, choice, and tradition. As you studied these passages and student work samples, you gained insights and views about these ideas. The reading selections in this chapter provide a sense of continuity connecting previous chapters' themes—freedom and choice. These themes give you the opportunity to address ideas making connections across expository text and imaginative literature.

The Declaration of Independence, July 4, 1776, of the United States of America—a powerful document, unprecedented in its prose for the eighteenth century, sets the groundwork for emerging democracies. For the readings in this chapter, this document serves as a defining basis for freedom and choice. Although references to "men" in the Declaration of Independence is interpreted to mean "white men owning property," in recent times, it has transcended this limited definition and has the inherent capacity to include all humankind. Thus, the Declaration of Independence continues to inspire new emerging democracies. Appropriately, the Declaration of Independence introduces the readings as a defining basis for the themes, freedom and choice. These essays indicate how individuals from different walks of life resolve conflicting points of views in attempts to advance freedom and choice. In addition, events described happen across different time periods, showing how the movement toward a democracy can be a slow march.

Overview

Approximately one hundred years after the Declaration of Independence Native Americans—indigenous peoples of North America—African slaves, and women were all engaged in a concerted effort using various tactics to gain their freedoms for which they had so long been denied. The first essay, a speech delivered by Elizabeth Cady Stanton at Seneca Falls, New York, July 19, 1848, addressed the rights to which women were entitled—this included the right to vote. Frederick Douglass, an ex-slave, brilliant orator, writer, and tireless fighter for freedom of African slaves as well as women, addressed the Rochester Ladies' Antislavery Society in Rochester, New York, July 4, 1852. His presentation reminded the audience that the Declaration of Independence was a promise yet to be fulfilled. The next speech, made during the same time period, is an eloquent speech by Chief Seattle of the Duwamish and Suquamish Nations of the Northwest. He delivered this speech after being notified by the Governor of Washington that the federal government of the United States wanted to buy the land his people resided on and they were to be moved to a reservation. Chief Seattle's speech clearly identifies a different worldview of the Native American than that of white men.

Moving on to the twentieth century, John F. Kennedy, President of the United States of America (January 1961–November 1963), optimistic, visionary, at his Inaugural Address, January 20, 1961, laid the foundation for a new vision for America, asking citizens to make the choice: "Ask not what your country can do for you—ask what you can do for your country." At the same time, there were those Americans who were asking different questions, which needed answers to participate fully in the vision President Kennedy aspired to. None have expressed these concerns more powerfully than Martin Luther King, Jr., a political activist and minister fighting for the rights of all, trying to secure rights for African Americans for which they had so long fought. The last essay of this section is that of the Honourable Shirley Chisholm, member of the New York House of Representatives. Shirley Chisholm was an African American educator, perceptive politician, and tireless fighter for women and minority rights. In 1972 she declared her candidacy for president of the United States and won 151 delegate votes thereby giving her the opportunity to address the Democratic Convention.

As we have done throughout *Reading Between the Lines*, in this section selections from imaginative literature are included to consider ideas of freedom and choice. To provide background information, we open this section with an essay by Doris Lessing, *Group Minds*, in which she presents ideas on how an individual's choice is greatly influenced by the group to which one identifies—family, ethnic group, class, social groups, and the like. Although Lessing clearly wants to inform us of the pitfalls of group think, it may result in positive choices as we have seen in the Declaration of Independence, which was agreed upon and signed by 56 representatives of "like mind." Lessing's essay reminds us, however, that our choices are ultimately our own. *The Lottery* by Shirley Jackson (1947) and excerpts from George Orwell's *1984* illustrate how group mind may function and the choices individuals make under its influence, whether by tradition or in the absence of freedom. Through the eyes of the characters we may ask, "Under similar circumstances, how would I choose?" or "What choices would I make in the absence of freedom or when individuals choose differently?"

At the end of each reading selection, you are encouraged to make connections across selections, and evaluate and critique essays. At the end of all selections, suggestions have been given to write a synthesis. The questions you choose to answer is your choice: your analysis, your opinions have value—and yet—your ideas about freedom and choice may change as you read and interpret the essays. On the other hand, as any reader, you may choose to withold judgment until you have the opportunity to read additional information.

Preparation Before Reading

Before reading the essays, begin your journal entries by creating two concept webs: one on "freedom" and one on "choice." Then write a paragraph on freedom; do the same for choice. You may wish to combine the paragraphs. Place these paragraphs aside to review and reflect upon as you read the selections.

Concept Webs for Freedom and Choice

- In your journal, write "Freedom" and begin to record words and phrases that you associate with "freedom"; continue the process for three to five minutes.
- Record additional words and phrases to further explain your initial recordings.
- On the second journal page write "choice" in the center.
- Record words and phrases for choices you wish to make.
- Under the choices you have recorded, connect the freedom you need in order to make the choice.
- Number each circle on both webs to determine how you will write your essay: 1 = to begin the essay; 2 = for your discussion; 3 = for your conclusions.
- Using your webs, write an essay on freedom and choice.

Review the following reading strategies before reading the selections:

- Select an article and preview it.
- Formulate questions or use questions at the end of the article.

- Divide the article into segments at points which you will read and review and record annotations.
- Make marginal notes, note signal words, and identify unfamiliar vocabulary, terms, and phrases.
- Identify paragraph patterns to follow the thinking of the author; for example, cause-effect, opinion-reason, simple listing, and so on. Remember, more than one pattern may be included in an essay.
- In your own words write a declarative sentence for main ideas.
- Distinguish between facts and opinions.
- Monitor your thinking and emotional reactions.
- Journal entries—use alternative thinking strategies; summary annotations, commentary, and questions.
- Contextualize your analysis—when is this happening? What does the author want me to believe and why?

The Declaration of Independence
United States of America
July 4, 1776

When in the Course of human Events, it becomes necessary for one People to dissolve the Political Bands which have connected them with another, and to assume among the Powers of the Earth, the separate and equal Station to which the Laws of Nature and of Nature's God entitle them, a decent Respect to the Opinions of Mankind requires that they should declare the causes which impel them to the Separation.

We hold these Truths to be self-evident that all men are created equal, that they are endowed by their Creator with certain unalienable rights, that among these are Life, Liberty and the Pursuit of Happiness—That to secure these Rights, Governments are instituted among Men, deriving their just Powers from the Consent of the Governed, that whenever any Form of Government becomes destructive of these Ends, it is the Right of the People to alter or to abolish it, and to institute new Government, laying its Foundation on such Principles, and organizing its Powers in such Form, as to them shall seem most likely to effect their Safety and Happiness. Prudence, indeed, will dictate that Governments long established should not be changed for light and transient Causes; and accordingly all Experience hath shewn, that Mankind are more disposed to suffer, while Evils are sufferable, than to right themselves by abolishing the Forms to which they are accustomed. But when a long Train of Abuses and Usurpations, pursuing invariably the same Object, evinces a Design to reduce them under absolute Despotism, it is their Right, it is their Duty, to throw off such Government, and to provide new Guards for their future Security. Such has been the patient Sufferance of these Colonies; and such is now the Necessity which constraints them to alter their former Systems of Government. The History of the present King of Great-Britain is a History of repeated Injuries and Usurpations, all having in direct Object the Establishment of an absolute Tyranny over these States. To prove this, let Facts be submitted to a candid World.

- He has refused his Assent to Laws, the most wholesome and necessary for the public Good.
- He has forbidden his Governors to pass Laws of immediate and pressing Importance, unless suspended in their Operation till his Assent should be obtained; and when so suspended, he has utterly neglected to attend to them.
- He has refused to pass other Laws for the Accommodation of large Districts of People, unless those People would relinquish the Right of Representation in the Legislature, a Right inestimable to them, and formidable to Tyrants only.
- He has called together Legislative Bodies at Places unusual, uncomfortable, and distant from the Depository of their public Records, for the sole Purpose of fatiguing them into Compliance with his Measures.
- He has dissolved Representative Houses repeatedly, for opposing with many Firmness his Invasions on the Rights of the People.
- He has refused for a long Time, after such Dissolutions, to cause others to be elected; whereby the Legislative Powers, incapable of the Annihilation, have returned to the People at large for their exercise; the State remaining in the mean time exposed to all the Dangers of Invasion from without, and the Convulsions within.
- He has endeavoured to prevent the Population of these States; for that Purpose obstructing the Laws of naturalization of foreigners; refusing to pass others to encourage their Migrations hither, and raising the Conditions of new Appropriations of Lands.
- He has obstructed the Administration of Justice, by refusing his Assent to Laws for establishing Judiciary Powers.
- He has made judges dependent on his Will alone, for the Tenure of their Offices, and the Amount and Payment of their Salaries.
- He has erected a Multitude of new Offices, and sent hither Swarms of Officers to harass our People, and eat out their Substance.
- He has kept among us, in Times of Peace, Standing Armies, without the consent of our Legislatures.

- He has affected to render the Military independent of and superior to the Civil Power.
- He has combined with others to subject us to a Jurisdiction foreign to our Constitution, and unacknowledged by our Laws; giving his Assent to their Acts of pretended Legislation:

    For quartering large Bodies of Armed Troops among us;

    For protecting them, by a mock Trial, from Punishment for any Murders which they should commit on the Inhabitants of these States:

    For cutting off our Trade with all Parts of the World:

    For imposing Taxes on us without our Consent:

    For depriving us, in many Cases, of the Benefits of Trial by Jury:

    For transporting us beyond Seas to be tried for pretended Offences:

    For abolishing the free System of English Laws in a neighbouring Province, establishing therein an arbitrary Government, and enlarging its Boundaries, so as to render it at once an Example and fit Instrument for introducing the same absolute Rules into thee Colonies:

    For taking away our Charters, abolishing our most valuable Laws, and altering fundamentally the Forms of our Governments:

    For suspending our own Legislatures, and declaring themselves invested with Power to legislate for us in all Cases whatsoever.
- He has abdicated Government here, by declaring us out of his Protection and waging War against us.
- He has plundered our Seas, ravaged our Coasts, burnt our Towns, and destroyed the Lives of our People.
- He is, at this Time, transporting large Armies of foreign Mercenaries to compleat the Works of Death, Desolation, and Tyranny, already begun with circumstances of Cruelty and Perfidy, scarcely paralleled in the most barbarous Ages, and totally unworthy of the Head of a civilized Nation.
- He has constrained our fellow Citizens taken Captive on the high Seas to bear Arms against their Country, to become the Executioners of their Friends and Brethren, or to fall themselves by their Hands.
- He has excited domestic Insurrections amongst us, and has endeavoured to bring on the Inhabitants of our Frontiers, the merciless Indian Savages, whose known Rule of Warfare, is an undistinguished Destruction of all Ages, Sexes and Conditions.

In every stage of these Oppressions we have Petitioned for Redress in the most humble Terms: Our repeated Petitions have been answered only by repeated Injury. A Prince, whose character is thus marked by every act which may define a Tyrant, is unfit to be the Ruler of a free People.

Nor have we been wanting in Attentions to our British Brethren. We have warned them from Time to Time of Attempts by their Legislature to extend an unwarrantable Jurisdiction over us. We have reminded them of the Circumstances of our Emigration and Settlement here. We have appealed to their native Justice and Magnanimity, and we have conjured them by the Ties of our common Kindred to disavow these Usurpations, which, would inevitably interrupt our Connections and Correspondence. They too have been deaf to the Voice of Justice and of Consanguinity. We must, therefore, acquiesce in the Necessity, which denounces our Separation, and hold them, as we hold the rest of Mankind, Enemies in War, in Peace, Friends.

We, therefore, the Representatives of the United States Of America, in General Congress, Assembled, appealing to the Supreme Judge of the World for the Rectitude of our Intentions, do, in the Name, and by Authority of the good People of these Colonies are, solemnly Publish and Declare, That these United Colonies are, and of Right ought to be, Free and Independent States; and they are absolved from all Allegiance to the British Crown, and that all political Connection between them and the State of Great-Britain, is and ought to be totally dissolved; and that as Free and Independent States, they have full Power to levy War, conclude Peace, contract Alliances, establish Commerce, and to do all other Acts and Things which Independent States may of right do. And for the support of this Declaration, with a firm Reliance on the Protection of divine Providence, we mutually pledge to each other our Lives, our Fortunes, and our sacred Honor.

Signed by ORDER and in BEHALF of the CONGRESS,

John Hancock, PRESIDENT
Attest. Charles Thomas, Secretary

Reading and Studying the Text

1. Preview
2. Formulate questions
3. Identify unfamiliar vocabulary

Journal Annotations

1. Record your thinking and emotional responses to the text; record terms and phrases which had a strong emotional impression.

2. Record summary annotations, commentary, and questions.
3. Reread to clarify points.

Analysis: Lateral Thinking and Writing Connection

1. Choose three of the grievances outlined in the Declaration of Independence and write a journal entry to determine how it provides you the freedom to choose in your daily life. For example, how would it affect your daily life if the government cut off trade from all parts of the world?
2. Review your essays on freedom and choose and determine which rights under the Declaration of Independence enable you to exercise the freedoms you have included in your paragraphs.
3. Now that you have read the Declaration of Independence, expand your paragraphs on freedom and choice and add additional information which you would include in your ideas.

*Use concept webs to aid in your writing.

Elizabeth Cady Stanton
Declaration of Sentiments and Resolutions
Seneca Falls Convention, July 19, 1848

When, in the course of human events, it becomes necessary for one portion of the family of man to assume among the people of the earth a position different from that which they have hitherto occupied, but one to which the laws of nature and of nature's God entitle them, a decent respect to the opinions of mankind requires that they should declare the causes that impel them to such a course.

We hold these truths to be self-evident: that all men and women are created equal; that they are endowed by their Creator with certain inalienable rights; that among these are life, liberty, and the pursuit of happiness; that to secure these rights governments are instituted, deriving their just powers from the consent of the governed. Whenever any form of government becomes destructive of these ends, it is the right of those who suffer from it to refuse allegiance to it, and to insist upon the institution of a new government, laying its foundation on such principles, and organizing its powers in such form, as to them shall seem most likely to effect their safety and happiness. Prudence indeed, will dictate that governments long established should not be changed for light and transient causes and accordingly all experience hath shown that mankind are more disposed to suffer, while evils are sufferable, than to right themselves by abolishing the forms to which they were accustomed. But when a long train of abuses and usurpations, pursuing invariably the same object evinces a design to reduce them under absolute despotism, it is their duty to throw off such government, and to provide new guards for their future security. Such has been the patient sufferance of the women under this government, and such is now the necessity which constrains them to demand the equal station to which they are entitled.

The history of mankind is a history of repeated injuries and usurpations on the part of man toward woman, having in direct object the establishment of an absolute tyranny over her. To prove this, let facts be submitted to a candid world.

He has never permitted her to exercise her inalienable right to the elective franchise.

He has compelled her to submit to laws, in the formation of which she had no voice.

He has withheld from her rights which are given to the most ignorant and degraded men—both natives and foreigners.

Having deprived her of this first right of a citizen, the elective franchise, thereby leaving her without representation in the halls of legislation, he has oppressed her on all sides.

He has made her, if married, in the eye of the law, civilly dead.

He has taken from her all right in property, even to the wages she earns.

He has made her, morally, an irresponsible being, as she can commit many crimes with impunity, provided they be done in the presence of her husband. In the covenant of marriage, she is compelled to promise obedience to her husband, he becoming, to all intents and purposes, her master—the law giving him power to deprive her of her liberty, and to administer chastisement.

He has so framed the laws of divorce, as to what shall be the proper causes, and in case of separation, to whom the guardianship of the children shall be given, as to be wholly regardless of the happiness of women—the law, in all cases, going upon a false supposition of the supremacy of man, and giving all power into his hands.

After depriving her of all rights as a married woman, if single, and the owner of property, he has taxed her to support a government which recognizes her only when her property can be de profitable to it.

He has monopolized nearly all the profitable employments, and from those she is permitted to follow, she receives but a scanty remuneration. He closes against her all the avenues to wealth and distinction which he considers most honorable to himself. As a teacher of theology, medicine, or law, she is not known.

He has denied her the facilities for obtaining a thorough education, all colleges being closed against her.

He allows her in Church, as well as State, but a subordinate position, claiming Apostolic authority for her exclusion from the ministry, and, with some exceptions, from any public participation in the affairs of the Church.

He has created a false public sentiment by giving to the world a different code of morals for men and women, by which moral delinquencies which exclude women from society, are not only tolerated, but deemed of little account in man.

He has usurped the prerogative of Jehovah himself, claiming it as his right to assign for a sphere of action, when that belongs to conscience and to her God.

He has endeavored, in every way that he could, to destroy her confidence in her own powers, to lessen her self-respect, and to make willing to lead a dependent and abject life. Now, in view of this entire disfranchisement one-half the people of this country, their social and religious degradation—in view of the unjust laws above mentioned, and because women do feel themselves aggrieved, oppressed, and fraudulently deprived of their most sacred rights, we insist that they have immediate admission to all the rights and privileges which long to them as citizens of the United States.

In entering upon the great work before us, we anticipate no small amount of misconception, misrepresentation, and ridicule; but we shall use every instrumentality within our power to effect our object. We shall employ agents, circulate tracts, petition the State and National legislatures, and endeavor to enlist the pulpit and the press in our behalf. We hope this Convention will be followed by a series of Conventions embracing every part of the country. (Lucretia Mott, Thomas and Mary Ann McClintock, Amy Post, Catharine A. F. Stebbins, and others, discussed these resolutions, which were later adopted.)

WHEREAS, The great precept of nature is conceded to be, that "man shall pursue his own true and substantial happiness." Blackstone in his Commentaries remarks, that this law of Nature being coeval with mankind, and dictated by God himself, is of course superior in obligation to any other. It is binding over all the globe, in all countries and at all times; no human laws are of any validity if contrary to this, and such of them as are valid, derive all their force, and all their validity, and all their authority, immediately and immediately, from this original; therefore,

Resolved, That such laws as conflict, in any way, with the true and substantial happiness of woman, are contrary to the great precept of nature and of no validity, for this is "superior in obligation to any other."

Resolved, That all laws which prevent woman from occupying such a station in society as her conscience shall dictate, or which place her in a position inferior to that of man, are contrary to the great precept of nature, and therefore of no force or authority.

Resolved, That woman is man's equal—was intended to be so by the Creator, and the highest good of the race demands that she should be recognized as such.

Resolved, That the women of this country ought to be enlightened in regard to the laws under which they live, that they may no longer publish their degradation by declaring

themselves satisfied with their present position, nor their ignorance, by asserting that they have all the rights they want.

Resolved, That inasmuch as man, while claiming for himself intellectual superiority, does accord to woman moral superiority, it is pre-eminently his duty to encourage her to speak and teach, as she has an opportunity, in all religious assemblies.

Resolved, That the same amount of virtue, delicacy, and refinement of behavior that is required of woman in the social state, should also be required of man, and the same transgressions should be visited with equal severity on both man and woman.

Resolved, That the objection of indelicacy and impropriety, which is so often brought against woman when she addresses a public audience, comes with a very ill-grace from those who encourage, by their attendance, her appearance on the stage, in the concert, or in feats of the circus.

Resolved, That woman has too long rested satisfied in the circumscribed limits which corrupt customs and a perverted application of the scriptures have marked out for her, and that it is time she should move in the enlarged sphere which her great Creator has assigned her.

Resolved, That it is the duty of the women of this country to secure to themselves their sacred right to the elective franchise.

Resolved, That the equality of human rights results necessarily from the fact of the identity of the race in capabilities and responsibilities.

Resolved, therefore, That, being invested by the Creator with the same capabilities, and the same consciousness of responsibility for their exercise, it is demonstrably the right and duty of woman, equally with man, to promote every righteous cause by every righteous means, and especially in regard to the great subjects of morals and religion, it is self-evidently her right to participate with her brother in teaching them, I both in private and in public, by writing and by speaking, by any instrumentalities proper to be used, and any assemblies proper to be held; and this being a self-evident truth growing out of the divinely implanted principles of human nature, any custom or authority adverse to it, whether modern or wearing the hoary sanction of antiquity, is to be regarded as a self-evident falsehood, and at war with mankind.

Resolved, That the speedy success of our cause depends upon the zealous and untiring efforts of both men and women, for the overthrow of the monopoly of the pulpit, and for the securing to woman an equal participation with men in the various trades, professions, and commerce.

Reading and Studying the Text

1. Preview
2. Formulate questions
3. Identify unfamiliar vocabulary, terms, and phrases

Journal Annotations

1. Record your thinking and emotional responses to the text; record terms and phrases which had a strong emotional impression.
2. Reread to clarify points.
3. Record summary annotations, commentary, and questions.
4. Summarize the speech.

Analysis: Lateral Thinking and Writing Connection

1. Why did Stanton begin her essay with the Declaration of Independence with the following change from "that all men are created equal" to "that all men and women are created equal"?
2. Compare and contrast the grievances set forth in the Declaration of Independence with the resolutions drafted at the Seneca Falls Convention.
3. Reread the resolutions and determine whether Indigenous and African women were included. Write a critique in your journal to include the resolutions which support your conclusions.

*Use concept webs to aid in your writing.

Frederick Douglass
"What to the Slave Is the Fourth of July?"
July 1852

Mr. President, Friends and Fellow Citizens: He, who could address this audience without a quailing sensation, has stronger nerves than I have. I do not remember ever to have appeared as a speaker before any assembly more shrinkingly, or with greater distrust of my ability, that I do this day. A feeling has crept over me, quite unfavorable to the exercise of my limited powers of speech. The task before me is one which requires much previous thought and study for its proper performance. I know that apologies of this sort are generally considered flat and unmeaning. I trust, however, that mine will not be so considered. Should I seem at ease, my appearance would much misrepresent me. The little experience I have had in addressing public meetings, in country schoolhouses, avails me nothing on the present occasion.

The papers and placards say, that I am to deliver a 4th [of] July oration. This certainly sounds large, and out of the common way, for it is true that I have often had the privilege to speak in this beautiful Hall, and to address many who now honor me with their presence. But neither their familiar faces, nor the perfect gage I think I have of Corinthian Hall, seems to free me from embarrassment.

The fact is, ladies and gentlemen, the distance between this platform and the slave plantation, from which I escaped, is considerable—and the difficulties to be overcome in getting from the latter to the former, are by no means slight. That I am here to-day is, to me, a matter of astonishment as well as of gratitude. You will not, therefore, be surprised, if in what I have to say, I evince no elaborate preparation, nor grace my speech with any high sounding exordium. With little experience and with less learning, I have been able to throw my thoughts hastily and imperfectly together; and trusting to your patient and generous indulgence, I will proceed to lay them before you.

This, for the purpose of this celebration, is the 4th of July. It is the birthday of your National Independence, and of your political hope that high freedom. This, to you, is what the Passover was to the emancipated people of God. It carries your minds back to the day, and to the act of your great deliverance; and to the signs, and to the wonders, associated with that fact, and that day. This celebration also marks the beginning of another year of your national life; and reminds you that the Republic of America is now 76 years old. I am glad, fellow-citizens, that your nation is so young. Seventy-six years, though a good old age for a man, is but a mere speck in the life of a nation. Three score years and ten is the allotted time for individual men; but nations number their years by thousands. According to this fact, you are, even now, only in the beginning of your national career, still lingering in the period of childhood. I repeat, I am glad this is so. There is hope in the thought, and hope is much needed, under the dark clouds which lower above the horizon....

Fellow-citizens, I shall not presume to dwell at length on the associations that cluster about this day. The simple story of it is that, 76 years ago, the people of this country were British subjects. The style and title of your "sovereign people" (in which you now glory) was not then born. You were under the British Crown. Your fathers esteemed the English Government as the home government; and England as the fatherland. This home government, you know, although a considerable distance from your home, did, in the exercise of its parental prerogatives, impose upon its colonial children, such restraints, burdens and limitations, as, in its mature judgement, it deemed wise, right and proper.

But, your fathers, who had not adopted the fashionable idea of this day, of the infallibility of government, and the absolute character of its acts, presumed to differ from the home government in respect to the wisdom and the justice of some of those burdens and restraints. They went so far in their excitement as to pronounce the measures of government unjust, unreasonable, and oppressive, and altogether such as ought not to be quietly submitted to. I scarcely need say, fellow-citizens, that my opinion of those measures fully accords with that of your fathers. Such a declaration of agreement on my part would not be worth much to anybody. It would, certainly, prove nothing, as to what part I might have taken, had I lived during the great controversy of 1776. To say now that America was right, and England wrong, is exceedingly easy. Everybody can say it; the dastard, not less than the noble brave, can flippantly discant on the tyranny of England towards the American Colonies. It is fashionable to do so; but there was a time when to pronounce against England, and in favor of the cause of the colonies tried men's souls. They who did so were accounted in their day, plotters of mischief, agitators and rebels, dangerous men. To side with the right, against the wrong, with the weak against the strong, and with the oppressed against the oppressor! Here lies the merit, and the one which, of all others, seems unfashionable in our day. The cause of liberty may be stabbed by the men who glory in the deeds of your fathers. But, to proceed.

Feeling themselves harshly and unjustly treated by the home government, your fathers, like men of honesty, and men of spirit, earnestly sought redress. They petitioned and remonstrated; they did so in a decorous, respectful, and loyal manner. Their conduct was wholly unexceptionable. This, however, did not answer the purpose. They saw themselves treated with sovereign indifference, coldness and scorn. Yet they persevered. They were not the men to look back.

On the 2nd of July 1776, the old Continental Congress, to the dismay of the lovers of ease, and the worshipers of property, clothed that dreadful idea with all the authority of national sanction. They did so in the form of a resolution; and as we seldom hit upon resolutions, drawn up in our day, whose transparency is at all equal to this, it may refresh your minds and help my story if I read it.

"Resolved, That these united colonies are, and of right, ought to be free and Independent States; that they are absolved from all allegiance to the British Crown; and that all political connection between them and the State of Great Britain is, and ought to be dissolved."

Citizens, your fathers made good that resolution. They succeeded; and to-day you reap the fruits of their success. The freedom gained is yours; and you, therefore, may properly celebrate this anniversary. The 4th of July is the first great fact in your nation's history—the very ring-bolt in the chain of your yet undeveloped destiny.

Pride and patriotism, not less than gratitude, prompt you to celebrate and to hold it in perpetual remembrance. I have said that the Declaration of Independence is the ring-bolt to the chain of your nation's destiny; so, indeed, I regard it. The principles contained in that instrument are saving principles. Stand by those principles, be true to them on all occasions, in all places, against all foes, and at whatever cost.

* * * * * *

The coming into being of a nation, in any circumstances, is an interesting event. But, besides general considerations, there were peculiar circumstances, which make the advent of this republic an event of special attractiveness.

The whole scene, as I look back to it, was simple, dignified and sublime.

The population of the country, at the time, stood at the insignificant number of three million. The country was poor in the munitions of war. The population was weak and scattered, and the country a wilderness unsubdued. There were then no means of concert and combination, such as exist now. Neither steam nor lightning had then been reduced to order and discipline. From the Potomac to the Delaware was a journey of many days. Under these, and innumerable other disadvantages, your fathers declared for liberty and independence and triumphed.

Fellow Citizens, I am not wanting in respect for the fathers of this republic. The signers of the Declaration of Independence were brave men. They were great men too—great enough to give fame to a great age. It does not often happen to a nation to raise, at one time such a number of truly great men. The point from which I am compelled to view them is not, certainly, the most favorable; and yet I cannot contemplate their great deeds with less than admiration. They were statesmen, patriots and heroes, and for the good they did, and the principles they contended for, I will unite with you to honor their memory.

They loved their country better than their own private interests; and, though this is not the highest form of human excellence, all will concede that it is a rare virtue, and that when it is exhibited, it ought to command respect. He who will, intelligently, lay down his life for his country, is a man whom it is not in human nature to despise. Your fathers staked their lives, their fortunes, and their sacred honor, on the cause of their country. In their admiration of liberty, they lost sight of all other interests.

They were peace men; but they preferred revolution to peaceful submission to bondage. They were quiet men; but they did not shrink from agitating against oppression. They showed forbearance; but that they knew its limits. They believed in order; but not in the order of tyranny. With them, nothing was "settled" that was not right. With them, justice, liberty and humanity were "final"; not slavery and oppression. You may well cherish the memory of such men. They were great in their day and generation. Their solid manhood stands out the more as we contrast it with these degenerate times.

* * * * * *

Friends and citizens, I need not enter further into the causes which led to this anniversary. Many of you understand them better than I do. You could instruct me in regard to them. That is a branch of knowledge in which you feel, perhaps, a much deeper interest than your speaker. The causes which led to the separation of the colonies from the British crown have never lacked for a tongue. They have all been taught in your common schools, narrated at your firesides, unfolded from your pulpits, and thundered from your legislative halls, and are as familiar to you as household words. They form the staple of your national poesy and eloquence.

I remember, also, that, as a people, Americans are remarkably familiar with all facts which make in their own favor. This is esteemed by some as a national trait—perhaps a national weakness. It is a fact, that whatever makes for the wealth or for the reputation of Americans, and can be had cheap! will be found by Americans. I shall not be charged with slandering Americans, if I say I think the American side of any question may be safely left in American hands.

* * * * * *

We have to do with the past only as we can make it useful to the present and to the future. To all inspiring motives, to noble deeds which can be gained from the past, we are welcome. But now is the time, the important time. Your fathers have lived, died, and have done their work, and have done much of it well. You live and must die, and you must do your work. You have no right to enjoy a child's share in the labor of your fathers, unless your children are to be blest by your labors. You have no right to wear out and waste the hard-earned fame of your fathers to cover your indolence. Sydney Smith tells us that men seldom eulogize the wisdom and virtues of their fathers, but to excuse some Folly or wickedness of their own. This truth is not a doubtful one.

* * * * * *

...The blessings in which you, this day, rejoice, are not enjoyed in common. The rich inheritance of justice, liberty, prosperity and independence, bequeathed by your fathers, is shared by you, not by me. The sunlight that brought life and healing to you, has brought stripes and death to me. This Fourth [of] July is yours, not mine. You may rejoice, I must mourn. To drag a man in fetters into the grand illuminated temple of liberty, and call upon him to join you in joyous anthems, were inhuman mockery and sacrilegious irony. Do you mean, citizens, to mock me, by asking me to speak to-day? If so, there is a parallel to your conduct. And let me warn you that it is dangerous to copy the example of a nation whose crimes, lowering up to heaven, were thrown down by the breath of the Almighty, burying that nation in irrecoverable ruin! I can to-day take up the plaintive lament of a peeled and woe-smitten people!

* * * * * *

Fellow-citizens; above your national, tumultuous joy, I hear the mournful wail of millions! Whose chains, heavy and grievous yesterday, are, to-day, rendered more intolerable by the jubilee shouts that reach them. If I do forget, if I do not faithfully remember those bleeding children of sorrow this day, "may my right hand forget her cunning, and may my tongue cleave to the roof of my mouth!" To forget them, to pass lightly over their wrongs, and to chime in with the popular theme, would be treason most scandalous and shocking, and would make me reproach before God and the world. My subject, then fellow-citizens, is AMERICAN SLAVERY. I shall see, this day, and its popular characteristics, from the slave's point of view. Standing, there, identified with the American bondman, making his wrongs mine, I do not hesitate to declare, with all my soul, that the character and conduct of this nation never looked blacker to me than on this 4th of July! Whether we turn to the declarations of the past, or to the professions of the present, the conduct of the nation seems equally hideous and revolting. America is false to the past, false to the present, and solemnly binds herself to be false to the future. Standing with God and the crushed and bleeding slave on this occasion, I will, in the name of humanity which is outraged, in the name of liberty which is fettered, in the name of the constitution and the Bible, which are disregarded and trampled upon, dare to call in question and to denounce, with all the emphasis I can command, everything that serves to perpetuate slavery—the great sin and shame of America! "I will not equivocate; I will not excuse"; I will use the severest language I can command; and yet not one word shall escape me that any man, whose judgment is not blinded by prejudice, or who is not at heart a slaveholder, shall not confess to be right and just.

* * * * * *

Would you have me argue that man is entitled to liberty? that he is the rightful owner of his own body? You have already declared it. Must I argue the wrongfulness of slavery? Is that a question for Republicans? Is it to be settled by the rules of logic and argumentation, as a matter beset with great difficulty, involving a doubtful application of the principle of justice, hard to be understood'? How should I look to-day, in the presence of Americans, dividing, and subdividing a discourse, to show that men have a natural right to freedom? speaking of it relatively, and positively, negatively and affirmatively. To do so, would be to make myself ridiculous, and to offer an insult to your understanding. There is not a man beneath the canopy of heaven, that does not know that slavery is wrong for him.

What, am I to argue that it is wrong to make men brutes, to rob them of their liberty, to work them without wages, to keep them ignorant of their relations to their fellow men, to beat them with sticks, to flay their flesh with the lash, to load their limbs with irons, to hunt them with dogs, to sell them at auction, to sunder their families, to knock out their teeth, to burn their flesh, to starve them into obedience and submission to their masters? Must I argue that a system thus marked with blood, and stained with pollution, is wrong? No! I will not. I have better employments for my time and strength, than such arguments would imply.

What, then, remains to be argued? Is it that slavery is not divine; that God did not establish it; that our doctors of divinity are mistaken? There is blasphemy in the thought. That which is inhuman, cannot be divine! Who can reason on such a proposition? They that can, may; I cannot. The time for such argument is past.

At a time like this, scorching irony, not convincing argument, is needed. O! had I the ability, and could I reach the nation's ear, I would, to-day, pour out a fiery stream of biting ridicule, blasting reproach, withering sarcasm, and stern rebuke. For it is not light that is needed, but fire; it is not the gentle shower, but thunder. We need the storm, the whirlwind, and the earthquake. The feeling of the nation must be quickened; the conscience of the nation must be roused; the propriety of the nation must be startled; the hypocrisy of the nation must be exposed; and its crimes against God and man must be proclaimed and denounced.

What, to the American slave, is your 4th of July? I answer: a day that reveals to him, more than all other days in the year, the gross injustice and cruelty to which he is the constant victim. To him, your celebration is a sham; your boasted liberty, an unholy license; your national greatness, swelling vanity; your sounds of rejoicing are empty and heartless; your denunciations of tyrants, brass fronted impudence; your shouts of liberty and equality, hallow mockery; your prayers and hymns, your sermons and thanksgivings, with all your religious parade, and solemnity, are, to him, mere bombast, fraud, deception, impiety, and hypocrisy—a thin veil to cover up crimes which would disgrace a nation of savages. There is not a nation on the earth guilty of practices, more shocking and bloody, than are the people of these United States, at this very hour.

Allow me to say, in conclusion, notwithstanding the dark picture I have this day presented of the state of the nation, I do not despair of this country. There are forces in operation, which must inevitably work The downfall of slavery. "The arm of the Lord is not shortened," and the doom of slavery is certain. I, therefore, leave off where I began, with hope. While drawing encouragement from the Declaration of Independence, the great principles it contains, and the genius of American Institutions, my spirit is also cheered by the obvious tendencies of the age.

Reading and Studying the Text

1. Preview
2. Formulate questions
3. Identify unfamiliar vocabulary, terms, and phrases

Journal Annotations

1. Record you thinking and emotional responses to the text; record terms and phrases which had a strong emotional impression.
2. Record summary annotations, commentary, and questions.

Analysis: Lateral Thinking and Writing Connection

1. Summarize the speech—what were your emotional responses to the text? Compare and contrast the tone of the introduction with (1) the discussion regarding the Colonist's decision to break with England

and (2) the arguments around slavery. Include those aspects of the Declaration of Independence that Douglass employs.
2. Describe Douglass' assessment of the character of the men who penned the Declaration of Independence.

*Use concept webs to facilitate your writing.

Chief Seattle's 1854 Oration
Delivered to the Governor of the Washington Territory

Yonder sky that has wept tears of compassion upon my people for centuries untold, and which to us appears changeless and eternal, may change. Today is fair. Tomorrow it may be overcast with clouds. My words are like the stars that never change. Whatever Seattle says, the great chief at Washington can rely upon with as much certainty as he can upon the return of the sun or the seasons. The white chief says that Big Chief at Washington sends us greetings of friendship and good will. This is kind of him for we know he has little need of our friendship in return. His people are many. They are like the grass that covers vast prairies. My people are few. They resemble the scattering trees of a storm-swept plain. The great, and I presume also good, White Chief sends us word that he wishes to buy our land but is willing to allow us enough to live comfortably. This indeed appears just, even generous, for the Red Man no longer has rights that he need respect, and the offer may be wise, also, as we are no longer in need of an extensive country.

There was a time when our people covered the land as the waves of a wind-ruffled sea cover its shell-paved floor, but that time long since passed away with the greatness of tribes that are now but a mournful memory. I will not dwell on, nor mourn over, our untimely decay, nor reproach my paleface brothers with hastening it, as we too may have been somewhat to blame.

Youth is impulsive. When our young men grow angry at some real or imaginary wrong, and disfigure their faces with black paint, it denotes that their hearts are black, and that they are often cruel and relentless and our old men and old women are unable to restrain them. Thus it has ever been. Thus it was when the white man began to push our forefathers ever westward. But let us hope that the hostilities between us may never return. We would have everything to lose and nothing to gain. Revenge by young men is considered gain, even at the cost of their own lives, but old men who stay at home in times of war, and mothers who have sons to lose, know better.

Our great father in Washington, for I presume he is now our father as well as yours, since King George has moved his boundaries further north; our great and good father, I say, sends us word that if we do as he desires he will protect us. His brave warriors will be to us a bristling wall of strength, and his wonderful ships of war will fill our harbors, so that our ancient enemies far to the northward—the Haidas and Tsimshians—will cease to frighten our women, children, and old men. Then in reality he will be our father and we his children. But can that ever be? Your God is not our God! Your God loves your people and hates mine; he folds his strong protecting arms lovingly about the paleface and leads him by the hand as a father leads an infant son. But, He has forsaken His Red children, if they really are His. Our God, the Great Spirit, seems also to have forsaken us. Your God makes your people wax stronger every day. Soon they will fill all the land. Our people are ebbing away like a rapidly receding tide that will never return. The white man's God cannot love our people or He would protect them. They seem to be orphans who can look nowhere to help. How then can we be brothers? How can your God become our God and renew our prosperity and awaken in us dreams of returning greatness? If we have a common Heavenly Father, He must be partial, for He came to His paleface children. We never saw Him. He gave you laws but had no word for His red children whose teeming multitudes once filled this vast continent as stars fill the firmament. No, we are two distinct races with separate origins and separate destinies. There is little in common between us.

To us the ashes of our ancestors are sacred and their resting place is hallowed ground. You wander far from the graves of your ancestors and seemingly without regret. Your religion was written upon tablets of stone by the iron finger of your God so you could not forget. The Red Man could never comprehend or remember it. Our religion is the traditions of our ancestors—the dreams of our old men, given them in solemn hours of the night by the Great Spirit; and the visions of our sachems, and is written in the hearts of our people.

Your dead cease to love you and the land of their nativity as soon as they pass the portals of the tomb and wander away beyond the stars. They are soon forgotten and never return. Our dead never forget this beautiful world that gave them being. They still love its verdant valleys, its murmuring rivers, its magnificent mountains, sequestered vales and verdant lined lakes and bays, and ever yearn in tender fond affection over the lonely hearted living, and often return from the happy hunting ground to visit, guide, console and comfort them.

Day and night cannot dwell together. The Red Man has ever fled the approach of the White Man, as the morning mist flees before the morning sun. However, your proposition seems fair and I think that my people will accept it and will retire to the reservation you offer them. Then we will dwell apart in peace, for the words of the Great White Chief seem to be the worse of nature speaking to my people out of dense darkness.

It matters little where we pass the remnant of our days. They will not be many. The Indian's night promises to be dark. Not a single star of hope hovers above his horizons. Sad-voiced winds moan in the distance. Grim fate seems to be on the Red Man's trail, and wherever he will hear the approaching footsteps of his fell destroyer and prepare stolidly to meet his doom, as does the wounded doe that hears the approaching footsteps of the hunter.

A few more moons, a few more winters, and not one of the descendants of the mighty hosts that once moved over this broad land or lived in happy homes, protected by the Great Spirit, will remain to mourn over the graves of a people once more powerful and hopeful than yours. But why should I mourn at the untimely fate of my people? Tribe follows tribe, and nation follows nation, like the waves of the sea. It is the order of nature, and regret is useless. Your time of decay may be distant, but it will surely come, for even the White Man whose God walked and talked with him as friend to friend, cannot be exempt from the common destiny. We may be brothers after all. We will see.

We will ponder your proposition and when we decide we will let you know. But should we accept it, I here and now make this condition that we will not be denied the privilege without molestation of visiting at any time the tombs of our ancestors, friends, and children. Every part of this soil is sacred in the estimation of my people. Every hillside, every valley, every plan and grove, has been hallowed by some sad or happy event in days long vanished. Even the rocks, which seem to be dumb and dead as they swelter in the sun along the silent shore, thrill with memories of stirring events connected with the lives of my people, and the very dust upon which you now stand responds more lovingly to their footsteps than yours, because it is rich with the blood of our ancestors, and our bare feet are conscious of the sympathetic touch. Our departed braves, fond mothers, glad, happy hearted maidens, and even the little children who lived here and rejoiced here for a brief season, will love these somber solitudes and at eventide they greet shadowy returning spirits. And when the last Red Man shall have perished, and the memory of my tribe shall have become a myth among the White Men, these shores will swarm with the invisible dead of my tribe, and when your children's children think themselves alone in the field, the store, the shop, upon the highway, or in the silence of the pathless woods, they will not be alone. In all the earth there is no place dedicated to solitude. Tonight when the streets of your cities and villages are silent and you think them deserted, they will throng with the returning hosts that once filled them and still love this beautiful land. The White Man will never be alone.

Let him be just and deal kindly with my people, for the dead are not altogether powerless. Dead did I say? There is no death, only a change of worlds.

Reading and Studying the Text

1. Preview
2. Formulate questions
3. Identify unfamiliar vocabulary, terms, and phrases

Journal Annotations

1. Record your thinking and emotional responses; record terms and phrases which had a strong emotional impression.
2. Record summary annotations, commentary, and questions.
3. Summarize the speech.

Analysis: Lateral Thinking and Writing Connection

1. What is the tone of this speech?
2. According to Chief Seattle, what ideas and beliefs of the red man are directly in conflict with the ideas of the white man?
3. Critique Chief Seattle's speech.
4. Choose one of the following and write an essay:
   a. Choose three ideas presented by Chief Seattle and explain which ideas in the Declaration of Independence have been violated.
   b. Given the conflicts Chief Seattle describes, write a journal entry to explain if the Declaration of Independence can resolve the conflicts.

*Use concept webs to generate ideas.

John F. Kennedy, President, United States of America (January 1961 – November 1963) 1961, Inaugural Address

We observe today not a victory of party but a celebration of freedom—symbolizing an end as well as a beginning—signifying renewal as well as change. For I have sworn before you and Almighty God the same solemn oath our forebears prescribed nearly a century and three quarters ago.

The world is very different now. For man holds in his mortal hands the power to abolish all forms of human poverty and all forms of human life. And yet the same revolutionary beliefs for which our forebears fought are still at issue around the globe—the belief that the rights of man come not from the generosity of the state but from the hand of God.

We dare not forget today that we are the heirs of that first revolution. Let the word go forth from this time and place, to friend and foe alike, that the torch has been passed to a new generation of Americans—born in this century, tempered by war, disciplined by a hard and bitter peace, proud of our ancient heritage—and unwilling to witness or permit the slow undoing of those human rights to which this nation has always been committed, and to which we are committed today at home and around the world.

Let every nation know, whether it wishes us well or ill, that we shall pay any price, bear any burden, meet any hardship, support any friend, oppose any foe to assure the survival and the success of liberty.

This much we pledge—and more.

To those old allies whose cultural and spiritual origins we share, we pledge the loyalty of faithful friends. United, there is little we cannot do in a host of co-operative ventures. Divided, there is little we can do—for we dare not meet a powerful challenge at odds and split asunder.

To those new states whom we welcome to the ranks of the free, we pledge our word that one form of colonial control shall not have passed away merely to be replaced by a far more iron tyranny. We shall not always expect to find them supporting our view. But we shall always hope to find them strongly supporting their own freedom—and to remember that, in the past, those who foolishly sought power by riding the back of the tiger ended up inside.

To those people in the huts and villages of half the globe struggling to break the bonds of mass misery, we pledge our best efforts to help them help themselves, for whatever period is required—not because the Communists may be doing it, not because we seek their votes, but because it is right. If a free society cannot help the many who are poor, it cannot save the few who are rich.

To our sister republics south of the border, we offer a special pledge—to convert our good words into good deeds—in a new alliance for progress—to assist free men and free governments in casting off the chains of poverty. But this peaceful revolution of hope cannot become the prey of hostile powers. Let all our neighbors know that we shall join with them to oppose aggression or subversion anywhere in the Americas. And let every other power know that this hemisphere intends to remain the master of its own house.

To that world assembly of sovereign states, the United Nations, our last best hope in an age where the instruments of war have far outpaced the instruments of peace, we renew our pledge of support—to prevent it from becoming merely a forum for invective—to strengthen its shield of the new and the weak—and to enlarge the area in which its writ may run.

Finally, to those nations who would make themselves our adversary, we offer not a pledge but a request: that both sides begin anew the quest for peace, before the dark powers of destruction unleashed by science engulf all humanity in planned or accidental self-destruction.

We dare not tempt them with weakness. For only when our arms are sufficient beyond doubt can we be certain beyond doubt that they will never be employed.

But neither can two great and powerful groups of nations take comfort from our present course—both sides overburdened by the cost of modern weapons, both rightly alarmed by the steady spread of the deadly atom, yet both racing to alter that uncertain balance of terror that stays the hand of mankind's final war.

So let us begin anew—remembering on both sides that civility is not a sign of weakness, and sincerity is always subject to proof. Let us never negotiate out of fear. But let us never fear to negotiate.

Let both sides explore what problems unite us instead of belaboring those problems which divide us.

Let both sides, for the first time, formulate serious and precise proposals for the inspection and control of arms—and bring the absolute power to destroy other nations under the absolute control of all nations.

Let both sides seek to invoke the wonders of science instead of its terrors. Together let us explore the stars, conquer the deserts, eradicate disease, tap the ocean depths, and encourage the arts and commerce.

Let both sides unite to heed in all corners of the earth the command of Isaiah—to "undo the heavy burdens...and let the oppressed go free."

And if a beachhead of co-operation may push back the jungle of suspicion, let both sides join in creating a new endeavor, not a new balance of power, but a new world of law, where the strong are just and the weak secure and the peace preserved.

All this will not be finished in the first one hundred days. Nor will it be finished in the first one thousand days, not in the life of this administration, nor even perhaps in our lifetime on this planet. But let us begin.

In your hands my fellow citizens, more than mine, will rest the final success or failure of our course. Since this country was founded, each generation of Americans has been summoned to give testimony to its national loyalty. The graves of young Americans who answered the call to service surround the globe.

Now the trumpet summons us again—not as a call to bear arms, though arms we need—not as a call to battle, though embattled we are—but a call to bear the burden of a long twilight struggle, year in and year out, "rejoicing in hope, patient in tribulation"—a struggle against the common enemies of man: tyranny, poverty, disease, and war itself.

Can we forge against these enemies a grand and global alliance. North and South, East and West that can assure a more fruitful life for all mankind? Will you join in that historic effort?

In the long history of the world, only a few generations have been granted the role of defending freedom in its hour of maximum danger. I do not shrink from this responsibility—I welcome it. I do not believe that any of us would exchange places with any other people or any other generation. The energy, the faith, the devotion which we bring to this endeavor will light our country and all who serve it—and the glow from that fire can truly light the world.

And so, my fellow Americans: ask not what your country can do for you—ask what you can do for your country.

My fellow citizens of the world: ask not what America will do for you, but what together we can do for the freedom of man.

Finally, whether you are citizens of America or citizens of the world, ask of us here the same high standards of strength and sacrifice which we ask of you. With a good conscience our only sure reward, with history the final judge of our deeds, let us go forth to lead the land we love, asking His blessing and His help, but knowing that here on earth God's work must truly be our own.

Reading and Studying the Text

1. Preview
2. Formulate questions
3. Identify unfamiliar vocabulary, terms, and phrases

Journal Annotations

1. Record your thinking and emotional responses; record terms and phrases which had a strong emotional impression.
2. Record summary annotations, commentary, and questions.
3. Summarize the major points in the speech.

Analysis: Lateral Thinking and Writing Connection

1. Describe the tone and intent of Kennedy's speech.
2. Kennedy addressed the American people and he also addressed other nations. Describe the challenge and the vision in which he invites the citizens of America and other nations to participate. In your opinion, why is Kennedy's vision compelling?
3. Explain statements which infer the rights of individuals and nations as outlined in The Declaration of Independence.
4. Write a critique of this speech.

*Use concept webs to facilitate your writing.

Martin Luther King, Jr.
Letter From Birmingham City Jail
April 16, 1963

To: Bishop C.C. Carpenter, Bishop Joseph A. Durick, Rabbi Milton L. Grafman, Bishop Paul Hardin, Bishop Nolan B. Harmon, The Rev. George M. Murray, The Rev. Edward V. Ramage, The Rev. Earl Stallings

MY DEAR FELLOW CLERGYMEN:

While confined here in the Birmingham city jail, I came across your recent statement calling my present activities "unwise and untimely." Seldom, if ever, do I pause to answer criticism of my work and ideas. If I sought to answer all the criticisms that cross my desk, my secretaries would be engaged in little else in the course of the day and I would have no time for constructive work. But since I feel that you are men of genuine good will and that your criticisms are sincerely set forth, I would like to answer your statement in what I hope will be patient and reasonable terms.

I think I should give the reason for my being in Birmingham, since you have been influenced by the argument of "outsiders coming in." I have the honor of serving as president of the Southern Christian Leadership Conference, an organization operating in every southern state, with headquarters in Atlanta, Georgia. We have some eighty-five affiliated organizations all across the South—one being the Alabama Christian Movement for Human Rights. Whenever necessary and possible we share staff, educational, and financial resources with our affiliates. Several months ago our local affiliate here in Birmingham invited us to be on call to engage in a nonviolent direct action program if such were deemed necessary. We readily consented and when the hour came we lived up to our promises. So I am here, along with several members of my staff, because we were invited here. I am here because I have basic organizational ties here. Beyond this, I am in Birmingham because injustice is here. Just as the eighth century prophets left their villages and carried their "thus saith the Lord" far beyond the boundaries of their home town, and just as the Apostle Paul left his village of Tarsus and carried the gospel of Jesus Christ to practically every hamlet and city of the Greco-Roman world, I too am compelled to carry the gospel of freedom beyond my particular home town. Like Paul, I must constantly respond to the Macedonian call for aid.

Moreover, I am cognizant of the interrelatedness of all communities and states. I cannot sit idly by in Atlanta and not be concerned about what happens in Birmingham. Injustice anywhere is a threat to justice everywhere. We are caught in an inescapable network of mutuality, tied in a single garment of destiny. Whatever affects one directly, affects all indirectly. Never again can we afford to live with the narrow, provincial "outside agitator" idea. Anyone who lives inside the United States can never be considered an outsider anywhere in this country.

You deplore the demonstrations that are presently taking place In Birmingham. But I am sorry that your statement did not express a similar concern for the conditions that brought the demonstrations into being. I am sure that each of you would want to go beyond the superficial social analysis who looks merely at effects, and does not grapple with underlying causes. I would not hesitate to say that it is unfortunate that so-called demonstrations are taking place in Birmingham at this time, but I would say in more emphatic terms that it is even more unfortunate that the white power structure of this city left the Negro community with no other alternative.

In any nonviolent campaign there are four basic steps: (1) collection of the facts to determine whether injustices are alive; (2) negotiation; (3) self-purification; and (4) direct action. We have gone through all these steps in Birmingham. There can be no gainsaying of the fact that racial injustice engulfs this community. Birmingham is probably the most thoroughly segregated city in the United States. Its ugly record of brutality is widely known. Its unjust treatment of Negroes in the courts is a notorious reality. There have been more unsolved bombings of Negro homes and churches in Birmingham than in any city in the nation. These are the hard, brutal, and unbelievable facts. On the basis of these conditions, Negro leaders sought to negotiate with the city fathers. But the political leaders consistently refused to engage in good faith negotiation.

Then came the opportunity last September to talk with some of the leaders of the economic community. In these negotiations sessions certain promises were made by the merchants—such as the promise to remove the humiliating racial signs from the stores. On the basis of these promises, the Reverend Fred Shuttlesworth and the leaders of the Alabama Christian Movement for Human Rights agreed to call a moratorium on any type of demonstrations. As the weeks and months unfolded, we realized that we were the victims of a broken promise. Signs remained. As in so many experiences of the past, we were confronted with blasted hopes, and the dark shadow of a deep disappointment settled upon us. So we had no alternative except that of preparing for direct action, whereby we would present our very bodies as a means of laying our case before the conscience of the local and national community. We are not unmindful of the difficulties involved. So we decided to go through a process of self-purification. We started having workshops on nonviolence, and repeatedly asked ourselves questions: "Are you able to accept blows without retaliating?" "Are you able to endure the ordeal of jail?"

We decided to schedule our direct-action program around the Easter season, realizing that with the exception of Christmas, this was the largest shopping period of the year. Knowing that a strong economic withdrawal program would be the by-product of direct action, we felt that this would be the best time to bring pressure on the merchants for the needed changes. Then it occurred to us that the March election was ahead, and so we speedily decided to postpone action until after Election Day. When we discovered that Mr. Connor was in the run-off, we decided again to postpone action so that the demonstrations could not be used to cloud the issues. At this time we agreed to begin our nonviolent witness the day after the run-off. This reveals that we did not move irresponsibly into direct action. We too wanted to see Mr. Connor defeated; so we went through postponement after postponement to aid in this community need. After this we felt that direct action could be delayed no longer.

You may well ask: "Why direct action? Why sit-ins, marches and so forth? Isn't negotiation a better path?" You are exactly right in your call for negotiation. Indeed, this is the very purpose of direct action. Nonviolent direct action seeks to create such a crisis and establish such creative tension that a community that a community that has constantly refused to negotiate is forced to confront the issue. It seeks to dramatize the issue that it can no longer be ignored. I just referred to the creation of tension as a part of the work of the nonviolent resister. This may sound rather shocking. But I must confess that I am not afraid of the word "tension." I have earnestly worked and preached against violent tension, but there is a type of constructive nonviolent tension which is necessary for growth. Just as Socrates felt that it was necessary to create a tension in the mind so that individuals could rise from the bondage of myths and half-truths to the unfettered realm of creative analysis and objective appraisal, we must we see the need for nonviolent gadflies to create the kind of tension in society that will help men rise from the dark depths of prejudice and racism to the majestic heights of understanding and brotherhood. So the purpose of our direct-action program is to create a situation so crisis-packed that it will inevitably open the door to negotiation. We, therefore, concur with you in your call for negotiation. Too long has our beloved Southland been bogged down in a tragic attempt to live in monologue rather than dialogue.

One of the basic points in your statement is that our acts are untimely. Some have asked: "Why didn't you give the new city administration time to act?" The only answer that I can give to this inquiry is that the new Birmingham administration must be prodded about as much as the outgoing one before it acts. We will be sadly mistaken if we feel that the election of Mr. Boutwell will bring the millennium to Birmingham. While Mr. Boutwell is a much more gentle than Mr. Connor, they are both segregationists, dedicated to the task of maintenance the status quo. The hope I see in Mr. Boutwell is that he will be reasonable enough to see the futility of massive resistance to desegregation. But he will not see this without pressure from the devotees of civil rights. My friends, I must say to you that we have not made single gain civil rights without determined legal and nonviolent pressure. History is the long and tragic story of the fact that privileged groups seldom give up their privileges voluntarily. Individuals may see the moral light and voluntarily give up their unjust posture; but as Reinhold Niebuhr has reminded us, groups are more immoral than individuals.

We know through painful experience that freedom is never voluntarily given by the oppressor; it must be demanded by the oppressed. Frankly, I have yet to engage in a direct-action campaign that was "well timed" in the view of those who have not suffered unduly from the disease of segregation. For years now I have heard the word "Wait!" It rings in the ear of every Negro with piercing familiarity. This "Wait" has almost always meant 'Never." We must come to see, with one of our distinguished jurists, that "justice too long delayed is justice denied."

You express a great deal of anxiety over our willingness to break laws. This is certainly a legitimate concern. Since we so diligently urge people to obey the Supreme Court's decision of 1954 outlawing segregation in the public schools, at first glance it may seem rather paradoxical for us consciously to break laws. One may won ask: "How can you advocate breaking some laws and obeying others?" The answer lies in the fact that there fire two types of laws: there are just laws and unjust laws. I would be the first to advocate obeying just laws. One has not only a legal but moral responsibility to obey just laws. Conversely, one has a moral responsibility to disobey unjust laws. I would agree with St. Augustine "an unjust law is no law at all"

Now, what is the difference between the two? How does one determine whether a law is just or unjust? A just law is a man-made code that squares with the moral law or the law of God. An unjust law is a code that is out of harmony with the moral law. To put it in the terms of St. Thomas Aquinas: An unjust law is a human law that is not rooted in eternal law and natural law. Any law that uplifts human personality is just. Any law that degrades human personality is unjust. All segregation statutes are unjust because segregation distorts the soul and damages the personality. It gives the segregator a false sense of superiority and the segregated a false sense of inferiority. Segregation, to use the terminology of the Jewish philosopher Martin Buber, substitutes an "I-it" relationship for an "I-thou" relationship and ends up relegating persons to the status of things. So segregation is politically, economically and sociologically unsound, it is morally wrong and sinful. Paul Tillich said that sin is separation. Is not segregation an existential expression of man's tragic separation, his awful estrangement, his terrible sinfulness? So I can urge men to obey the 1954 decision of the Supreme Court, because it is morally right; and I can urge them to disobey segregation ordinances, for they are morally wrong.

Let me give another explanation. An unjust law is a code inflicted upon a minority which that minority had no part in enacting or reacting because they did not have the unhampered right to vote. Who can say that the legislature of Alabama which set up the segregation laws was democratically elected? Throughout Alabama all sorts of conniving methods are used to prevent Negroes from becoming registered voters, and there are some counties without a single Negro registered to vote despite the fact that the Negro constitute a majority of the population. Can any law se up in such a state be considered democratically structured?

Of course, there is nothing new about this kind of civil disobedience. It was evidenced sublimely in the refusal of Shadrach, Meshach and Abednego to obey the laws of Nebuchadnezzar, on the ground that a higher moral law was at stake. It was practiced superbly by the early Christians, who were willing to face hungry lions and the excruciating pain of chopping blocks rather than submit to certain unjust laws of the Roman Empire. To a degree, academic freedom is a reality today because Socrates practiced civil disobedience.

We should never forget that everything Adolf Hitler did in Germany was "legal" and everything the Hungarian freedom fighters did in Hungary was "illegal." It was "illegal" to aid and comfort a Jew in Hitler's Germany. But I am sure that, had I lived in Germany at the time, I would have aided and comforted my Jewish brothers. If I lived in a Communist country where certain principles dear to the Christian faith are suppressed, I would openly advocate disobeying that country's antireligious laws.

In your statement you assert that our actions, even though peaceful, must be condemned because they precipitate violence. But can this assertion be logically made? Isn't this like condemning a robbed man because his possession of money precipitated the evil act of robbery? Isn't this like condemning Socrates because his unswerving commitment to truth and his philosophical inquiries precipitated the act by the misguided popular mind to make him drink the hemlock? Isn't this like condemning Jesus because his unique God-consciousness and never-ceasing devotion to God's will precipitated the evil act of crucifixion? We must come to see that, as the federal courts have consistently affirmed, it is immoral to urge an individual to withdraw his efforts to gain his basic constitutional rights because the quest may precipitate violence. Society must protect the robbed and punish the robber.

Oppressed people cannot remain oppressed forever. The urge for freedom eventually comes. This is what has happened to the American Negro. Something within has reminded him of his birthright of freedom, and something without has reminded him that he can gain it. Consciously or unconsciously, he has been caught up by what the Germans call Zeitgeist, and with his black brothers of Africa and his brown and yellow brothers of Asia, South America and the Caribbean, the United States Negro is moving with a sense of cosmic urgency toward the promised land of racial justice. Recognizing this vital urge that has engulfed the Negro community, one should readily understand public demonstrations. The Negro has many pent-up resentments and latent frustrations. He has to get them out. So let him march; let him make prayer pilgrimages to the city hall; understand why he must have sit-ins and freedom rides. If his repressed emotions do come out in thee nonviolent ways, they will come out in ominous expressions of violence. This is not a threat; it is a fact of history. So I have not said to my people: "Get rid of your discontent." But, I have tried to say that this normal and healthy discontent can be channeled through the creative outlet of nonviolent direct action. Now this approach is being dismissed as extremist. I must admit that I was initially disappointed in being so categorized.

But as I continued to think about the matter I gradually gained a bit of satisfaction from being considered an extremist. Was not Jesus an extremist in love? "Love your enemies, bless them that curse you, do good to them that hate you, and pray for them which despitefully use you, and persecute you." Was not Amos an extremist for justice: "Let justice roll down like waters and righteousness like an ever-flowing stream." Was not Paul an extremist for the Christian gospel: "I bear in my body the marks of the Lord Jesus." Was not Martin Luther an extremist: "Here I stand; I cannot do otherwise, so help me God." And John Bunyan: "I will stay in jail to the end of my days before I make a butchery of my conscience." And Abraham Lincoln: "This nation cannot survive half slave and half free." And Thomas Jefferson: "We hold these truths to be self-evident, that an men are created equal ..." So the question is not whether we will be extremists, but what kind of extremists will we be. Will we be extremists for hate or will we be extremists for love? Will we be extremist for the preservation of injustice—or will we be extremists for the cause of justice? In that dramatic scene on Calvary's hill three men were crucified. We must never forget that all three were crucified for the same crime—the crime of extremism. Two were extremists for immorality, and thus fell below their environment. The other, Jesus Christ, was an extremist for love, truth and goodness, and thereby rose above his environment. So, after all, maybe the South, the nation and the world are in dire need of creative extremists.

When I was suddenly catapulted into the leadership of the bus protest in Montgomery, Alabama, a few years ago, I felt we would be supported by the white church felt that the white ministers, priests and rabbis of the South would be among our strongest allies. Instead, some have been outright opponents, refusing to understand the freedom movement and misrepresenting its leader era; and too many others have been more cautious than courageous and have remained silent behind the anesthetizing security of stained-glass windows.

I have traveled the length and breadth of Alabama, Mississippi and all the other southern states. On sweltering summer days and crisp autumn mornings I have looked at her beautiful churches with their lofty spires pointing heavenward. I have beheld the impressive outlay of her massive religious-education buildings. Over and over I have found myself asking: "What kind of people worship here? Who is their God? Where were their voices when the lips of Governor Barnett dripped with words of interposition and nullification? Where were they when Governor Walleye gave a clarion call for defiance and hatred? Where were their voices of support when bruised and weary Negro men and women decided to rise from the dark dungeons of complacency to the bright hills of creative protest?"

Yes, these questions are still in my mind. In deep disappointment I have wept over the laxity of the church. But be assured that my tears have been tears of love. There can be no deep disappointment where there is not deep love. Yes, I love the church. How could I do otherwise? I am in the rather unique position of being the son, the grandson and the great-grandson of preachers. Yes, I see the church as the body of Christ. But, oh! How we have blemished and scarred that body through social neglect and through fear of being nonconformists.

I must close now. Before closing I feel impelled to mention one other point in your statement that has troubled me profoundly. You warmly commend the Birmingham police force for keeping "order" and "preventing violence." I don't think that you would have so warmly commended the police force if you had seen its angry, violent dogs literally biting six unarmed nonviolent Negroes. I don't believe you would so quickly commend the policemen if you would observe their ugly and inhuman treatment of Negroes here in the city jail; if you would watch them push and curse old Negro women and young Negro girls; if you would see them slap and kick old Negro men and young Negro boys; if you will observe them, as they did on two occasions, refuse to give us food because we wanted to sing our grace together. I'm sorry that I can't join in your praise for the police department.

It is true that they have been rather disciplined in their public handling of the demonstrators. In this sense they have been rather publicly "nonviolent." But for what purpose? To preserve the evil system of segregation. Over the past few years I have consistently preached that nonviolence demands the means we use must be as pure as the ends we seek. I have tried to make clear that it is wrong to use immoral means to attain moral ends. But now I must affirm that it is just as wrong, or even more so, to use moral means to preserve immoral ends. Maybe Mr. Connor and his policemen have been rather publicly nonviolent, as was Chief Pritchett in Albany, Georgia but they have used the moral means of nonviolence to maintain the immoral end of racial injustice. As T. S. Eliot has said: "The last temptation is the greatest treason: To do the right deed for the wrong reason."

I wish you had commended the Negro sit-inners and demonstrators of Birmingham for their sublime courage, their willingness to suffer and their amazing discipline in the midst of great provocation. One day the South will recognize its real heroes. They will be the James Merediths, courageously and with a majestic sense of purpose, facing jeering and hostile mobs and the agonizing loneliness that characterizes the life of the pioneer. They will be old, oppressed, battered Negro women, symbolized in a seventy-two-year-old woman in Montgomery, Alabama, who rose up with a sense of dignity and with her people decided not to ride segregated buses, and responded to one who inquired about her tiredness with ungrammatical profundity: "My feets is tired, but my soul is rested." They will be the young high school and college students, the young ministers of the gospel and a host of the elders, courageously and nonviolently sitting in at lunch counters and willingly going to jail for conscience sake. One day the South will know that when these disinherited children of God sat down at lunch counters, they were in reality standing up for the best in the American dream and for the most sacred values in our Judeo-Christian heritage, and thus carrying our whole nation back to great wells of democracy which were dug deep by the founding fathers in the formulation of the Constitution and the Declaration of Independence.

If I have said anything in this letter that is an overstatement of the truth and indicative of an unreasonable impatience, I beg you to forgive me. If I have said anything in this letter that is an understatement of the truth and is indicative is of my having a patience that makes me patient with anything less than brotherhood, I beg God to forgive me.

MARTIN LUTHER KING, JR.

Reading and Studying the Text

1. Preview
2. Formulate questions
3. Identify unfamiliar vocabulary, terms and phrases

Journal Annotations

1. Record your thinking and emotional responses to the text; record terms and phrases which had a strong emotional impression.
2. Reread to clarify points.
3. Record summary annotations, commentary, and questions.
4. Summarize the speech.

Analysis: Lateral Thinking and Writing Connection

1. Cite the reasons King gives for breaking the law.
2. Cite how the Declaration of Independence supports his position.
3. Explain how King distinquishes between a just and unjust law.
4. Explain how King reconciles being labeled an extremist.
5. Explain how Kennedy's vision supports King's goals.

*Use concept webs to facilitate your writing.

Equal Rights for Women
by Shirley Chisholm
U.S. House of Representatives of New York

Address to the United States House of Representatives
Washington, DC: May 21, 1969

Mr. Speaker, when a young woman graduates from college and starts looking for a job, she is likely to have a frustrating and even demeaning experience ahead of her. If she walks into an office for an interview, the first question she will be asked is, "Do you type?"

There is a calculated system of prejudice that lies unspoken behind that question. Why is it acceptable for women to be secretaries, librarians, and teachers, but totally unacceptable for them to be managers, administrators, doctors, lawyers, and Members of Congress.

The unspoken assumption is that women are different. They do not have executive ability, orderly minds, stability, leadership skills, and they are too emotional.

It has been observed before, that society for a long time, discriminated against another minority, the blacks, on the same basis—that they were different and inferior. The happy little homemaker and the contented "old darkey" on the plantation were both produced by prejudice.

As a black person, I am no stranger to race prejudice. But the truth is that in the political world I have been far oftener discriminated against because I am a woman than because I am black.

Prejudice against blacks is becoming unacceptable although it will take years to eliminate it. But it is doomed because, slowly, white America is beginning to admit that it exists. Prejudice against women is still acceptable. There is very little understanding yet of the immorality involved in double pay scales and the classification of most of the better jobs as "for men only."

More than half of the population of the United States is female. But women occupy only 2 percent of the managerial positions. They have not even reached the level of tokenism yet. No women sit on the AFL-CIO council or Supreme Court. There have been only two women who have held Cabinet rank, and at present there are none. Only two women now hold ambassadorial rank in the diplomatic corps. In Congress, we are down to one Senator and 10 Representatives.

Considering that there are about 3 1/2 million more women in the United States than men, this situation is outrageous.

It is true that part of the problem has been that women have not been aggressive in demanding their rights. This was also true of the black population for many years. They submitted to oppression and even cooperated with it. Women have done the same thing. But now there is an awareness of this situation particularly among the younger segment of the population.

As in the field of equal rights for blacks, Spanish-Americans, the Indians, and other groups, laws will not change such deep-seated problems overnight. But they can be used to provide protection for those who are most abused, and to begin the process of evolutionary change by compelling the insensitive majority to reexamine its unconscious attitudes.

It is for this reason that I wish to introduce today a proposal that has been before every Congress for the last 40 years and that sooner or later must become part of the basic law of the land—the equal rights amendment.

Let me note and try to refute two of the commonest arguments that are offered against this amendment. One is that women are already protected under the law and do not need legislation. Existing laws are not adequate to secure equal rights for women. Sufficient proof of this is the concentration of women in lower paying, menial, unrewarding jobs and their incredible scarcity in the upper level jobs. If women are already equal, why is it such an event whenever one happens to be elected to Congress?

It is obvious that discrimination exists. Women do not have the opportunities that men do. And women that do not conform to the system, who try to break with the accepted patterns, are stigmatized as "odd" and "unfeminine." The fact is that a woman who aspires to be chairman of the board, or a Member of the House, does so for exactly the same reasons as any man. Basically, these are that she thinks she can do the job and she wants to try.

A second argument often heard against the equal rights amendment is that is would eliminate legislation that many States and the Federal Government have enacted giving special protection to women and that it would throw the marriage and divorce laws into chaos.

As for the marriage laws, they are due for a sweeping reform, and an excellent beginning would be to wipe the existing ones off the books. Regarding special protection for working women, I cannot understand why it should be needed. Women need no protection that men do not need. What we need are laws to protect working people, to guarantee them fair pay, safe working conditions, protection against sickness and layoffs, and provision for dignified, comfortable retirement. Men and women need these things equally. That one sex needs protection more than the other is a male supremacist myth as ridiculous and unworthy of respect as the white supremacist myths that society is trying to cure itself of at this time.

Reading and studying the Text

1. Preview
2. Formulate questions
3. Identify unfamiliar vocabulary, terms, and phrases

Journal Annotations

1. Record your thinking and emotional responses to the text; record terms and phrases which had a strong emotional impression.
2. Reread to clarify points.
3. Record summary annotations, commentary and questions.
4. Summarize the speech.

Analysis: Lateral Thinking and Writing Connection

1. What is the tone of this speech? Cite phrases in support of your position.
2. Compare and contrast the difference between Chisholm's arguments for women's right and the arguments of Stanton posed over one hundred years before.
3. Critique Chisholm's speech and state if you agree and/or disagree with the positions on the Equal Rights Amendment for Women.

*Use your concept webs to facilitate your writing.

Group Minds
Doris Lessing (1987)

People living in the West, in societies that we describe as Western, or as the free world, may be educated in many different ways, but they will all emerge with an idea about themselves that goes something like this: I am a citizen of a free society, and that means I am an individual, making individual choices. My mind is my own, my opinions are chosen by me, I am free to do as I will, and at the worst the pressures on me are economic, that is, I may be too poor to do as I want.

This set of ideas may sound something like a caricature, but it is not so far off how we see ourselves. It is a portrait that may not have been acquired consciously, but is part of a general atmosphere or set of assumptions that influence our ideas about ourselves.

People in the West therefore may go through their entire lives never thinking to analyze this very flattering picture, and as a result are helpless against all kinds of pressures on them to conform in many kinds of ways.

The fact is that we all live our lives in groups—the family, work groups, social, religious and political groups. Very few people indeed are happy as solitaries, and they tend to be seen by their neighbours as peculiar or selfish or worse. Most people cannot stand being alone for long. They are always seeking groups to belong to, and if one group dissolves, they look for another. We are group animals still, and there is nothing wrong with that. But what is dangerous is not the belonging to a group, or groups, but not understanding the social laws that govern groups and govern us.

When we're in a group, we tend to think as that group does: we may even have joined the group to find "like-minded" people. But we also find our thinking changing because we belong to a group. It is the hardest thing in the world to maintain an individual dissident opinion, as a member of a group.

It seems to me that this is something we have all experienced—something we take for granted, may never have thought about it, but a great deal of experiment has gone on among psychologists and sociologists on this very theme. If I describe an experiment or two, then anyone listening who may be a sociologist or psychologist will groan, oh God not *again*—for they will have heard of these classic experiments far too often. My guess is that the rest of the people will never have heard of these experiments, never have had these ideas presented to them. If my guess is true, then it aptly illustrates my general thesis, and the general idea behind these talks, that we (the human race) are now in possession of a great deal of hard information about ourselves, but we do not use it to improve our institutions and therefore our lives.

A typical test, or experiment, on this theme goes like this. A group of people are taken into the researchers' confidence. A minority of one or two are left in the dark. Some situation demanding measurement or assessment is chosen. For instance, comparing lengths of wood that differ only a little from each other, but enough to be perceptible, or shapes that are almost the same size. The majority in the group—according to instruction—will assert stubbornly that these two shapes or lengths are the same length, or size, while the solitary individual, or the couple, who have not been so instructed will assert that the pieces of wood or whatever are different. But the majority will continue to insist speaking metaphorically—that black is white, and after a period of exasperation, irritation, even anger, certainly incomprehension, the minority will fall into line. Not always, but nearly always. There are indeed glorious individualists who stubbornly insist on telling the truth as they see it, but most give into the majority opinion, obey the atmosphere.

When put as baldly, as unflatteringly, as this, reactions tend to be an incredulous: "I certainly wouldn't give in, I speak my mind. . . ." But would you?

People who have experienced a lot of groups, who perhaps have observed their own behaviour, may agree that the hardest thing in the world is to stand out against one's group, a group of one's peers. Many agree that among our most shameful memories is this, how often we said black was white because other people were saying it.

In other words, we know that this is true of human behaviour, but how do we know it? It is one thing to admit it, in a vague uncomfortable sort of way (which probably includes the hope that one will never again be in such a testing situation) but quite another to make that cool step into a kind of objectivity, where one may say, "Right, if that's what human beings are like, myself included, then let's admit it, examine and organize our attitudes accordingly."

This mechanism, of obedience to the group, does not only mean obedience or submission to a small group, or one that is sharply determined, like a religion or political party. It means, too, conforming to those large, vague, ill-defined collections of people who may never think of themselves as having a collective mind because they are aware of differences of opinion—but which, to people from outside, from another culture, seem very minor. The underlying assumptions and assertions that govern the group are never discussed, never challenged, probably never noticed, the main one being precisely this: that it is a group mind, intensely resistant to change, equipped with sacred assumptions about which there can be no discussion.

Since my field is literature, it is there I most easily find my examples. I live in London, and the literary community there would not think of itself as a collective mind, to put it mildly, but that is how I think of it. A few mechanisms are taken for granted enough to be quoted and expected. For instance, what is called "the ten-year rule," which is that usually when a writer dies, her or his work falls out of favour, or from notice, and then comes back again. It is one thing to think vaguely that this is likely to happen, but is it useful? Does it have to happen? Another very noticeable mechanism is the way a writer may fall out of favour for many years—while still alive, be hardly noticed—then suddenly be noticed and praised. An example is Jean Rhys, who lived for many years in the country. She was never mentioned, she might very well have been dead, and most people thought she was. She was in desperate need of friendship and help and did not get it for a long time. Then, due to the efforts of a perspicacious publisher, she finished *The Cruel Sargasso Sea*, and at once as it were became visible again. But—and this is my point—all her previous books, which had been unmentioned and unhonoured, were suddenly remembered and praised. Why were they not praised at all during that long period of neglect? Well, because the collective mind works like that—it is follow-my-leader, people all saying the same thing at the same time.

One can say of course that this is only "the way of the world." But does it have to be? If it does have to be, then at least we could expect it, understand it, and make allowances for it. Perhaps if it is a mechanism that is known to be one then it might be easier for reviewers to be braver and less like sheep in their pronouncements.

Do they have to be so afraid of peer group pressure? Do they really not see how they repeat what each other says?

One may watch how an idea or an opinion, even a phrase, springs up and is repeated in a hundred reviews, criticisms, conversations—and then vanishes. But meanwhile each individual who has bravely repeated this opinion or phrase has been the victim of a compulsion to be like everyone else, and that has never been analyzed, or not by themselves. Though people outside can easily see it.

This is of course the mechanism that journalists rely on when they visit a country. They know if they interview a small sample of a certain kind, or group, or class of people, these two or three citizens will represent all the others, since at any given time, all the people of any group or class or kind will be saying the same things, in the same words.

My experience as Jane Somers illustrates these and many other points. Unfortunately there isn't time here to tell the story properly. I wrote two books under another name, Jane Somers, which were submitted to publishers as if by an unknown author. I did this out of curiosity and to highlight certain aspects of the publishing machine. Also, the mechanisms that govern reviewing. The first, *The Diary of a Good Neighbor*, was turned down by my two main publishers. It was accepted by a third and also by three European publishers.

The book was deliberately sent to all the people who regard themselves as experts of my work and they didn't recognize me. Eventually, it was reviewed, as most new novels are, briefly and often patronizingly, and would have vanished forever leaving behind a few fan letters. Because Jane Somers did get fan letters from Britain and the United States, the few people in on the secret were amazed that no one guessed. Then I wrote the second, called *If the Old Could*, and still no one guessed. Now people keep saying to me, "How is it possible that no one guessed? I would have guessed at once." Well, perhaps. And perhaps we're all more dependent on brand names and on packaging than we'd like to think. Just before I came clean, I was asked by an interviewer in the States what I thought would happen. I said that the British literary establishment would be angry and say the books were no good, but that everyone else would be delighted. And this is exactly what happened. I got lots of congratulatory letters from writers and from readers who had enjoyed the joke—and very sour and bitchy reviews. However, in France and in Scandinavia the books came out as *The Diaries of Jane Somers* by Doris Lessing. I have seldom had as good reviews as I did in France and in Scandinavia for the Jane Somers books. Of course, one could conclude that the *reviewers* in France and Scandinavia have no taste but that the British reviewers have!

It has all been very entertaining but it has also left me feeling sad and embarrassed for my profession. Does everything always have to be so predictable? Do people really have to be such sheep?

Of course, there are original minds, people who do take their own line, who do not fall victim to the need to say, or do, what everyone else does. But they are few. Very few. On them depends the health, the vitality of all our institutions, not only literature, from which I have been drawing my examples.

It has been noticed that there is this 10 per cent of the population, who can be called natural leaders, who do follow their own minds into decisions and choices. It has been noted to the extent that this fact has been incorporated into instructions for people who run prisons, concentration camps, prisoner of war camps: remove the 10 per cent, and your prisoners will become spineless and conforming.

Of course, we are back here with the notion of elitism, which is so unfashionable, so unlikeable to the extent that in large areas of politics, even education, the idea that some people may be naturally better equipped than others is resisted. But I will return to the subject of elitism later. Meanwhile, we may note that we all rely on, and we respect, this idea of the lonesome individualist who overturns conformity. It is the recurrent subject of archetypal American films—*Mr. Smith Goes to Washington*, for instance.

Take the way an attitude towards a certain writer or a book will be held by everyone, everyone saying the same things, whether for praise or for blame, until opinion shifts: this can be part of some wider social shift. Let us take the Women's Movement, as an example. There is a lively, courageous publishing house called Virago, run by women. A great many women writers who have been ignored or not taken seriously have been re-evaluated by them. But sometimes the shift is because one person stands out against the prevailing tide of opinion, and the others fall into line behind him, or her, and the new attitude then becomes general.

This mechanism is of course used all the time by publishers. When a new writer, a new novel, has to be launched, the publisher will look for an established writer to praise it. Because one "name" says it is good, the literary editors take notice and the book is launched. It is easy to see this bit of machinery at work in oneself: if someone one respects says such and such a thing is good, when you think it isn't, it is hard to differ. If several people say it is good, then it is correspondingly harder.

At a time when one set of attitudes is in the process of changing to another, it is easy to see the hedging-your-bets mechanism. A reviewer will write a piece nicely balanced between one possibility and another. A light, knowing, urbane tone often goes with this. This particular tone is used a great deal on radio and television, when doubtful subjects are under discussion. For example, when it was believed that it was impossible for us to put men on the moon, which is what the Astronomer Royal said a few years before it was done. This light, mocking, dismissive tone divorces the speaker from the subject: he or she addresses the listener, the viewer, as if it were over the head of the stupid people who believe that we could put men on the moon, or that there may be monsters in Loch Ness or Lake Champlain, or that . . . but fill in your own pet possibility.

Once we have learned to see this mechanism in operation, it can be seen how little of life is free of it. Nearly all the pressures from outside are in terms of group beliefs, group needs, national needs, patriotism and the demands of local loyalties, such as to your city and local groups of all kinds. But more subtle and more demanding—more dangerous—are the pressures from inside, which demand that you should conform, and it is these that are the hardest to watch and to control.

Many years ago I visited the Soviet Union, during one of their periods of particularly severe literary censorship. The groups of writers we met was saying that there was no need for their works to be censored, because they had developed what they called "inner censorship." That they said this with pride shocked us Westerners. What was shocking was that they were so naive about it, cut off as they are from information about psychological and sociological development. This "inner censorship" is what the psychologists call "internalizing" an exterior pressure—such as a parent—and what happens is that a previously resisted and disliked attitude becomes your own.

This happens all the time, and it is often not easy for the victims themselves to know it.

There are other experiments done by psychologists and sociologists that underline that body of experience to which we give the folk-name, "human nature." They are recent; that is to say, done in the last twenty or thirty years. There have been some pioneering and key experiments that have given birth to many others along the same lines—as I said before, over-familiar to the professionals, unfamiliar to most people.

One is known as the Milgram experiment. I have chosen it precisely because it was and is controversial, because it was so much debated, because all the professionals in the field probably groan at the very sound of it. Yet, most ordinary people have never heard of it. If they did know about it, were familiar with the ideas behind it, then indeed we'd be getting somewhere. The Milgram experiment was prompted by curiosity into how it is that ordinary, decent, kindly people, like you and me, will do abominable things when ordered to do them—like the innumerable officials under the Nazis who claimed as an excuse that they were "only obeying orders."

The researcher put into one room people chosen at random who were told that they were taking part in an experiment. A screen divided the room in such a way that they could hear but not see into the other part. In this second part volunteers sat apparently wired up to a machine that administered electric shocks of increasing severity up to the point of death, like the electric chair. This machine indicated to them how they had to respond to the shocks—with grunts, then groans, then screams, then pleas that the experiment should terminate. The person in the first half of the room believed the person in the second half was in fact connected to the machine. He was told that his or her job was to administer increasingly severe shocks according to the instructions of the experimenter and to ignore the cries of pain and pleas from the other side of the screen. Sixty-two per cent of the people tested continued to administer shocks up to the 450 volts level. At the 285 volts level the guinea pig had given an agonized scream and become silent. The people administering what they believed were at the best extremely painful doses of electricity were under great stress, but went on doing it. Afterwards most couldn't believe they were capable of such behaviour. Some said, "Well I was only carrying out instructions."

This experiment, like the many others along the same lines, offers us the information that a majority of people, regardless of whether they are black or white, male or female, old or young, rich or poor, will carry out orders, no matter how savage and brutal the orders are. This obedience to authority, in short, is not a property of the Germans under the Nazis, but a part of general human behaviour. People who have been in a political movement at times of extreme tension, people who remember how they were at school, will know this anyway . . . but it is one thing carrying a burden of knowledge around, half conscious of it, perhaps ashamed of it, hoping it will go away if you don't look too hard, and another saying openly and calmly and sensibly "Right. This is what we must expect under this and that set of conditions."

Can we imagine this being taught in school, imagine it being taught to children? "If you are in this or that type of situation, you will find yourself, if you are not careful, behaving like a brute and a savage if you are ordered to do it. Watch out for these situations. You must be on your guard against your own most primitive reactions and instincts."

Another range of experiments is concerned with how children learn best in school. Some results go flat against some of most cherished current assumptions such as, for instance, that they learn best not when "interested" or "stimulated" but when they are bored. But putting that aside—it is known that children learn best from teachers who expect them to learn well. And most will do badly if not much is expected of them. Now, we know that in classes of mixed boys and girls, most teachers will—quite unconsciously—spend more time on the boys than on the girls, expect much more in scope from the boys, will consistently underestimate the girls. In mixed classes, white teachers will—again quite unconsciously—denigrate the non-white children, expect less from them, spend less time on them. These facts are known—but where are they incorporated, where are they used in schools? In what town is it said to teachers something like this, "As teachers you must become aware of this, that attention is one of your most powerful teaching aids. Attention—the word we give to a certain quality of respect, an alert and heedful interest in a person—is what will feed and nourish your pupils." (To which of course I can already hear the response: "But what would you do if you had thirty children in your class, how much attention could you give to each?") Yes I know, but if these are the facts, if attention is so important, then at some point the people who allot the money for schools and for training programmes must, quite simply, put it to themselves like this: children flourish if they are given attention—and their teachers' expectations are that they will succeed. Therefore we must pay out enough money to the educators so that enough attention may be provided.

Another range of experiments was carried out extensively in the United States, and for all I know, in Canada too. For instance, a team of doctors cause themselves to be admitted as patients into a mental hospital, unknown to the staff. At once they start exhibiting the symptoms expected of mentally ill people, and start behaving within the range of behaviour described as typical of mentally ill people. The hospital doctors all, without exception, say they are ill, and classify them in various ways according to the symptoms described by them. It is not the psychiatrists or the nurses who see that these so-called ill people are quite normal; it is the other patients who see it. They aren't taken in; it is they who can see the truth. It is only with great difficulty that these well people convince the staff that they are well, and obtain their release from hospital.

Again: a group of ordinary citizens, researchers, [who] cause themselves to be taken into prison, some as if they were ordinary prisoners, a few in the position of warders. Immediately both groups start behaving appropriately: those as warders begin behaving as if they were real warders, with authority, badly treating the prisoners, who for their part show typical prison behaviour, become paranoid, suspicious, and so forth. Those in the role of warders confessed afterwards they could not prevent themselves enjoying the position of power, enjoying the sensation of controlling the weak. The so-called prisoners could not believe, once they were out, that they had in fact behaved as they had done.

But suppose this kind of thing were taught in schools?

Let us just suppose it, for a moment.... But at once the nub of the problem is laid bare.

Imagine us saying to children, "In the last fifty or so years, the human race has become aware of a great deal of information about its mechanisms; how it behaves, how it must behave under certain circumstances. If this is to be useful, you must learn to contemplate these rules calmly, dispassionately, disinterestedly, without emotion. It is information that will set people free from blind loyalties, obedience to slogans, rhetoric, leaders, group emotions." Well, there it is.

What government, anywhere in the world, will happily envisage its subject, learning to free themselves from governmental and state rhetoric amid pressures? Passionate loyalty and subjection to group pressure is what every state relies on. Some, of course, more than others. Khomeini's Iran, and the extreme Islamic sects, the Communist countries, are at one end of the scale. Countries like Norway, whose national day is celebrated by groups of children in fancy dress carrying, flowers, singing and dancing, with not a tank or a gun in sight, are at the other. It is interesting to speculate: what country, what nation, when, and where, would have undertaken a programme to teach its children to be people to resist rhetoric, to examine the mechanisms that govern them? I can think of only one—America, in that heady period of the Gettysburg Address.

And that time could not have survived the Civil War, for when war starts, countries cannot afford disinterested examination of their behaviour. When a war starts, nations go mad—and have to go mad, in order to survive. When I look back at the Second World War, I see something I didn't more than dimly suspect at the time. It was that everyone was crazy. Even people not in the immediate arena of war. I am not talking of the aptitudes for killing, for destruction, which soldiers are taught as part of their training, but a kind of atmosphere, the invisible poison, which spreads everywhere. And then people everywhere begin behaving as they never could in peace-time. Afterwards we look back, amazed. Did I really do that? Believe that? Fall for that bit of propaganda? Think that all our enemies were evil? That all our own nation's acts were good? How could I have tolerated that state of mind, day after day, month after month—perpetually stimulated, perpetually whipped up into emotions that my mind was meanwhile quietly and desperately protesting against?

No, I cannot imagine any nation—or not for long—teaching its citizens to become individuals able to resist group pressures.

And no political party, either. I know a lot of people who are socialists of various kinds, and I try this subject out on them, saying: all governments these days use social psychologists, experts on crowd behaviour, and mob behaviour, to advise them. Elections are stage-managed, public issues presented according to the rules of mass psychology. The military uses this information. Interrogators, secret services and the police use it. Yet these issues are never even discussed, as far as I am aware, by those parties and groups who claim to represent the people.

On one hand there are governments who manipulate, using expert knowledge and skills; on the other hand people who talk about democracy, freedom, liberty and all the rest of it, as if these values are created and maintained by simply talking about them, by repeating them often enough. How is it that so-called democratic movements don't make a point of instructing their members in the laws of crowd psychology, group psychology?

When I ask this, the response is always an uncomfortable, squeamish reluctance, as if the whole subject is really in very bad taste, unpleasant, irrelevant. As if it will all just go away if it is ignored.

So at the moment, if we look around the world, the paradox is that we may see this new information being eagerly studied by governments, the possessors and users of power—studied and put into effect. But the people who say they oppose tyranny literally don't want to know.

Reading and Studying the Text

1. Preview
2. Formulate questions
3. Identify unfamiliar vocabulary

Journal Annotations

1. Record your thinking and emotional responses to the text; record words and phrases which are particularly striking.
2. Record summary annotations, commentary, and questions.
3. Reread to clarify points.

Analysis: Lateral Thinking and Writing Connection

1. What is the purpose of Lessing's essay. Write a thesis sentence.
2. What evidence does she provide to support her thesis?
3. How does your membership in a group (family, social, other) affect the choices you make.
4. Lessing describes a number of experiments that explains how group mind works. In your journal describe an incident in your life and explain a choice you made to go with the group even when you wanted to do otherwise. Or describe and explain a choice you made which went against group think.

*Use concept webs to aid in your writing.

The Lottery
Shirley Jackson (1947)

THE MORNING of June 27th was clear and sunny, with the fresh warmth of a full-summer day; the flowers were blossoming profusely and the grass was richly green. The people of the village began to gather in the square, between the post office and the bank, around ten o'clock; in some towns there were so many people that the lottery took two days and had to be started on June 26th, but in this village, where there were about three hundred people, the whole lottery took less than two hours, so it could begin at ten o'clock in the morning and still be through in time to allow the villagers to get home for noon dinner.

The children assembled first, of course. School was recently over for the summer, and the feeling of liberty sat uneasily on most of them; they tended to gather together quietly for a while before they broke into boisterous play, and their talk was still of the classroom and the teacher, of books and reprimands. Bobby Martin had already stuffed his pockets full of stones and the other boys soon followed his example, selecting the smoothest and roundest stones; Bobby and Harry Jones and Dickie Delacroix—the villagers pronounced this name "Dellacroy"—eventually made a great pile of stones in one corner of the square and guarded it against the raids of the other boys. The girls stood aside, talking among themselves, looking over their shoulders at the boys, and the very small children rolled in the dust or clung to the hands of their older brothers or sisters. Soon the men began to gather, surveying their own children, speaking of planting and rain, tractors and taxes. They stood together, away from the pile of stones in the corner, and their jokes were quiet and they smiled rather than laughed. The women, wearing faded house dresses and sweaters, came shortly after their menfolk. They greeted one another and exchanged bits of gossip as they went to join their husbands. Soon the women, standing by their husbands, began to call to their children, and the children came reluctantly, having to be called four or five times. Bobby Martin ducked under his mother's grasping hand and ran, laughing, back to the pile of stones. His father spoke up sharply, and Bobby came quickly and took his place between his father and his oldest brother.

The lottery was conducted—as were the square dances, the teen-age club, the Halloween program—by Mr. Summers, who had time and energy to devote to civic activities. He was a round-faced, jovial man and he ran the coal business, and people were sorry for him, because he had no children and his wife was a scold. When he arrived in the square, carrying the black wooden box, there was a murmur of conversation among the villagers, and he waved and called, "Little late today, folks." The postmaster, Mr. Graves, followed him, carrying a three legged stool, and the stool was put in the center of the square and Mr. Summers set the black box down on it. The villagers kept their distance, leaving a space between themselves and the stool, and when Mr. Summers said, "Some of you fellows want to give me a hand?" there was a hesitation before two men, Mr. Martin and his oldest son, Baxter, came forward to hold the box steady on the stool while Mr. Summers stirred up the papers inside it.

The original paraphernalia for the lottery had been lost long ago, and the black box now resting on the stool had been put into use even before Old Man Warner, the oldest man in town, was born. Mr. Summers spoke frequently to the villagers about making a new box, but no one liked to upset even as much tradition as was represented by the black box. There was a story that the present box had been made with some pieces of the box that had preceded it, the one that had been constructed when the first people settled down to make a village here. Every year, after the lottery, Mr. Summers began talking again about a new box, but every year the subject was allowed to fade off without anything being done. The black box grew shabbier each year; by now it was no longer completely black but splintered badly along one side to show the original wood color, and in some places faded or stained.

Mr. Martin and his oldest son, Baxter, held the black box securely on the stool until Mr. Summers had stirred the papers thoroughly with his hand. Because so much of the ritual had been forgotten or discarded, Mr. Summers had been successful in having slips of paper substituted for the chips of wood that had been used for generations. Chips of wood, Mr. Summers had argued, had been all very well when the village was tiny, but now that the population was more than three hundred and likely to keep on growing, it was necessary to use something that would fit more easily into the black box. The night before the lottery, Mr. Summers and Mr. Graves made up the slips of paper and put them in the box, and it was then taken to the safe of Mr. Summers' coal company and locked up until Mr. Summers was ready to take it to the square next morning. The rest of the year, the box was put away, sometimes one place, sometimes another; it had spent one year in Mr. Graves' barn and another year underfoot in the post office, and sometimes it was set on a shelf in the Martin grocery and left there. There was a great deal of fussing to be done before Mr. Summers declared the lottery open. There were the lists to make up—of heads of families, heads of households in each family, members of each household in each family. There was the proper swearing of Mr. Summers by the postmaster, as the official of the lottery; at one time, some people remembered, there had been a recital of some sort, performed by the official of the lottery, a perfunctory, tuneless chant that had been rattled off duly each year; some people believed that the official of the lottery used to stand just so when he said or sang it, others believed that he was supposed to walk among the people; but years and years ago this part of the ritual had been allowed to lapse. There had been, also, a ritual salute, which the official of the lottery had had to use in addressing each person who came up to draw from the box, but this also had changed with time, until now it was felt necessary only for the official to speak to each person approaching. Mr. Summers was very good at all this; in his clean white shirt and blue jeans, with one hand resting carelessly on the black box, he seemed very proper and important as he talked interminably to Mr. Graves and the Martins.

Just as Mr. Summers finally left off talking and turned to the assembled villagers, Mrs. Hutchinson came hurriedly along the path to the square, her sweater thrown over her shoulders, and slid into place in the back of the crowd. "Clean forgot what day it was," she said to Mrs. Delacroix, who stood next to her and they both laughed softly.

"Thought my old man was out back stacking wood," Mrs. Hutchinson went on, "and then I looked out the window and the kids was gone, and then I remembered it was the twenty-seventh and came a-running." She dried her hands on her apron, and Mrs. Delacroix said, "You're in time, though. They're still talking away up there."

Mrs. Hutchinson craned her neck to see through the crowd and found her husband and children standing near the front. She tapped Mrs. Delacroix on the arm as a farewell and began to make her way through the crowd. The people separated good-humoredly to let her through; two or three people said, in voices just loud enough to be heard across the crowd, "Here comes your Missus, Hutchinson," and "Bill, she made it after all." Mrs. Hutchinson reached her husband, and Mr. Summers, who had been waiting, said cheerfully, "Thought we were going to have to get on without you, Tessie." Mrs. Hutchinson said, grinning, "Wouldn't have me leave m'dishes in the sink, now, would you, Joe?" and soft laughter ran through the crowd as the people stirred back into position after Mrs. Hutchinson's arrival.

"Well, now," Mr. Summers said soberly, "guess we better get started, get this over with, so's we can go back to work. Anybody ain't here?"

"Dunbar," several people said. "Dunbar, Dunbar."

Mr. Summers consulted his list. "Clyde Dunbar," he said. "That's right. He's broke his leg, hasn't he? Who's drawing for him?"

"Me. I guess," a woman said, and Mr. Summers turned to look at her. "Wife draws for her husband," Mr. Summers said. "Don't you have a grown boy to do it for you, Janey?" Although Mr. Summers and everyone else in the village knew the answer perfectly well, it was the business of the official of the lottery to ask such questions formally. Mr. Summers waited with an expression of polite interest while Mrs. Dunbar answered.

"Horace's not but sixteen yet," Mrs. Dunbar said regretfully. "Guess I gotta fill in for the old man this year."

"Right," Mr. Summers said. He made a note on the list he was holding. Then he asked, "Watson boy drawing this year?" A tall boy in the crowd raised his hand. "Here," he said. "I'm drawing for m'mother and me." He blinked his eyes nervously and ducked his head as several voices in the crowd said things like "Good fellow, Jack," and "Glad to see your mother's got a man to do it."

"Well," Mr. Summers said, "guess that's everyone. Old Man Warner make it?"

"Here," a voice said, and Mr. Summers nodded.

A sudden hush fell on the crowd as Mr. Summers cleared his throat and looked at the list. "All ready?" he called. "Now I'll read the names—heads of families first—and the men come up and take a paper out of the box. Keep the paper folded in your hand without looking at it until everyone has had a turn. Everything clear?"

The people had done it so many times that they only half listened to the directions; most of them were quiet, wetting their lips, not looking around. Then Mr. Summers raised one hand high and said, "Adams." A man disengaged himself from the crowd and came forward. "Hi, Steve," Mr. Summers said, and, Mr. Adams said, "Hi, Joe." They grinned at one another humorlessly and nervously. Then Mr. Adams reached into the black box and took out a folded paper. He held it firmly by one corner as he turned and went hastily back to his place in the crowd, where he stood a little apart from his family, not looking down at his hand.

"Allen," Mr. Summers said. "Anderson. . . . Bentham." "Seems like there's no time at all between lotteries any more," Mrs. Delacroix said to Mrs. Graves in the back row. "Seems like we got through with the last one only last week."

"Time sure goes fast," Mrs. Graves said.

"Clark. . . . Delacroix."

"There goes my old man," Mrs. Delacroix said. She held her breath while her husband went forward.

"Dunbar," Mr. Summers said, and Mrs. Dunbar went steadily to the box while one of the women said, "'Go on, Janey,'" and another said, "There she goes."

"We're next," Mrs. Graves said. She watched while Mr. Graves came around from the side of the box, greeted Mr. Summers gravely, and selected a slip of paper from the box. By now, all through the crowd there were men holding the small folded papers in their large hands, turning them over and over nervously. Mrs. Dunbar and her two sons stood together, Mrs. Dunbar holding the slip of paper.

"Harburt. . . . Hutchinson."

"Get up there, Bill," Mrs. Hutchinson said, and the people near her laughed.

"Jones."

"They do say," Mr. Adams said to Old Man Warner, who stood next to him, "that over in the north village they're talking of giving up the lottery."

Old Man Warner snorted. "Pack of crazy fools," he said. "Listening to the young folks, nothing's good enough for them. Next thing you know, they'll be wanting to go back to living in caves, nobody work any more, live that way for a while. Used to be a saying about 'Lottery in June, corn be heavy soon.' First thing you know, we'd all be eating stewed chickweed and acorns. There's *always* been a lottery," he added petulantly. "Bad enough to see young Joe Summers up there joking with everybody."

"Some places have already quit lotteries," Mrs. Adams said. "Nothing but trouble in that," Old Man Warner said stoutly. "Pack of young fools."

"Martin." And Bobby Martin watched his father go forward. "*Overdyke*. . . . Percy."

"I wish they'd hurry," Mrs. Dunbar said to her older son. "I wish they'd hurry."

"They're almost through," her son said.

"You get ready to run tell Dad," Mrs. Dunbar said. Mr. Summers called his own name and then stepped forward precisely and selected a slip from the box. Then he called, "Warner."

"Seventy-seventh year I been in the lottery," Old Man Warner said as he went through the crowd. "Seventy-seventh time."

"Watson." The tall boy came awkwardly through the crowd. Someone said, "Don't be nervous, Jack," and Mr. Summers said, "Take your time, son."

"Zanini."

After that, there was a long pause, a breathless pause, until Mr. Summers, holding his slip of paper in the air, said, "All right, fellows." For a minute, no one moved, and then all the slips of paper were opened. Suddenly, all the women began to speak at once, saying, "Who is it?", "Who's got it?", "Is it the Dunbars?", "Is it the Watsons?" Then the voices began to say, "It's Hutchinson. It's Bill." "Bill Hutchinson's got it."

"Go tell your father," Mrs. Dunbar said to her older son. People began to look around to see the Hutchinsons. Bill Hutchinson was standing quiet, staring down at the paper in his hand. Suddenly, Tessie Hutchinson shouted to Mr. Summers, "You didn't give him time enough to take any paper he wanted. I saw you. It wasn't fair!"

"Be a good sport, Tessie," Mrs. Delacroix called, and Mrs. Graves said, "All of us took the same chance."

"Shut up, Tessie," Bill Hutchinson said.

"Well, everyone," Mr. Summers said, "that was done pretty fast, and now we've got to be hurrying a little more to get done in time." He consulted his next list. "Bill," he said, "you draw for the Hutchinson family. You got any other households in the Hutchinsons?"

"There's Don and Eva," Mrs. Hutchinson yelled. "Make them take their chance!"

"Daughters draw with their husbands' families, Tessie," Mr. Summers said gently. "You know that as well as anyone else."

"It wasn't fair," Tessie said.

"I guess not, Joe," Bill Hutchinson said regretfully. "My daughter draws with her husband's family, that's only fair. And I've got no other family except the kids."

"Then, as far as drawing for families is concerned, it's you," Mr. Summers said in explanation, "and as far as drawing for households is concerned, that's you, too. Right?"

"Right," Bill Hutchinson said.

"How many kids, Bill?" Mr. Summers asked formally.

"Three," Bill Hutchinson said. "There's Bill, Jr., and Nancy, and little Dave. And Tessie and me."

"All right, then," Mr. Summers said. "Harry, you got their tickets back?"

Mr. Graves nodded and held up the slips of paper. "Put them in the box, then," Mr. Summers directed. "Take Bill's and put it in."

"I think we ought to start over," Mrs. Hutchinson said, as quietly as she could. "I tell you it wasn't *fair*. You didn't give him time enough to choose. Everybody saw that."

Mr. Graves had selected the five slips and put them in the box, and he dropped all the papers but those onto the ground, where the breeze caught them and lifted them off.

"Listen, everybody," Mrs. Hutchinson was saying to the people around her.

"Ready, Bill?" Mr. Summers asked, and Bill Hutchinson, with one quick glance around at his wife and children, nodded.

"Remember," Mr. Summers said, "take the slips and keep them folded until each person has taken one. Harry, you help little Dave." Mr. Graves took the hand of the little boy, who came willingly with him up to the box. "Take a paper out of the box, Davy," Mr. Summers said. Davy put his hand into the box and laughed. "Take just one paper," Mr. Summers said. "Harry, you hold it for him." Mr. Graves took the child's hand and removed the folded paper from the tight fist and held it while little Dave stood next to him and looked up at him wonderingly.

"Nancy next," Mr. Summers said. Nancy was twelve, and her school friends breathed heavily as she went forward, switching her skirt, and took a slip daintily from the box. "Bill, Jr.," Mr. Summers said, and Billy, his face red and his feet overlarge, nearly knocked the box over as he got a paper out. "Tessie," Mr. Summers said. She hesitated for a minute, looking around defiantly, and then set her lips and went up to the box. She snatched a paper out and held it behind her.

"Bill," Mr. Summers said, and Bill Hutchinson reached into the box and felt around, bringing his hand out at last with the slip of paper in it.

The crowd was quiet. A girl whispered, "I hope it's not Nancy," and the sound of the whisper reached the edges of the crowd.

"It's not the way it used to be," Old Man Warner said clearly. "People ain't the way they used to be."

"All right," Mr. Summers said. "Open the papers. Harry, you open little Dave's."

Mr. Graves opened the slip of paper and there was a general sigh through the crowd as he held it up and everyone could see that it was blank. Nancy and

Bill, Jr., opened theirs at the same time, and both beamed and laughed, turning around to the crowd and holding their slips of paper above their heads.

"Tessie," Mr. Summers said. There was a pause, and then Mr. Summers looked at Bill Hutchinson, and Bill unfolded his paper and showed it. It was blank.

"It's Tessie," Mr. Summers said, and his voice was hushed. "Show us her paper, Bill."

Bill Hutchinson went over to his wife and forced the slip of paper out of her hand. It had a black spot on it, the black spot Mr. Summers had made the night before with the heavy pencil in the coal-company office. Bill Hutchinson held it up, and there was a stir in the crowd.

"All right, folks," Mr. Summers said. "Let's finish quickly." Although the villagers had forgotten the ritual and lost the original black box, they still remembered to use stones. The pile of stones the boys had made earlier was ready; there were stones on the ground with the blowing scraps of paper that had come out of the box. Mrs. Delacroix selected a stone so large she had to pick it up with both hands and turned to Mrs. Dunbar. "Come on," she said. "Hurry up."

Mrs. Dunbar had small stones in both hands, and she said, gasping for breath, "I can't run at all. You'll have to go ahead and I'll catch up with you."

The children had stones already, and someone gave little Davy Hutchinson a few pebbles.

Tessie Hutchinson was in the center of a cleared space by now, and she held her hands out desperately as the villagers moved in on her. "It isn't fair," she said. A stone hit her on the side of the head.

Lottery

Old Man Warner was saying, "Come on, come on, everyone." Steve Adams was in the front of the crowd of villagers, with Mrs. Graves beside him.

"It isn't fair, it isn't right," Mrs. Hutchinson screamed, and then they were upon her.

Reading and Studying the Text

1. Preview
2. Formulate questions
3. Identify unfamiliar vocabulary, terms, and phrases.

Journal Annotations

1. Write a declarative sentence identifying the theme.

2. Record your thinking and emotional responses to the text; record terms and phrases which had a strong emotional impact.
3. Reread to clarify points.
4. Record summary annotations, commentary, and questions.

Character Analysis

1. Create character map(s)—include information which will help you make connections to understand the hierarchy in the village.

Analysis: Freedom and Choice

1. Explain how the concept of group minds functioned in this village.
2. Cite actions of villagers which would indicate that some were reluctant to participate in the stoning.
3. Under similar circumstances how would you respond? Write an account of a choice you may have made given which would have gone against your traditional way of doing things or in contradiction of a particular group to which you belong. Support your position using a life experience of your own to indicate why you made the choice to go along with the group or to choose differently. Examples of group includes your family, club, place of worship, and so on.

Excerpt from *1984*
Part I
George Orwell (1948)

IT WAS A BRIGHT COLD DAY IN APRIL, and the clocks were striking thirteen. Winston Smith, his chin nuzzled into his breast in an effort to escape the vile wind, slipped quickly through the glass doors of Victory Mansions, though not quickly enough to prevent a swirl of gritty dust from entering along with him.

The hallway smelt of boiled cabbage and old rag mats. At one end of it a colored poster, too large for indoor display, had been tacked to the wall. It depicted simply an enormous face, more than a meter wide: the face of a man about forty-five, with a heavy black mustache and ruggedly handsome features. Winston made for the stairs. It was no use trying the lift. Even at the best of times it was seldom working, and at present the electric current was cut off during daylight hours. It was part of the economy drive in preparation for Hate Week. The flat was seven flights up, and Winston, who was thirty-nine and had a varicose ulcer above his right ankle, went slowly, resting several times on the way. On each landing, opposite the lift shaft, the poster with the enormous face gazed from the wall. It was one of those pictures which are so contrived that the eyes follow you about when you move. BIG BROTHER IS WATCHING YOU, the caption beneath it ran.

Inside the flat a fruity voice was reading out a list of figures which had something to do with the production of pig iron. The voice came from an oblong metal plaque like a dulled mirror which formed part of the surface of the right-hand wall. Winston turned a switch and the voice sank somewhat, though the words were still distinguishable. The instrument (the telescreen, it was called) could be dimmed, but there was no way of shutting it off completely. He moved over to the window: a smallish, frail figure, the meagerness of his body merely emphasized by the blue overalls which were the uniform of the Party. His hair was very fair, his face naturally sanguine, his skin roughened by coarse soap and blunt razor blades and the cold of the winter that had just ended.

Outside, even through the shut window pane, the world looked cold. Down in the street little eddies of wind were whirling dust and torn paper into spirals, and though the sun was shining and the sky a harsh blue, there seemed to be no color in anything except the posters that were plastered everywhere. The black-mustachio'd face gazed down from every commanding corner. There was one on the house front immediately opposite. BIG BROTHER IS WATCHING YOU, the caption said, while the dark eyes looked deep into Winston's own. Down at street level another poster, torn at one corner, flapped fitfully in the wind, alternately covering and uncovering the single word INGSOC. In the far distance a helicopter skimmed down between the roofs, hovered for an instant like a blue-bottle, and darted away again with a curving flight. It was the Police Patrol, snooping into people's windows. The patrols did not matter, however. Only the Thought Police mattered.

Behind Winston's back the voice from the telescreen was still babbling away about pig iron and the overfulfillment of the Ninth Three-Year Plan. The telescreen received and transmitted simultaneously. Any sound that Winston made, above the level of a very low whisper, would be picked up by it; moreover, so long as he remained within the field of vision which the metal plaque commanded, he could be seen as well as heard. There was of course no way of knowing whether you were being watched at any given moment. How often, or on what system, the Thought Police plugged in on any individual wire was guesswork. It was even conceivable that they watched everybody all the time. But at any rate they could plug in your wire whenever they wanted to. You had to live—did live, from habit that became instinct—in the assumption that every sound you made was overheard, and, except in darkness, every movement scrutinized.

Winston kept his back turned to the telescreen. It was safer; though, as he well knew, even a back can be revealing. A kilometer away the Ministry of Truth, his place of work, towered vast and white above the grimy landscape. This, he thought with a sort of vague distaste—this was London, chief city of Airstrip One, itself the third most populous of the provinces of Oceania. He tried to squeeze out some childhood memory that should tell him whether London had always been quite like this. Were there always these vistas of rotting nineteenth century houses, their sides shored up with balks of timber, their windows patched with cardboard and their roofs with corrugated iron, their crazy garden walls sagging in all directions? And the bombed sites where the plaster dust swirled in the air and the willow herb straggled over the heaps of rubble; and the places where the bombs had cleared a larger path and there had sprung up sordid colonies of wooden dwellings like chicken houses? But it was no use, he could not remember: nothing remained of his childhood except a series of bright-lit tableaux, occurring against no background and mostly unintelligible.

The Ministry of Truth—Minitrue, in Newspeak*—was startlingly different from any other object in sight. It was an enormous pyramidal structure of glittering white concrete, soaring up, terrace after terrace, three hundred meters into the air. From where Winston stood it was just possible to read, picked out on its white face in elegant lettering, the three slogans of the Party:

WAR IS PEACE
FREEDOM IS SLAVERY
IGNORANCE IS STRENGTH.

The Ministry of Truth contained, it was said, three thousand rooms above ground level, and corresponding ramifications below. Scattered about London there were just three other buildings of similar appearance and size. So completely did they dwarf the surrounding architecture that from the roof of Victory Mansions you could see all four of them simultaneously. They were the homes of the four Ministries between which the entire apparatus of government was divided: the Ministry of Truth, which concerned itself with news, entertainment, education, and the fine arts; the Ministry of Peace, which concerned itself with war; the Ministry of Love, which maintained law and order; and the Ministry of Plenty, which was responsible for economic affairs. Their names, in Newspeak: Minitrue, Minipax, Miniluv, and Miniplenty.

---

*Newspeak was the official language of Oceania

The Ministry of Love was the really frightening one. There were no windows in it at all. Winston had never been inside the Ministry of Love, nor within half a kilometer of it. It was a place impossible to enter except on official business, and then only by penetrating through a maze of barbed-wire entanglements, steel doors, and hidden machine-gun nests. Even the streets leading up to its outer barriers were roamed by gorilla-faced guards in black uniforms, armed with jointed truncheons.

* * * * * *

... From the table drawer he took out a penholder, a bottle of ink, and a thick, quarto-sized blank book with a red back and a marbled cover.

* * * * * *

The thing that he was about to do was to open a diary. This was not illegal (nothing was illegal, since there were no longer any laws), but if detected it was reasonably certain that it would be punished by death, or at least by twenty-five years in a forced-labor camp.... He dipped the pen into the ink and then faltered for just a second. A tremor had gone through his bowels. To mark the paper was the decisive act. In small clumsy letters he wrote: April 4th, 1984.

Reading and Studying the Text

1. Preview
2. Formulate questions
3. Identify unfamiliar vocabulary, terms, and phrases

Journal Annotations

1. Record your thinking and emotional responses to the text: terms, phrases, passages which had a strong emotional impact.
2. Reread to clarify points.
3. Write a declarative sentence identifying the theme.
4. Record summary annotations, commentary, and questions.

Character Analysis

1. Create a character map of Winston and write an analysis

2. Explain why Winston's choice to write in his diary can be considered an act of courage. Include a choice you have made which also took courage to enact.

Analysis: Freedom and Choice

1. List the freedoms which were denied the citizens in Oceania and the methods to enforce conformity.
2. How is the language, Newspeak, used in Oceania to limit freedom and choice?

Syntheses of Readings

Choose one or more of the following essays to make connections across readings and record your thinking on the topic of freedom and choice.

1. Compare and contrast the arguments of Stanton (1848), Douglass (1852), and Chief Seattle (1854) in their efforts to help women, Africans, and Native American free to make choices.
2. Considering Kennedy's (1961) vision for America and the changes Martin Luther King, Jr. wanted, what freedoms would have to be in place for the vision to become a reality for all citizens to participate in this vision. Refer to the Declaration of Independence and your ideas on freedom and choice to guide you.
3. Compare and contrast the emphasis of the arguments Stanton (1848) makes for equal rights for women with the arguments made a century later by Shirley Chisholm (1969).
4. Compare and contrast the actions of the characters in *The Lottery* with Winston's actions in *1984*. Include your opinions and comments.

Bibliography

Adams, M., & Bertraum, B. (1980). *Background knowledge and reading comprehension* (Reading Ed. Rep. No. 13). Urbana: University of Illinois Press, Center for the Study of Reading. (ERIC Document Reproduction Service ED 181 431)

Alexander, P. A., & Jetton, T. L. (2000). Learning from text: A multidimensional and developmental perspective. In M. L. Kamil, P. B. Mosenthal, P. D. Pearson, & R. Barr (Eds.), *Handbook of reading research* (vol. 3, pp. 285–310). Mahwah, NJ: Lawrence Erlbaum Associates.

Alvermann, D. E., & Moore, D. W. (1991). Secondary school reading. In R. Barr, M. L. Kamil, P. B. Mosenthal, & P. D. Pearson (Eds.), *Handbook of reading research* (vol. 2, pp. 951–983). New York: Longman.

Alvermann, D. E., Smith, L. C., & Readence, J. E. (1985). Prior knowledge activation and the comprehension of compatible and incompatible text. *Reading Research Quarterly*, 20, 420–436.

Ames, C., & Archer, J. (1988). Achievement goals in the classroom: Students' learning strategies and motivational processes. *Journal of Educational Pysychology*, 80, 260–267.

Anders, P., & Bos, C. (1986). Semantic feature analysis: An interactive strategy for vocabulary development and text comprehension. *Journal of Reading*, 29, 610–616.

Anderson, R. C., & Freebody, P. (1981). Vocabulary knowledge. In J. T. Guthrie (Ed.), *Comprehension and teaching: Research reviews* (pp. 77–117). Newark, DE: International Reading Association.

Anderson, T. H., & Armbruster, B. B. (1984). Studying. In P. D. Pearson (Ed.), *Handbook of reading research* (pp. 657–679). New York: Longman.

Armbruster, B. B., Anderson, T. H., & Osterlag, J. (1989). Teaching text structure to improve reading and writing. *The Reading Teacher*, 43, 130–137.

Au, K. H., Carroll, J. H., & Scheu, J. A. (1997). *Balanced literacy instruction: A teacher's resource book*. Norwood, MA: Christopher-Gordon Publishers.

Ayan, J. (1997). *Aha! 10 ways to free your creative spirit and find your great ideas*. New York: Three Rivers Press.

Baker, L., & Brown, A. L. (1984a). Cognitive monitoring in reading. In. J. Flood (Ed.), *Understanding reading comprehension* (pp.21–44). Newark, DE: International Reading Association.

Baker, L., & Brown, A. L. (1984b). Metacognitive skills in reading. In P. D. Pearson (Ed.), *Handbook of reading research* (pp. 353–394). New York: Longman.

Bandura, A. (1997). *Self-efficacy: The exercise of control.* New York: W.H. Freeman.

Baumann, J. F. (1986). *Teaching main idea comprehension.* Newark, DE: International Reading Association.

Baumann, J. F., & Schmitt, M. C. (1986). The what, why, how, and when of comprehension instruction. *The Reading Teacher, 39,* 640–647.

Bean, T. W., & Steenwyk, F. L. (1984). The effect of three forms of summarization instruction on sixth graders' summary writing and comprehension. *Journal of Reading Behavior, 16,* 297–306.

Beck, I., & McKeown, M. (1981). Developing questions that promote comprehension: The story map. *Language Arts, 58,* 913–918.

Benson, H.M.D. (2000). *Beyond the relaxation response.* New York: Harper Collins.

Benson, H.M.D. (1980). *The relaxation response.* New York: Times Books.

Birnbaum, J. C. (1982). The reading and composing behavior of selected fourth- and seventh-grade students. *Research in the Teaching of English, 16,* 241–260.

Blachowicz, C. L. Z. (1986). Making connections: Alternatives to the vocabulary notebook. *Journal of Reading, 29,* 643–649.

Black, R. (1994). *Broken crayons: Break your crayons and draw outside the lines.* Dubuque, IA: Kendall-Hunt.

Bromley, K. D. (1989). Buddy journals make the reading writing connection. *The Reading Teacher, 36*(9), 884–891.

Buehl, D. (1996). Improving students' learning strategies through self-reflection. *Teaching and Change, 3*(3), 227–237.

Buzan, T. (1976). *Use both sides of the brain.* New York: Plume Book.

Buzan, T. (2001). *Head strong.* West Wales, UK: Cygnus Books.

Calkins, L. M. (1994). *The art of teaching writing* (new ed.). Portmouth, NH: Heinemann.

Carr, M. (1987). Clustering with nonreaders/writers. In C. B. Olson (Ed.), *Practical ideas for teaching writing as a process* (pp. 20–21). Sacramento: California State Department of Education.

Chief Seattle. Speech delivered to the Governor of the Washington Territory, 1854. Recorded by Dr. Henry A. Smith.

Chisholm, Shirley. Equal rights for women. The United States House of Representatives, Washington, D.C. May 21, 1969.

Ciardiello, A. V. (1998). Did you ask a good question today? Alternative cognitive and metacognitive strategies. *Journal of Adolescent & Adult Literacy, 42*(3), 210–219.

Coger, L. E., & White, M. R. (1982). *Readers theatre handbook: A dramatic approach to literature.* Glenview, IL: Scott, Foresman.

Conference, Cognitive and Social Perspectives for Literacy Research and Instruction (pp. 345–352). Chicago: The National Reading Conference.

Davey, B., & McBride, S. (1986). Effects of question generating training on reading comprehension. *Journal of Educational Psychology, 78*(4), 256–262.

Davis, M., & Fanning, P. (1981). *Thoughts & feelings: The art of cognitive stress intervention.* Richmond, CA: New Harbinger Publications.

Davis, M., Eshelman, E. R., & McKay, M. (1980). *The relaxation & stress reduction workbook.* Richmond, CA: New Harbinger Publications.

de Bono, E. (1990). *Lateral thinking: Creativity step by step.* New York: Perennial Library.

de Bono, E. (1994). *Parallel thinking: From Socratic thinking to De Bono thinking.* New York: Viking.

Denner, P. R., & Rickards, J. P. (1987). A developmental comparison of the effects of provided and generated questions on text recall. *Contemporary Educational Psychology, 12,* 135–146.

Dole, J. A., & Smith, E. L. (1989). Prior knowledge and learning from science text: An instructional study. In the *Thirty-Eighth Yearbook of the National Reading Conference, Cognitive and Social Perspectives for Literacy Reasearch and Instruction*, (pp. 342–352). Chicago, IL: The National Reading Conference.

Douglass, Frederick. "What to the Slave is the Fourth of July?" 5 July 1852.

Duffy, G. G., Roehler, L. R., Sivan, E., Rackliffe, G., Book, C., Meloth, M., Vavrus, L. G., Wesselman, R., Putnam, J., & Bassiri, D. (1987). Effects of explaining the reasoning associated with using reading strategies. *Reading Research Quarterly, 22*, 347–368.

Edwards, B. (1999). *The new drawing on the right side of the brain*. New York: Harper Collins.

Facione, P. (1998). *Critical thinking: What it is and why it counts*. Milibrae, CA: California Academic Press.

Flood, J., & Lapp, D. (1988). Conceptual mapping strategies for information texts. *The Reading Teacher, 41*, 780–783.

Freeman, D. E., & Freeman, Y. S. (2000). *Teaching reading in multilingual classrooms*. Portsmouth, NH: Heinemann.

Goleman, D. (1991). *The meditative mind*. New York: St. Martin's Press.

Goleman, D. (1995), *Emotional intelligence*. New York: Bantam Books.

Goodman, K. S. (1994). Reading, writing and written texts: A transactional sociopsycholinguistic view. In R. B. Ruddell, M. R. Ruddell, & H. Singer, (Eds.), *Theoretical models and processes of reading*, (4th ed.) Newark, DE: International Reading Association.

Guthrie, J.T., & Alao, S. (1997). Designing contexts to increase motivation for reading. *Educational Psychologist, 32*, 95–105.

Jackson, Shirley (1947). *The lottery*. New York: Farrar, Straus and Giroux.

Jiménez, R. T., García, G. E., & Pearson, P. D. (1996). The reading strategies of bilingual Latina/o students who are successful English readers: Opportunities and obstacles. *Reading Research Quarterly, 31*(1), 90–112.

Kennedy, John F. Inaugural Address. Washington, D. C. January 20, 1961. John F. Kennedy Library and Museum. July, 2004: http://www.c.v.umb.edu/jfklibrary/j012061.htm

King, Martin Luther, Jr. Letter from Birmingham City Jail, April 16, 1963. Philadelphia, PA: American Friends Service Committee

Kintsch, W. (1994). The role of knowledge in discourse comprehension: A construction-integration model. In, R. B. Ruddell, M. R. Ruddell, & H. Singer (Eds.), *Theoretical models and processes of reading* (4th ed.) (pp. 951–995). Newark, DE: International Reading Association.

Kirby, K. (1986). The reading journal: A bridge between reading and writing. *Forum for Reading*, fall/winter, 13–19.

Kucan, L., & Beck, I. L. (1997). Thinking aloud and reading comprehension research: Inquiry, instruction, and social interaction. *Review of Educational Research, 67*(3), 271–299.

Langer, J. A. (1986). Reading, writing and understanding: An analysis of the Construction of meaning. Written Communication, 3, 219–267.

Lesgold, A. M., & Curtis, M. E. (1981). Learning to read words efficiently. In A. M. Lesgold & A. Perfetti (Eds.) *Interactive processes in reading*. Hillsdale, NJ: Lawrence Erlbaum Associates.

Lessing, Doris. (1987). "Group minds," in *Prisons we choose to live inside*. New York: Harper and Row.

Lipson, M. N.(1995). The effect of semantic mapping instruction on prose Comprehension of below-level college readers. *Reading Research and Instruction, 34*, 367–378.

Lipson, M. Y. (1982). Learning new information from text. The role of prior knowledge and reading ability. *Journal of Reading Behavior, 14*, 243–261.

Lynch, M. N. (1981). Unblocking writers block for reading students, National Conference on College Learning Assistance Centers, Nassau Community College, May 1981.

Lynch, M. N. (1984). Clustering: Improving analytical thinking, reading and writing, Third Conference on Developmental Education, Brooklyn College, April, 1984.

Lynch, M. N. (1985). Right brain activities to improve analytical thinking, 30th Annual International Reading Association Convention, May, 1985.

Lynch, M. N. (1986). Non-traditional methods for outlining, *Learning Styles Network*, 7 (2):3.

Lynch, M. N. (1990). The reader as writer: Using journals in college reading, in *College Reading and the New Majority: Improving Instruction in Multicultural Education*, Al Frager, (Ed.) Oxford, OH: College Reading Association.

Lynch, M. N. (1981). Test Anxiety and the Underprepared College Student: Implications For Reading Instruction, Developmental Education Conference, Brooklyn College, April 1981 (updated 1986/1990/1995).

Lynch, M. N. (1984). Improving reading, writing and diction, Nassau Reading Council, Annual Spring Conference, March 1984.

Lynch, M. N. (1985). Effective study habits and skills, New York City Technical College Lecture Series, Spring 1985.

Lynch, M. N. (1985). Overcoming test anxiety, New York City Technical College, Fall, 1985.

Lynch, M. N. (1988). Using reading journals to develop analytical skills, 32nd Annual Conference of the College Reading Association, Atlanta, GA.

Lynch, M. N. (1997). Using journals in the college classroom. First Annual Faculty Conference, Brooklyn College, May, 1997.

Lynch, M. N. (1986). Reading aloud to college freshmen, Thirtieth College Reading Association Conference, October 23-25, 1986.

Mewes, W. (1976). From Linear to Cybernetic Thinking. http://www.strategic.net/internat/english/linear

Moore, D. W., Readence, J. E., & Rickelman, R. J. (1989). *Prereading activities for content area reading and learning* (2nd ed.). Newark, DE: International Reading Association.

Morrow, L. (1985). Retelling stories: A strategy for improving children's comprehension, concept of story structure, and oral language complexity. *Elementary School Journal*, 85, 647–661.

Noyce, R. M., & Christie, J. F. (1989). *Intergrating reading and writing instruction in grades K–8*. Boston: Allyn & Bacon.

Orwell, G. (1948). Part I, 1984. In *George Orwell Animal Farm and 1984*. London: A. M. Heath.

Pearson, P. D., & Tierney, R. J. (1984). On becoming a thoughtful reader: Learning to read like a writer. In A. C. Purves & O. Niles (Eds.), *Eighty-third yearbook of the National Society of the Study of Education, Becoming readers in a complex society* (pp. 144–173). Chicago: University of Chicago Press.

Pinnell, G. S., & Fountas, G. S. (1998). *Word matters*. Portsmouth, NH: Heinenmann.

Pressley, M., & Harris, K. R. (1990). What we really know about strategy instruction. *Educational Leadership*, 48, 31–34.

Ramage, A., & Holland, A. (2000). Thinking outside of the (black) box. *Brain and Language*, 71(1): 93-5.

Rico, G. L. (2000). *Writing the natural way*. Los Angeles: J.P. Tarcher.

Riding, R., & Rayner, E. (Eds.) (1998). *Cognitive styles and learning strategies: Understanding style differences in learning and behavior*. London: David Fulton Publishers.

Stanton, Elizabeth Cady. Declaration of sentiments and resolutions, Seneca Falls Convention, July 19, 1848. Online. Gifts of Speech. Available: http://gos.sbc.edu/s/stanton.html. 21 July 2004.

Sutcliffe, J. (1995). *The complete book of relaxation techniques*. Allentown, PA: People's Medical Society.
The Declaration of Independence A Transcription. IN CONGRESS, July 4, 1776. The unanimous declaration of the thirteen united States of America. Online. United States Archives & Records Administration. Available: http://ww.archives.gov/nationa_archives_experience/charters/print_friendly.html
Wlodkowski, R. (1985). *Enhancing adult motivation to learn*. San Francisco: Jossey-Bass.

eXtreme teaching
rigorous texts for troubled times

Joe L. Kincheloe and Danny Weil
General Editors

Books in this series will provide practical ideas on classroom practice for teachers and teacher educators that are grounded in a profound understanding of the social, cultural, political, economic, historical, philosophical, and psychological contexts of education as well as in a keen sense of educational purpose. Within these contextual concerns contributors will address the ferment, uncertainty, and confusion that characterize the troubles of contemporary education. The series will focus specifically on the act of teaching. While the topics addressed may vary, EXtreme Teaching is ultimately a book series that addresses new, rigorous, and contextually informed modes of classroom practice. Authors will bring together a commitment to educational and social justice with a profound understanding of a rearticulation of what constitutes compelling scholarship. The series is based on the insight that the future of progressive educational reform rests at the intersection of socio-educational justice and scholarly rigor. Authors will present their conceptions of this rigorous new pedagogical frontier in an accessible manner that avoids the esoteric language of an "in group." In this context, the series editors will make use of their pedagogical expertise to introduce pedagogical ideas to student, teacher, and professional audiences. In this process, they will explain what they consider the basic concepts of a field of study, developing their own interpretive insights about the domain and how it should develop in the future. Very few progressive texts exist to introduce individuals to rigorous and complex conceptions of pedagogical practice: thus, authors will be expected to use their contextualized interpretive imaginations to introduce readers to a creative and progressive view of pedagogy in the field being analyzed.

For additional information about this series or for the submission of manuscripts, please contact:

> Joe L. Kincheloe & Danny Weil
> c/o Peter Lang Publishing, Inc.
> 275 Seventh Avenue, 28th floor
> New York, New York 10001

To order other books in this series, please contact our Customer Service Department:
> (800) 770-LANG (within the U.S.)
> (212) 647-7706 (outside the U.S.)
> (212) 647-7707 FAX

Or browse online by series at *www.peterlangusa.com*